Politics
and
Popular Culture

JOHN STREET

Polity Press

First published in 1997 by Polity Press in association with Blackwell Publishers Ltd.

Editorial office:
Polity Press
65 Bridge Street
Cambridge CB2 1UR, UK

Marketing and production:
Blackwell Publishers Ltd
108 Cowley Road
Oxford OX4 1JF, UK

ISBN 0-7456-1213-X
ISBN 0-7456-1214-8 (pbk)

A CIP catalogue record for this book is available from the British Library.

Typeset in 10.5 on 12.5 pt Palatino
by Ace Filmsetting Ltd, Frome, Somerset
Printed in Great Britain by Hartnolls Ltd, Bodmin, Cornwall

This book is printed on acid-free paper.

For Marian

Contents

Acknowledgements

This book argues that the divide between the pleasures and the passions of politics and of popular culture is almost entirely artificial, and it tries to show how intimately they are, in fact, connected.

Politics and Popular Culture has taken a long time to write, much longer than I promised it would, and as a result I have incurred a large number of debts. The first is to my editor at Polity, Rebecca Harkin, who was very patient, and then very helpful when eventually I broke my silence. I am also very grateful to the people who saw the book through to publication, especially Justin Dyer, Julia Harsant and Annabelle Mundy.

The bulk of the work was done while I was on study leave granted me by the University of East Anglia. Such free time is a wonderful privilege, but it does impose costs on others – in my case, my colleagues in the Politics and Sociology Sector, and our secretary Anne Martin.

Many people have been – often unwittingly – the sounding-boards for the ideas contained here. They include the students on my Politics and Popular Culture unit and my fellow members of the International Association for the Study of Popular Music (IASPM); they also include several friends, in particular: Marian Brandon, Ian Forbes, Marion Forsyth, Steve Foster, Shaun Hargreaves Heap, John Orman, Alan Scott, Mike Stephens and John Wulfsohn. I have been lucky to have had the opportunity to try out some ideas in occasional reviews for *The Times*. I have learnt a great deal from the experience, and I owe thanks to Richard Morrison, Debra Craine and above all David Sinclair. Steve Smith, who helped to get me started, and Simon Frith, who gave encouragement at the end, are also owed much, but should be spared any blame.

Finally, I must mention my family – Marian, Alex, Jack and Tom – because they wouldn't forgive me if I didn't, and because they provide the best kind of distraction.

Earlier versions of some of the arguments here were published elsewhere: 'Local Differences? Popular Music and the Local State', *Popular Music*, 12(1), 1993, pp. 43–55; 'In Praise of Packaging', *Press/ Politics*, 1(2), 1996, pp. 126–33; 'Musicologists, Sociologists and Madonna', *Innovation in Social Science Research*, 6(3), 1993, pp. 277–89; 'Political Culture – From Civic Culture to Mass Culture', *British Journal of Political Science*, 24(1), 1993, pp. 95–114; '(Dis)located? Rhetoric, Politics, Meaning and the Locality', in W. Straw, S. Johnson, R. Sullivan and P. Friedlander (eds), *Popular Music – Style and Identity*, Montreal: IASPM/Centre for Research on Canadian Cultural Industries and Institutions, pp. 255–64.

The author and publisher are grateful to the following for permission to reproduce extracts from copyright material: Guardian Newspapers Ltd: extracts from *The Guardian*, © *The Guardian* and *The Observer*, © *The Observer*; Harvard University Press: extract from Ithiel de Sola Pool: *Technologies Without Borders*, copyright © 1990 by the President and Fellows of Harvard College; The Harvill Press: lines from Jonathan Raban: *Hunting Mr Heartbreak* (first published in Great Britain by Collins Harvill, 1990), copyright © Jonathan Raban 1990; Picasso Administration: words of Pablo Picasso, © Succession Picasso 1997, quoted in *Art and Power: Images of the 1930s* (Hayward Gallery, London, 1995); Laurence Pollinger Ltd and Viking Penguin, a division of Penguin Books USA Inc.: extract from Hannah Arendt: *Between Past and Future*, copyright © 1954, 1956, 1957, 1958, 1960, 1961 by Hannah Arendt; Routledge: extract from Duncan Webster: *Looka Yonder! The Imaginary America of Popular Culture* (1988); Telegraph Group Ltd: extract from article by Tom Utley in *The Daily Telegraph*, © Telegraph Group Limited, London, 1996; Verso: extract from George Lipsitz: *Dangerous Crossroads: Popular Music, Postmodernism and the Poetics of Place* (1995).

PART ONE

The Political and the Popular

CHAPTER ONE

Passion, populism, politics

If we were real, then what we saw on CNN was fiction; if
it was real, then we must be tricks of the light.
                    Jonathan Raban, *Hunting Mr Heartbreak*

In March 1981 John Hinckley shot President Reagan in order to
impress the film star Jodie Foster. With this single act, politics and
popular culture were linked inextricably. Hinckley's 'love' of Foster derived only from her screen image, but it was enough to inspire his attempt to assassinate the President of the United States
of America. It might, of course, be reasonable to consign such acts
to the realms of clinical psychology, to see them as having no real
relevance to either politics or popular culture. But even if the
Hinckley case is an extreme one, I still want to claim that it is an
example of the intimacy in which politics and popular culture co-
exist. This relationship is founded on the passions that are generated both by politics and by popular culture.

   This connection is not, of course, a simple one. It is not just a
matter of popular culture 'reflecting' or 'causing' political thoughts
and actions. Popular culture cannot be treated as a peg on which
to hang glib generalizations about the state of the world or about
popular feeling. Equally, popular culture does not make people
think and act in particular ways. Oliver Stone's film *Natural Born
Killers*, whatever the rhetoric and panic that it provoked, cannot
be treated as the cause of acts of mindless violence.

Following the 1992 British General Election, *The Sun* newspaper declared that it had secured the Conservatives' victory. This view was widely shared. It fitted with many general preconceptions about the political power of the tabloid press and of the ambitions of its owners, men like Rupert Murdoch. But such tempting conclusions have proved hard to substantiate. Credible claims have been made for both sides, for those who said the *Sun* was decisive (Linton, 1996), and for those who said it made no difference (Curtice and Semetko, 1994). The argument between the two sides is couched in terms of separating 'cause' and 'effect', of distinguishing between the papers as reflections of popular opinion and the papers as shapers of it. But, I want to suggest, the problem may actually lie in posing the debate like this in the first place. Our relationship to popular culture and the popular press cannot be seen simply as a relationship of cause and effect. Instead, popular culture has to be understood as *part* of our politics.

This is not to deny the political importance of the popular press, but rather to understand it as part of the wider and more complex relationship we have with popular culture. This is to link popular culture directly to our histories and experiences. Reflecting on Elvis Presley's afterlife, Greil Marcus (1991: xiii–xiv) writes about how Elvis is still part of 'a great, common conversation . . . made out of songs, art works, books, movies, dreams; sometimes more than anything cultural noise, the glossolalia of money, advertisements, tabloid headlines, best sellers, urban legends, nightclub japes'. And in this conversation, suggests Marcus, people 'find themselves caught up in the adventure of remaking his [Elvis'] history, which is to say their own'. This, I think, better captures our relationship to popular culture than any crude notion of culture as cause or as reflection. Popular culture neither manipulates nor mirrors us; instead we live through and with it. We are not compelled to imitate it, any more than it has to imitate us. None the less our lives are bound up with it. This is what Iain Chambers (1986: 13) implies when he talks of popular culture as offering a 'democratic prospect for appropriating and transforming everyday life'. We might quibble over how 'democratic' the relationship is, how much power fans and audiences have compared to that wielded by the producers of popular culture, but Chambers' key point is about the way we live through that culture. This, it seems to me, is what Jon Savage (1991: 361) means when he records in his diary how it felt to hear punk music in the late 1970s:

The Sex Pistols play for their lives. Rotten pours out all his resentments, his frustration, his claustrophobia into a cauldron of rage that turns this petty piece of theatre into something massive. . . . The audience is so close that the group are playing as much to fight them off, yet at the same time there is a strong bond: we feel what they feel. We're just as cornered.

Thirty years earlier, a similar account was given of seeing the film *The Blackboard Jungle*: 'I went three times to see that film. Then we'd be dancing coming home, in the middle of the road with all our friends, remembering the footsteps and everything' (Everett, 1986: 24).

If this view of popular culture is right, then there are important implications for politics. Let me suggest what these might be. Political thoughts and actions cannot be treated as somehow separate or discrete from popular culture. Marcus (1975: 204) writes of Elvis Presley as embodying 'America' and its political principles: 'Elvis takes his strength from the liberating arrogance, pride, and the claim to be unique that grow out of a rich and commonplace understanding of what "democracy" and "equality" are all about.' The connection between politics and popular emerges too in the way we choose our pleasures and judge our political masters, in the way the aesthetic blends into the ethical. Simon Frith (1996: 72) writes: 'not to like a record is not just a matter of taste; it is a matter of morality.' Criticism is often couched in ethical terms. In a review of Michael Cimino's *The Deer Hunter*, Pauline Kael wrote in the *New Yorker* that the film had 'no more moral intelligence than the Eastwood action pictures', and that it was a 'small-minded film'. The core of the problem lay in its hero, Michael, played by Robert De Niro. She complains that 'he is a hollow figure. There is never a moment when we feel, Oh My God, I know that man, I am that man' (Kael, 1980: 513, 518 and 519). This is as much a moral judgement as an aesthetic one. This is how the US critic Dave Marsh expressed his dislike of the rock band Oasis: 'Noel and Liam Gallagher seem, in the end, to be the kind of quasimoralists that Maggie and Ron were, content with their privileges because they think they earned them' (Marsh, 1996: 71). And just as moral judgements operate within culture, so cultural values operate in politics. We 'read' our politicians through their gestures and their faces, in the same way that we read performers on television. One of the key themes in this book is the way in which popular culture becomes – through the uses to which it is put and through the judgements made of it – a form of political activity. An accompanying theme is the thought that contemporary politics is itself conducted through the language and the formats of popular culture.

These themes do not, however, exhaust the relationship between politics and popular culture. The same politicians who exploit popular culture are also engaged in shaping popular culture, and, in doing so, making possible some experiences and denying access to others. Copyright laws, trade policy, censorship, education policy, broadcasting regulations, all these things produce a popular culture that profoundly affects what is heard and seen. And this matters: it matters if people cannot enjoy certain films or books or musics because of the way they live through this culture. The political management of popular culture is, therefore, another key theme.

In an attempt to defend the claim that politics and popular culture are intimately linked, and to explore its implications, this book adopts two perspectives. The first is that of a student of politics, the point of view of someone who wants to understand political processes, political thoughts and political actions. The book is driven by the idea that, if we fail to take popular culture seriously, we impoverish our understanding of the conflicting currents and aspirations which fuel politics. But this book is not just about our understanding of politics. It is also about making sense of popular culture. This is the second perspective, and it derives from one particular question: how do political processes shape the form and content of popular culture? The pleasures and effects of popular culture do not derive straightforwardly from our visits to the cinema or club. Rather they are a consequence of the access we have to popular culture, the opportunity we have to discover its pleasures. And these are the results of political processes. The content and character of popular culture is a legacy of a complex chain of events, marked by the operation of the political institutions and political ideologies that organize them. My approach, and my focus on politics, is not intended to rule out other ways of understanding popular culture, rather it is to emphasize the fact that in thinking about popular culture, we need to recognize the political processes that forge it. They are crucial to determining the importance it has and the stories it tells.

Before looking in detail at the two perspectives, I want to say something about what is meant by 'popular culture'. In particular, I want to show that even here, in defining popular culture, political institutions and political judgements are inescapably involved.

Defining popular culture

There are countless ways of defining popular culture (see Storey, 1993: 6–17). Many focus upon the means of its production, distribution and consumption. Popular culture is a form of entertainment that is mass produced or is made available to large numbers of people (for example, on television). Availability may be measured by the opportunity to enjoy the product or by the absence of social barriers to enjoyment of it (no particular skills or knowledge are required; no particular status or class is barred from entry). The implicit contrast in this definition of popular culture is to be made with another form of culture: high culture, which is more exclusive, which is less accessible both practically and socially. Chambers (1986: 12) expands upon this distinction:

> Official culture, preserved in art galleries, museums and university courses, demands cultivated tastes and a formally imparted knowledge. It demands moments of attention that are separated from the run of daily life. Popular culture, meanwhile, mobilizes the tactile, the incidental, the expendable, the visceral. It does not involve an abstract aesthetic research amongst privileged objects of attention, but invokes mobile orders of sense, taste and desire.

The same contrast can be made between plays in the theatre and television soap operas, between the novels of John Grisham and those of Jeanette Winterson.

Although there is an appealing formality about defining popular culture in terms of the mechanisms that organize its production and consumption, it raises problems in its failure to say anything about the character of the culture itself. What this means is that a play that is seen by a few people off-Broadway or in London's Royal Court Theatre would not be popular culture in this setting, but were it to be transmitted on a major television channel at peak hours it would become popular culture. In the same way, a novel's status as popular culture is defined by its sales rather than its style. To avoid these problems, other definitions resort to a more explicitly evaluative approach, focusing on style as much as sales. Here a work of opera, by virtue of the demands it makes upon listener and performer, is deemed to be 'high' culture, irrespective of the number of people who see or hear it. This definition of popular culture is established by references to styles and genres of cultural activity. Rock is popular culture, opera is not. Popular (or 'low') culture is defined by the fact that it appeals physically (as dance) rather than cerebrally (as contemplation). Other definitions again dwell upon the role and character of the audience, the way it is formed and addressed. This allows distinctions to be made within cultural forms, so that rock that is aimed at (or attracts) a small audience may not count as popular culture; or Beethoven's symphonies may be popular culture, while his string quartets are not; or Chopin may be popular culture while Stockhausen is not.

It will be immediately apparent that none of these attempts to define popular culture are altogether successful. In the first instance, they are not consistent with each other. For example, popular culture defined by its form (for example, pop music) can clash with the intuition that 'popular' also means 'liked by a large number of people'. Classical music can be 'popular' (for example, Pavarotti, Vanessa Mae or Michael Nyman); and some pop music may command a very small audience. Similar problems emerge in using evaluative criteria: can we make sensible and useful distinctions between the songs of Rosanne Cash, Elvis Costello, Ma Rainey, Stephen Sondheim and Benjamin Britten? Terms like 'complexity' or 'sophistication' are unlikely to get us far, since they can be applied, albeit in different ways, to music in any genre (see Middleton, 1990).

It is from within these confusions that the politics of 'popular culture' begin to emerge. Each of the competing accounts is underpinned by a set of political judgements which implicitly separate high from low culture, the elite from the popular. Each definition, by its nature, entails *selecting* particular cultural forms from amongst others, and making evaluations of their worth. It is not, of course, that such judgements can be avoided, only that they tend to be made implicitly, disguising their underlying values. All definitions of popular culture encode a set of political judgements, or, if acted upon, a set of political consequences. To describe something as popular culture is, for some, to suggest that it is less worthy than other forms of culture. And one implication of this will be to devote fewer resources to it or accord it less status. Only 'high' culture is supposed to require state support, because it is deemed to be worthwhile but unable to sustain itself through the market. Equally, to call something popular culture may be, from another point of view, to see it as representing a democratic voice. So, for example, Stuart Hall (1981: 238) sees definitions of popular culture as being juxtaposed to some notion of the 'power bloc'. Popular culture is defined *against* dominant culture. These two different definitions of popular culture derive from different political positions. Their differences emerge in the way they identify 'the people' and in the way people relate to popular culture. This contingent view of popular culture chimes with Morag Shiach's (1989: 2) observation that the definition of popular culture is never settled, but is the product of a 'complex series of responses to historical developments within communications technologies, to increased literacy, or to changes in class relations'. If what we mean by popular culture is conditioned by history, by ideology and by institutions, and if these also affect people's relationship to popular culture, then we need to look more closely at how popular culture can engage with politics, and vice versa. We need, in short, to return to the two perspectives that I referred to earlier.

Perspective 1: from popular culture to politics

What I want to do here is to sketch briefly the ways in which popular culture seems to engage with politics, the way its pleasures are linked to political thoughts and actions. Think of the way we respond to favourite films or songs or television programmes: the way we laugh and cry, dance and dream. Popular culture makes us feel things, allows us to experience sensations, that are both familiar and novel. It does not simply echo our state of mind, it moves us. Simon Frith (1988a: 123) once wrote: 'Pop songs do not "reflect" emotions . . . but give people romantic terms in which to articulate their emotions.' And in articulating emotions, popular culture links us into a wider world. Part of the pleasure of soap operas is their endless playing out of everyday moral dilemmas, posing questions and suggesting answers to our worries about what we should do. Here is the voice of a woman explaining the pleasure of watching TV soaps: 'I go round my mate's and she'll say, "Did you watch *Coronation Street* last night? What about so and so?" ... We always sit down and it's "Do you think she's right last night, what she's done?" Or, "I wouldn't have done that," or "Wasn't she a cow to him?" ' (Morley, 1986: 156). The vicarious thrill of seeing people behaving badly is animated by our sense of what is right and our understanding of the urge to do wrong. These tensions are not just a matter of private morality; they also extend into our public lives. This, for example, is how some writers have understood the success of *film noir* of the 1940s. Films like *Double Indemnity* touched upon the anxieties that confronted a post-war world. George Lipsitz (1982: 177) argues that 'The popularity of the film noir scenario in postwar America represents more than a commercial trend or an artistic cliché. In its portrayal of a frustrated search for community, film noir addressed the central political issues of American life in the wake of World War II.' Often this anxiety focused, in such films as *The Lady from Shanghai*, on male fears about the new social mobility enjoyed by women as a consequence of wartime demands (Chambers, 1986: 101). That popular culture can articulate such thoughts is not merely a matter of academic interest. It can have direct, political consequences. In nineteenth-century France the café singer Thérèsa was immensely popular, but her popularity was seen as subversive and threatening. 'People believed', writes T. J. Clark (1984: 227), 'that Thérèsa posed some sort of threat to the propertied order, and certainly the empire appeared to agree with them. It policed her every line and phrase, and its officers made no secret of the fact that they considered the café-concert a public nuisance.'

Popular culture's ability to produce and articulate feelings can become the basis of an identity, and that identity can be the source of political thought and action. We know who we are through the feelings and responses we have, and who we are shapes our expectations and our preferences. This sort of argument is advanced by Frith and Horne (1987: 16), who begin by claiming that identity is a founding aspect of politics: 'People's sense of themselves has always come from the use of images and symbols (signs of nation, class and sexuality, for example). How else do politics and religion, and art itself work?' And they go on to argue that identity is itself a product of our encounters with popular culture: 'We become who we are – in terms of taste and style and political interest and sexual preference – through a whole series of responses to people and images, identifying with some, distinguishing ourselves from others, and through the interplay of these decisions with our material circumstances (as blacks or whites, males or females, workers or non-workers)' (Frith and Horne, 1987: 16). Behind this argument is the thought that, if politics is the site within which competing claims are voiced and competing interests are managed, there is an important question to be addressed: why do people make such claims or see themselves as having those interests? The answer is that they are the consequence of us seeing ourselves as being certain sorts of people, as having an identity, which in turn establishes our claim upon the political order. These identities emerge in relation to the ways in which nations are defined in their rituals and pageants, in their sporting contests, in their daily newspapers. The press in particular is a crucial actor: in the divisions that get drawn between 'us' and 'them', whether within countries or between countries. There is an endless attempt to locate people in order to tell stories about them and to provide explanations for their behaviour.

The constant stream of representations in popular culture only paints part of the picture. It matters what people do with the barrage of images and identities. This is revealed in people's passionate investment in popular culture (representations matter little if no one cares about them). The sports fan is perhaps the most obvious example. Consider this description of Italian football fans:

> The AC Roma supporters sang in the stadium for five hours before the kick off. After defeat, fires lit up all around the ground in the balmy dusk. A riot? No, it was the fans burning every flag, scarf and hat they had, in complete silence: an extraordinary ritual. In the streets outside, true, some threw bottles at the English. But many more – grown men – wept on their knees in gutters. (Quoted in Redhead, 1986: 109)

This kind of passionate involvement can take on political significance. In 1990, the politician Norman Tebbit suggested the introduction of a 'nationality test'. To tell whether someone was truly British you had to see whom they supported in international sporting contests. Recalling a visit to a match between England and the West Indies at Lord's, the home of English cricket, Mike Marqusee (1994: 227) writes:

> All of us would have disgracefully failed Norman Tebbit's cricket test. Alex had been born in Jamaica, so I suppose he had an excuse,

but all five of the boys had spent their entire lives in north London. They did not follow cricket with any real zeal, but they had made the West Indian side their own. For them, the West Indies' combination of raw power and refined skills served as a magisterial reply to a racist society. Whatever they may have liked to think, they were not West Indians. They were not like their parents. Their loyalty and pride in the West Indian side was a political choice.

Popular culture can, in the way it offers forms of identity, become engaged with politics, in particular with the politics of citizenship, the right to belong and to be recognized.

Popular culture can also become a form of resistance. It can provide a form of defiance, a weapon with which to deny power. For the writer Greil Marcus (1989a: 90), the Sex Pistols' last performance (before they reformed in 1996) was a living embodiment of just such a political gesture: 'Walking the aisles of the Winterland as the Sex Pistols played, I felt a confidence and a lust that were altogether new. Thirty-two years had not taught me what I learned that night: when you're pushed, push back; when a shove negates your existence, negate the shove.' It is exactly this role, as a source of political resistance, that has marked popular culture throughout history. Tracing this tradition, John Scott (1990: 37–8) talks of the way that popular culture provides a 'hidden transcript' in which is written 'the anger and reciprocal aggression denied by the presence of domination'. The hidden transcript can be found in 'rumor, gossip, folktales, jokes, songs, rituals, codes, and euphemism – a good part of the folk culture of subordinate groups' (Scott, 1990: 19). Such culture becomes part of a political struggle to establish a particular view of the world, one which challenges the conventions of the dominant common sense. Simon Schama (1989: 181) reports on just such a struggle during the French Revolution, when the competing factions fought to tell their story:

> . . . it was unbound literature – almanacs and the posting of notices and placards – that would have increasingly connected the common people of the French towns with the world of public events. Every morning in Paris forty bill stickers would paste the city with news of battles won or lost; edicts of the King and the government; public festivities to mark some auspicious event; timely indications about the transport of ordure or the removal of graves. At moments of crisis they would be defaced or (illegally) supplanted by notices parodying government orders or pillorying ministers. And the exuberance of their visual broadcasting was matched by the flam-

boyance of the oral world of the Parisian, tuned as it was to a whole universe of songs. . . . Songs were sold by strolling vendors on the boulevards, bridges and quais and were sung at the cafés, their themes spanning a whole universe from the predictable airs of songs of courtship, seduction and rejection, to others that caroled the sons of Liberty in America, the profligacy of the court, the impotence of the King and the naughtiness of the Queen.

Such acts of political resistance are commonly played out within popular culture, in the way figures of authority are mocked in satire and comedy – from *The Simpsons* to *Spitting Image*. They are not just statements or suppressed emotions, they are a kind of action, although as Scott (1990: 191) insists, we need to think of the hidden transcript 'as a condition of practical resistance rather than a substitute for it'.

Popular culture's ability to focus passion and to express defiance also allows it to become a form of political management. This opportunity can, of course, be used to malign and benign effect, just as the identities constructed through popular culture can be liberating or oppressive. We have only to recall the propaganda machines of Nazi Germany and Stalinist Russia to remember the ways in which the machinery of culture can be deployed to legitimate a political order and to orchestrate popular sentiment. And some would argue that the same insidious forces are still at work in the popular culture of liberal democratic states of the West (Harker, 1980). Both by acts of censorship as well as by acts of propaganda, the state tries to make popular culture a device for securing deference and marginalizing dissent. What the state is doing is drawing upon culture's ability to move us. Equally, of course, such effects can be put to better use by encouraging compassion and charity. One of the most famous examples of this was Live Aid in 1985. Bob Geldof used popular culture to organize a spirit of universal humanitarianism. Geldof was able to employ sounds and images to prick our collective conscience. There have been other examples of such use of popular culture (George Harrison's Concert for Bangladesh, for instance), but Live Aid was the biggest. Here was a pop star acting as a global statesman, not speaking for 'youth', but for 'us' all. Here was someone using the full array of media organizations and technologies to create an international audience. But these innovations should not obscure the fact that Geldof was also doing what politicians and pop stars have always tried to do: to create a following, to put together a 'people' (to create an identity) and to give them a focus for their passion. And it is at this point that the other perspective on the politics of popular culture emerges, when popular culture becomes the object of politics, rather than its subject.

In this section, I have looked at some of the ways in which the pleasures of popular culture become engaged with politics – through the feelings it articulates, the identities it offers, the passions it elicits and in the responses it prompts. These encounters with politics do not, however, describe an inevitable state of affairs. Popular culture does not always provide a source of defiance or whatever. Not every film 'works', and the way film moves us is different from the way music or television affects us. Many other factors come into play, from the text to the context, from the audience to the industry. One of the key elements is the way popular culture is organized, because it is this that shapes what is enjoyed and how it is enjoyed. This thought is crucial to the argument of this book, and I shall return to it towards the end of this chapter. But for the moment, I want to turn attention to the other perspective that links politics to popular culture.

Perspective 2: from politics to popular culture

It is more than an interesting coincidence that film stars or media moguls become political leaders. Ronald Reagan and Silvio Berlusconi are not exceptions. They are part of a general rule which recognizes that popular culture constitutes part of the way we communicate with each other, and that political communication depends upon symbols and gestures as much as on words and sentences. When South American chat-show hosts move – apparently effortlessly – from the studio to the hustings, or when the musician and actor Ruben Blades becomes a leading contender for the Panamanian presidency, we are witnessing a logic that inhabits both popular culture and politics. These are people who are expert in modern forms of communication, but they are also expert in 'representing' the people. Politicians increasingly borrow the techniques and skills of popular entertainment to communicate their message or promote their image. Boris Yeltsin solicited a parade of celebrities in his 1996 presidential election campaign in an attempt to acquire a starry glister; Bill Clinton not only played the saxophone on MTV, but he also studied carefully the ways in which television performers establish a rapport with their audience, and how they manage the emotions on display. Every party now deploys the language of the advertising executive and the skills of the pop video maker in their election campaigns. In Britain, this symbiosis was most dramatically represented in the 1987 Party Election Broadcast for Neil Kinnock, made by the director of *Chariots of Fire*, Hugh Hudson. The techniques of popular film and political image were captured in a series of sentimental memories, soft-focus shots and warm endorsements. The point was to sell Neil Kinnock, to sell his sensitivity and his warmth, just as videos and advertisements sell other products. As politicians desperately try to create a constituency for their parties and policies, they find themselves drawn ever closer to popular culture.

What popular culture represents is a mastery of popularity. The examples above are not isolated ones, but, as I have suggested, part of a pervasive logic. It is a logic that derives from a shared desire to generate popularity and to claim representation. As Marcus (1993: 293) once observed:

> Ronald Reagan has never said a public word about Prince or Madonna, only had Michael Jackson to the White House and appropriated Bruce Springsteen for a campaign speech. But by those acts and thousands like them, he validated the process by which stars are validated. He became bigger; so, for the moment, did they. The difference is that he is not in it for the moment.

The fact that we are seeing a new intimacy in the connection between politics and popular culture should not blind us to the realization that this link was always latent. Its current prominence tells us only that now it is an acknowledged fact, where before it was partially obscured by formal codes and artificial distinctions. British MPs resisted for years the televising of Parliament even as they increasingly exploited that same medium – in photo-opportunities and interviews – for their immediate political gain. Politicians have always sought popularity, and in their search they have always allied themselves with the cultural representations of 'the popular'. From the pre-war exploits of Governor Huey P. Long to Reagan's courtship of film stars and musicians, US politicians have made full use of the possibilities for self-promotion afforded by popular culture. Even the superficially reticent British have done the same. Over thirty years ago, Prime Minister Harold Wilson awarded the Beatles the MBE (Member of the British Empire). Nowadays pop stars become politicians, and politicians court pop stars. Together they exploit popular culture's ability to combine passion, politics and popularity.

Again, as with the first perspective, my claim is not that politics is inevitably linked to popular culture. Indeed, my argument is the same as before. The connection depends on the conditions and the context, on the type of popular culture and the type of political system. Once more, to understand the relationship between politics and popular culture we have to understand the ideas and institutions that organize them both. The connection does not just 'happen'; we have to see it as being created and administered. If we do not, the two perspectives – from popular culture to politics, from politics to popular culture – will seem to come together in a vague postmodern haze in which everyone is in the same business. As Brian Eno (1996: 251) wryly records in his diary: 'Now that artists, comedians, writers, poets, architects, newsreaders, religious leaders, politicians, industrialists, fashion designers and scientists are all acting like pop stars, there's nothing left for pop stars to do but award them all prizes.' This elision is seen as the consequence of the erosion of rigid hierarchies and of universal principles, of their replacement by amorphous networks and anonymous market forces. Our world is one in which, it seems, all choices – moral, political, aesthetic – are essentially consumer, lifestyle choices, arbitrated by the laws of supply and demand. This is the logic of populism, in politics and in culture. The only good policies, the only successful parties or politicians, are those that give the people what they want. The only test of cultural merit is to be found at the box office, or in the ratings or in the charts.

Both these varieties of populism – whether political or cultural – have a superficial appeal; they appear to guarantee neutrality and legitimacy. The popular choice is the democratic choice. It is not imposed; it is the product of free individuals responding to their preferences. Any alternative to this involves acts of judgement and interference, exercises of power that require the introduction of partial values and the prosecution of particular interests. But this is a false distinction. In reality, populism is itself as much the product of political judgements and interests as are imposed choices. The market is not a neutral instrument, it is a political arrangement. And in understanding the relationship of politics and popular culture, we need to be on guard against the easy option that 'populism' represents. It oversimplifies the ways in which popular culture takes on political significance, or the ways in which politics engages with popular culture. The relationship is itself dependent on political ideologies and institutions. I want, therefore, to spell out the problems of populism here, and to draw out the implications that these criticisms have for the connection between politics and popular culture.

Politics against populism

The blending of politics and popular culture runs the risk of seeing politicians as simply representing the people, and popular culture as being just a form of popular expression. I want to reject both of these views. Certainly, there is a strong desire on the part of the political order to claim that it represents the people, and for politicians to claim that they speak for the people. Running parallel to this political populism is a cultural populism, one that allows broadcasters, artists, cultural analysts and others to claim that popular culture expresses the wishes and desires of the people. Both political and cultural populism are, however, highly suspect ideas, at least in their unqualified form.

With the possible exception of fundamentalist regimes, which draw their legitimation from divine revelation, all forms of government – whether dictatorial or democratic, capitalist or communist – derive their authority from 'the people'. Their claim to rule is validated by the thought that they are 'the voice of the people' (and that this claim has itself been tested by elections and other constitutional devices). But in acknowledging this legitimating rhetoric, we cannot afford to forget that 'the people' are as much a rhetorical as a political fact. Politics is in large part an attempt to secure pre-eminence for one version of the people over another, to define the people in a way that serves a particular set of interests or practices. (Different electoral systems can produce quite different versions of the 'people's will'.) To lay claim to 'the people', argues Ernesto Laclau (1977: 167–73), is to engage in a political struggle in an attempt to secure victory for a dominant class. There is no final source of authority; there is no popular oracle. The 'people' are the product of politics, not its origin.

In achieving dominance, populist rhetoric adopts a variety of
codes and genres. It can, for example, appeal to past myths or
future fears; and it can dress them in different styles – it can be
hectoring or homely, grandiose or folksy. But what each is intended
to do is to link its audience to a vision which in turn legitimates a
particular course of action. This is, it needs to be stressed, a creative process. First, there is the question of who is to be included in
the idea of the people; and, secondly, there is the question of what
they want. The people do not have a 'voice'; they are given one by
opinion pollsters, commentators, journalists, politicians, interest
groups. The 'people' are created through the ways in which they
are represented and spoken for. The people are made; they do not
just exist.

Popular culture against populism

The same kind of scepticism has to be applied to popular culture.
Just as we may doubt the politician's claim to speak for the people, so we need to be equally wary of suggestions that popular
culture speaks for the people. There is a tradition of writing about
popular culture that links it directly to its 'times'. So sixties music
and films ('Streetfighting Man', *Easy Rider*) stand for the political
and social upheaval of those years, as punk expressed the economic downturn of the late seventies. Such readings tend to be
highly selective, depending, first, upon reading the culture in a
particular way (ignoring, for example, the immense popularity of
The Sound of Music [Harker, 1992]); and, secondly, upon highlight-
ing a particular set of experiences and lives (punk, after all, was
confined to relatively small metropolitan social networks). What
gets lost is all the other forms of popular culture and their follow-
ers. What is also missing is the way in which both the audiences
and the culture emerge from the complex network of bureaucra-
cies and agencies of the culture industries. The popular press may
pretend that it speaks for the people, but its values may not be
shared by its readers.

There is, though, another form of cultural populism, one which
recognizes the intervening power of the industry, but which invests audiences with the capacity to reinterpret and subvert its
messages. Here the culture *acquires* political significance through

the interpretations put upon it. This gives the audience power over the product and allows them to recruit the culture to their side in the political battle. It is this approach which makes it possible to find subversive social comment in *Baywatch* or radicalism in the Rambo films or authentic anger in Snoop Doggy Dogg. But in recognizing that cultural products are available to a number of different interpretations, there is a danger of adopting a populism which allows all popular culture to be treated as a form of political resistance. It is to assume that everywhere, in all acts of cultural consumption, subversive interpretations are being imposed which somehow empower audiences. To take this view is to ignore the differences between works of popular culture; it is to treat them as blank screens onto which any idea can be written. But as Jim McGuigan (1992) insists, this is to overlook the need for judgement and discrimination in understanding popular culture, the need to select between accuracy and distortion, the genuine and the phony. Some popular culture is better than others – as we acknowledge every time we choose a video or a film, every time we switch channels. It may be hard to explain our choice, but we do it, and someone – the television producer, the film distributor and many others – does it for us, every day. Such decisions cannot be avoided. The real question is who should take them and how. Whatever pleasures lie in the books of Jeffrey Archer, they hardly constitute the basis for a radical critique of capitalism, and there are better writers who could sell in the same quantity under a different publishing system. The populist reading of popular culture, just like the populist reading of politics, needs to be replaced by an approach which understands popular culture in terms of the institutions that create it and the political ideologies that inform it.

Beyond populism

What these criticisms of populism reveal is that there is another dimension to the relationship between politics and popular culture. It emerges in the way political institutions and ideas materially affect the character, content, production and consumption of popular culture. This is most evident in the practice of censorship or of propaganda, where the state (through its various agencies –

especially broadcasters) denies access to popular culture for fear
of its effects, or where it uses popular culture as propaganda in
order to maintain its authority and social order generally. But this
relationship between the political order and popular culture is also
present in a more subtle guise. It is there in the way the state creates the conditions under which popular culture is produced and
distributed. The state's role in broadcasting, education and industrial policy, among other areas, establishes the conditions, regulations and opportunities which help define what kind of popular
culture is available in any country or region. In other words, to
understand popular culture is to understand the conditions of its
production. It is not enough to look only at the text or its audience; we need also to look at the way popular culture is organized
and made available.

Equally, a state's constitutional and institutional structures can
also affect the ways in which popular culture becomes incorporated into political practice. Where parties control political career
paths, by the distribution of political patronage, the opportunities
offered by media exposure are less useful. But where parties are
weak, the media become crucial agents. This helps to explain the
greater prominence attached to the media in the USA; it also helps
to explain why, as formal party structures crumble, British politicians make ever greater use of media access. It also explains the
media-oriented political strategies of maverick campaigners like
Ross Perot or James Goldsmith (leader of the Referendum Party
in Britain). In the same way, social movements are more likely to
campaign through mass media than established interest groups.
Put differently control of media power will acquire greater political significance in some regimes, and not in others. Berlusconi's
rise in Italy was a product not simply of his media empire, but of
the Italian political system itself. A similar explanation is needed
for why people in showbusiness more easily rise to the top in politics in some countries than in others. Some systems reward
populism; others practise elitism.

The ability to claim to represent the people does not simply exist as a fact of life for either performers or politicians. They both
want to be popular, but what this means and how it is achieved
depend on many factors. Representatives have to be legitimated,
they have to be able to justify the claim to speak for their constituents or their country. To say that you speak for the people, that
you are a true representative, is not automatically established by

the political system; or, rather, even constitutionally validated representation is constantly challenged from within and from outside. Think of that moment when President Ceauşescu of Romania, head of a powerful authoritarian regime, was drowned out by the crowd in the square below. The revolution had begun; he could no longer even pretend to speak for the people. This was just another example of a politics in which there are competing claims about who or what constitutes the people. And this battle is waged around the symbolic representations of the people, around the devices that enable the people to be constituted in one form rather than another.

An obvious example of this constant struggle arises in the familiar arguments over popular culture itself. They are to be heard in the sound of politicians, priests and others lamenting the malign effects of popular culture on the minds and morals of those who fall under its spell. Whether it is *Neighbours* or raves, whether *Reservoir Dogs* or Roald Dahl, the argument is over what the public should see and hear, and how these things may change or influence them. The same questions inhabit debates about public funding of the arts, or about what children should be taught in school.

The arguments – about whether a particular piece of popular culture is suitable for public consumption – are not just about matters of 'taste' or about viewing figures or opinion polls. They are founded on judgements about what is to be admired or decried in popular culture, and they emerge from the different ways (and the different contexts) in which popular culture works. All of the arguments are the product of competing ideologies and competing interests, and their consequences are measured in the opportunities people have to engage with culture (and to benefit or suffer from it).

Passionate interests

The argument that we have sketched so far suggests that there is more to the link between politics and popular culture than their occasional borrowings and battles. There is an underlying logic which ropes them together. This logic springs from the way in which notions of representation, the people, popularity and identity are shared between them. Within and between politics and

popular culture, there is a constant struggle to articulate these identities, a battle that is, in one incarnation, fought over the claim to
'represent' those competing identities. The authority to speak for
the people is not simply given by a set of formal political rules. It
has to be established. And the ability to do this depends on the
ways in which political actors can be said to represent the people,
a claim that in turn rests upon the way 'the people' are themselves
defined and their 'representatives' connected to them.

This process takes place within a wider context in which political interests and values shape popular culture, just as the political
economy of popular culture determines the political possibilities
within that culture. The political shaping of popular culture is a
matter of both institutions and ideas. It is to be observed in the
organizations – transnational, national and regional – that order
the production and consumption of popular culture. It is also to
be observed in the judgements and values that underlie decisions
about how organizing principles are to be applied, as well as in
the way popular culture is used politically. But to argue for this
approach to understanding the relationship is to raise as many
questions as are answered – questions about the role of identity in
politics, about the relationship between 'material' interests and
perceptions, about how different forms of popular culture construct (or fail to construct) different senses of self, about the conditions under which popular culture operates. Accounts of politics
may often fail to explain or analyse the passions and pleasures
that make sense of popularity and which underlie political action,
but still we need to find a way of introducing such factors. Equally,
while cultural studies may tell us about how the popular works,
we need to supplement this with a sense of how political processes shape culture and our enjoyment of it. This book is an attempt to fill both these gaps.

Whatever next . . .

The rest of *Politics and Popular Culture* has a fairly straightforward
structure. It divides into three parts. The first develops further the
two perspectives (from popular culture to politics, from politics
to popular culture) that I discussed earlier. Chapter 2 looks at the
ways in which politics has been linked to popular culture, and

examines the claims that have been made for the political power of popular culture. The chapter ends with a brief discussion of what it means to talk of the 'politics' of popular culture. Chapter 3 turns attention to the ways in which conventional politics has increasingly drawn upon popular culture in order to promote its various causes. It focuses on 'dangers' associated with the packaging of politics. I argue that these are greatly exaggerated, but I also suggest that we need to recognize politics' dependence upon popular culture, and to judge it accordingly.

The second part of the book takes up the issue of the political management of popular culture. Central to this is the idea of the globalization of popular culture. Part II divides into three chapters, each of which deals with different levels in the political economy of popular culture: the transnational (chapter 4), the national (chapter 5) and the regional/local (chapter 6). In each, I look at the ways in which states organize popular culture and the effect this has upon that culture's own politics. It is important to see how political processes and political ideologies shape the form and content of popular culture. As such, this part constitutes an extended critique of some claims about the power and pervasiveness of globalization.

The final part addresses three key issues that underlie all discussion of the relationship between politics and popular culture. Chapter 7 examines the claims of cultural accounts of politics. There are, after all, several entirely respectable political science paradigms which regard culture as either peripheral, irrelevant or subservient. An argument for the political importance of popular culture must, therefore, establish some grounds for treating culture as a significant variable. In making the case for culture's explanatory role, I argue that we need also to think about the different political accounts that can be given of culture. Chapter 8 takes up this question, and looks at the political ideas that underpin competing understandings of popular culture. This leads to a chapter in which I look at the way in which political judgement is organized into the censorship and selection of popular culture. The concluding chapter argues that politics is deeply implicated in the way we choose and enjoy popular culture. In short, this book is an attempt to persuade political scientists to take popular culture seriously; and to persuade fans of popular culture of the importance of politics to their pleasures and passions (and maybe to make a little more sense of the bit of John Hinckley that lurks in all of us).

CHAPTER TWO

Popular culture
as politics

What do you think an artist is? An imbecile who has
only his eyes if he's a painter, or ears if he's a musician, or
a lyre at every level if he's a poet, or even, if he's a boxer,
just his muscles? On the contrary, he's at the same time
a political being, constantly alive to heartrending, fiery
or happy events, to which he responds in every way. . . .
No, painting is not done to decorate apartments. It is
an instrument of war for attack and defence against the
enemy.

Pablo Picasso, quoted in *Art and Power:*
Images of the 1930s

During the 1996 Brits awards ceremony, the British music industry's equivalent of the Oscars, Michael Jackson mimed to his hit
'Earth Song'. Jackson was there to receive the newly created 'Artist of a Generation' award from Bob Geldof. He appeared at the
top of a pyramid, surrounded by mists of dry ice. Slowly he de-
scended, mouthing words of despair at the plight of the world –
the famines, the refugees, the desecration of the planet. At the
bottom he was joined by a motley collection of children and adults,
extras dressed up to represent the destitute and the dispossessed.
It was like a scene from *Les Misérables*. As his evocation of human
tragedy reached its climax, Jackson tore off his outer clothes to
reveal an all-white suit. With his arms outstretched, as if cruci-
fied, he embraced his cast of waifs, before being borne aloft on a
hydraulic platform.

This spectacle proved too much for Jarvis Cocker, lead singer of the British pop group Pulp. He climbed on stage to mingle with Jackson's crowd of victims, and began to dance and gesture in mock sympathy. He was chased off by Jackson's security guards, who were also doing duty as extras. All of this was witnessed by the large audience and the television cameras (although it was not shown when highlights of the awards ceremony were broadcast the following night). Some time later Cocker was arrested and questioned for several hours at a local police station. Allegations were made that he had hurt one or two of the children on stage. Jackson and the Brits' organizers issued statements deploring Cocker's behaviour. The tabloid press, taking their cue from these briefings, pilloried Cocker. The broadsheet papers were less keen to condemn, and *The Guardian* newspaper actually solicited letters of support from other pop performers (Everything But The Girl, Bernard Butler). These correspondents celebrated Cocker's antics and complained of the vainglorious egotism of Jackson's performance. Cocker had expressed their revulsion at the sentiments of the song, at the style of the performance and at Jackson's attempt to use the ceremony as an opportunity to rehabilitate himself (following allegations of child abuse). Eventually, the police dropped the charges against Cocker, but the event itself passed into folklore. It was, in its way, a classic pop moment.

Not that everyone agreed as to what that moment signified. For some, Cocker's gesture represented a moment of splendid iconoclasm, a pricking of pop pomposity. For others, it was just the clash of two equally overblown egos, each desperate for attention. And there were others who condemned Cocker for behaving like a spoilt child at a grown-up party. Within this chatter of judgements, you can hear echoes of long-running debates about the politics of popular culture.

One strand of these was represented by Bob Geldof, Live Aid's mastermind, who was at the Brits to honour Jackson. Geldof is the embodiment of popular culture's ability to make a positive difference, to raise money for, and awareness of, a worthy cause. Geldof stands in that honourable tradition of people who have used their status and their work to raise money and awareness for good causes – from Jane Fonda's anti-war campaigns in the 1960s and 1970s, to Elizabeth Taylor's and Barbra Streisand's work for AIDS campaigns today. The other strand to the argument about popular culture's politics was pursued by Cocker, who, in his antics, was trying to undermine the event's respect-ability and to ignite a spirit of dissent. This is a tradition that flowered with the iconoclasm of punk, but has roots in Dadaism and situationism (Plant, 1992). What unites both strands is their shared sense that popular culture represents a site of politics, that you can say and do things with it that, in some way or other, matter politically. Or, at least, this is how pop-ular culture is understood to be 'political'. And it is with this thought – how popular culture is read as 'political' – that this chapter is concerned. I want to look at the ways in which popular culture takes a political guise, how it becomes a form of politics and how it fashions the landscape of the political imagi-nation.

This may seem like a broad brief, and I need to explain what is *not* involved as well as what is. In exploring popular culture's engagement with politics, I want to exclude the uses of popular culture by those whose prime aim is their own politi-cal advancement – the politicians who cosy up to film stars and rock icons. They are the topic of the next chapter. I do, however, want to discuss the ways in which the context of popular cul-ture may invest it with a political significance which, on the sur-face, it appears to lack. State intervention can turn a work of art into a political gesture. Censorship works like this. In a different way, the *fatwa* directed at Salman Rushdie as a result of his novel *The Satanic Verses* caused the author and his book to become the object of international diplomacy. But in noting such cases, I am here concerned not with why or how the state achieves these effects (that again is the task of another chapter), but rather with the way in which popular culture takes on a political character in different contexts. At heart, I am concerned with what it means to talk of popular culture as politics, to see where pleasure shades into political practice. This chapter is, therefore, a survey of some of the ways in which popular culture has been accorded the epi-thet 'political', how people have claimed that in producing or consuming popular culture we are engaging with politics, with the clash of ideas, identities and interests, with the distribution of resources and rewards.

Popular culture as political activism

It might be hard to credit the claim that East German rock musicians helped to bring down the Berlin Wall in 1989. But this is exactly the case made by Peter Wicke, who argues that certain musicians were indeed part of the political process that saw the collapse of communism. They were able to focus the anger and urgency that was decisive to the popular uprising. 'Rock musicians', writes Wicke (1992: 81), 'were instrumental in setting in motion the actual course of events which led to the destruction of the Berlin Wall and the disappearance of the GDR.'

That a group of musicians, however sophisticated their politics or their music, could be responsible for transforming an entire political system, especially a notoriously authoritarian one, may seem like the height of romantic naïvety. Politicians and political activists, or the forces that drive them, change political systems, not pop performers. But the claim that musicians *as musicians* were decisive is less bizarre than might at first appear.

The musicians' ability to make a difference stemmed from the way in which the state politicized East German popular music, giving every gesture and every symbol a political significance (Wicke, 1992: 88). There were two elements to this effect. The first was the constraints put upon political expression in the GDR. Political discussion and debate, protest and pressure, were subject to party control. But this established conditions for the second element. By imposing control on forms of expression, the party also *politicized* them. In 1965, the ruling Socialist Unity Party imposed controls on film directors, poets and musicians. Music was especially closely monitored: 'when beat groups came together in parks or marketplaces and drew crowds', Olaf Leitner (1994: 30) records, 'the crowds were broken up with dogs and water cannon.' Such treatment had the paradoxical effect of turning popular culture into a form of political rebellion. As Wicke (1992: 81) argues, 'it was precisely because the music was initially repressed that it became a medium of resistance which was more or less impossible to control.' Out of this failure of control came the authorities' decision to incorporate popular music within the state. Having failed to suppress it, the state made itself indispensable to popular music through its role as supplier of equipment and

regulator of performances, but still it did not make itself omni-
potent. Bands developed contacts with the West, which gave
them commercial and political independence, expressing the
latter in the lyrics of their songs. In doing so, they created a space
for political voices that were denied elsewhere by the state's control over political discussion.

That the musicians spoke with a similar voice was due to the
fact that the state had – unwittingly – provided them with a platform for their politics. In the early 1970s, the GDR state created
the Committee of Entertainment Arts to provide a way of managing cultural production and consumption (Wicke and Shepherd,
1993). 'Ironically,' remarks Wicke (1992: 87-8), 'it was the creation
of the structure necessary for this state-imposed discipline which
made it possible for the musicians to organize successfully. Without those structures, such organization would not have been possible.' And it was from their established institutional base and
through their command of political expression that the musicians
were able to articulate their concern about the system. One hun-
dred leading musicians signed a declaration that was read out
during a major public performance. It was to inspire a collective
protest against the old regime, a protest that was to bring down
the Berlin Wall (Wicke, 1992: 90–1).

I offer this example as one way of talking about the politics of
popular culture. It suggests that popular culture can function as
an instrument of political change, not merely reflecting reform,
but actually prompting it. It might be argued that the real instrument of change is the state, not the music or the musicians. It
was the state, rather than the musicians, which made the music
political; the musicians were merely pawns in a larger game. But
to take this line would be to overlook the options which the
musicians faced and the choices they made. It would be to ignore
the relationship they had with their audience, with the way in
which their performances and songs organized that relationship, and the ways in which they were able to generate a
response among their fans. It would be to overlook the very real
difficulties the state faced in trying to control them. And finally it
would be to forget that in the West popular culture can also become a source of resistance. This, for example, is how George
McKay portrays the rave movement in Britain. He describes the
Exodus Collective, which organizes dance events, as part of a larger
'culture of resistance' (McKay, 1996: 125). Simon Reynolds (1996)

invests the Jungle music scene with the same capacity to deny authority:

> Resistance doesn't necessarily take the 'logical' form of collective activism (unions, left-wing politics); it can be so distorted and im-aginatively impoverished by the conditions of capitalism itself, that it expresses itself as, say, the proto-fascist, anti-corporate nostalgia of America's right-wing militias, or as a hyper individualistic survivalism. In Hip Hop and, increasingly, Jungle, the response is a 'realism' that accepts a socially-constructed reality as natural. To 'get real' is to confront a state-of-nature where dog eats dog, where you're either a winner or a loser, and most will be losers. There's a cold rage seething in Jungle, but it's expressed within the terms of an anticapitalist yet non-socialist politics, and expressed defensively: as a determination that the underground will not be co-opted by the mainstream. . . . As music, as a form of cultural resistance, Jun-gle works by eroticising anxiety.

The point is, therefore, to recognize the ways in which popular culture – in this case, popular music – can become the site of po-litical resistance. The conditions and the forms may vary, but the possibility is always there. As John Shepherd (1993: 31) argues in the East German case:

> . . . although they [the authorities] might have decided to make life extremely difficult for musicians and their fans, it was always pos-sible for musicians to separate their music conceptually from those criteria which the state was harassing them with and to challenge state authorities to once again find ways to make life difficult for them. The 'nature of music,' in other words, made possible a game of cat and mouse between musicians and the authorities.

At the same time, the very fact of the music's popularity is a measure of its political potency: 'If music is "popular" within a particular cultural economy of desirability, then it will develop political and economic values symptomatic of that popularity' (Shepherd, 1993: 31). The important implication of Shepherd's ar-gument is that, in talking of the politics of popular culture, we are not just raising the question of what its politics are, but also what it means to talk about popular culture at all – what it is, and how people engage with it. The suggestion is, then, that popular cul-ture not only provides a site for the expression of political ideas, but that these ideas have some real impact.

Popular culture as political pressure

To use popular culture as a form of resistance, as a barrier against intrusion and an assertion of autonomy, is only one way in which it can engage with politics. Popular culture can also work within the system, putting pressure on it by exciting popular feelings of concern or compassion. The use of popular culture to raise money for charity or raise awareness is now so commonplace that we hardly bother to reflect upon it. Live Aid is the classic example, one which prompted many imitators: Farm Aid, Sun City, Comic Relief, Run the World, War Child and Rock the Vote. Even before Live Aid in 1985, there had been the Concert for Bangladesh and Rock against Racism, and there is, of course, a long tradition of making charity records or performing benefit gigs (Frith and Street, 1992). Music has no monopoly on such efforts. Film and television stars have associated themselves with any number of causes.

But to confine attention to these relatively high-profile benefactors and their particular charities would be to overlook the routine and regular ways in which popular sympathy is elicited by popular culture. Live Aid was prompted by a BBC news report from Ethiopia by the journalist Michael Buerk. Although it was not an entirely conventional news item (the images and the tone of Buerk's voice gave a note of dramatic desperation to the story), it still fell within the conventions of news broadcasting. And while this report was more than usually harrowing, the fact that it moved people did not make it unusual. All news stories dramatize their stories and organize our sympathies. To this extent, they make us care. What is true for news is equally true for documentaries, whether about natural history or current affairs. They work to engage the viewer through feelings of empathy and concern. And what is implicit in broadcasting is explicit in the press, where popular sympathies are daily organized into moods of disgust and delight, anger and compassion.

Popular culture's ability to create feelings of compassion can be measured – tangibly, by the hard cash they raise; less directly, by the shifting sands of popular anxiety, reflected in opinion polls and political agendas. But to what extent, and in what sense, can these achievements be attributed to popular culture and be used to demonstrate its political power? After all, it is possible to explain the sums raised by reference to the cause alone and the context in which it emerged. The obvious way to address these concerns is by comparing the occasions when popular culture is successfully deployed and when it fails.

The issue is whether success is ever a product of style, rather than of the cause. Eliciting people's compassion may depend on both the issue being addressed and the form in which our sympathy is being elicited. Some causes are easier to organize than others. The conventional reasons for this have to do with the money and the other resources that the activists possess; or with the structure of the problem: where the activists can achieve direct gains then there are stronger incentives to participate than if the benefits rebound upon everyone, irrespective of whether they participate or not (Olson, 1965). These factors may affect the success of popular culture's charitable acts. It is noticeable, for instance, that stars are much more likely to give their services if there is guaranteed coverage (on TV, in the press). But it is also possible to see that some causes fit more easily within the conventions of popular culture. It is easier to use popular culture to fuel compassion for individuals rather than for general political causes, for 'innocent victims' rather than for political parties. It is notable, for instance, that children are routinely beneficiaries of popular culture's campaigns.

Beneath the tendency to favour some causes over others lies a further political dimension. This concerns how these causes are represented, and the way we are encouraged to think about them. Popular culture's engagement with causes is bound up with an ideology that explains them and the audience's relationship to them. Greil Marcus (1989b), for instance, saw Live Aid as encoding a form of universal humanism that eliminated any sense of difference or of autonomy, which turned the globe into a mass market. Live Aid was, in this sense, a triumph of the commercial initiative of its sponsor, the Pepsi corporation. For Marcus (1993: 367), 'to make true political music, you have to say what decent people don't want to hear; that's something people fit for satellite benefit concerts will never understand.' By contrast, Dick Hebdige saw in Live Aid an ideological challenge to the emergent individualist consensus. 'Geldof's arrival', he wrote (1988: 219), 'introduced a new and different threat to Thatcherite populism: the articulation of a different version of "common-sense" drawing on traditions of co-operation and mutual support, rooted in the human(e) values of good fellowship and good neighbourliness, the ability to feel affinities across national, ethnic and cultural divisions, to imagine community beyond the boundaries of the known.' Other observers have found themselves torn between both positions (Eno, 1996: 310–11).

Whatever interpretation is adopted, the claim is that popular culture can not only fuel particular political actions, but that it can also give a distinct ideological significance to them. This is not to say that the cultural artefact in and of itself is the independent and sole cause of these thoughts and acts. They depend – like those of the musicians in the GDR – on the institutional and ideological context in which they operate. They have to be understood within the changing structure of the cultural industries, the notion of 'stardom' that they create, and the convention of broadcasting that they draw on to create a sympathetic audience. None the less, it still makes sense to talk of the 'politics of popular culture', where we mean by this the ability of popular culture to give shape to people's political sympathies and concerns. Not every cause and not every example of popular culture can work in this way; some can, though, and this success gives further credence to the link between politics and popular culture.

Popular culture as political control

Implicated in the idea that popular culture can inspire political action is the idea that it can or should be used as a mechanism of social control. Popular culture features here as, on the one hand, the source of dangerous or anti-social ideas and practices, and, on the other, as a way of inculcating more socially responsible or desirable behaviour.

In the first instance, popular culture becomes enmeshed with politics through censorship. The case for censoring popular culture is made on the grounds that it either causes offence (to moral or religious sensibilities) or that it is liable to lead to imitation of the behaviour it portrays (typically sexual or violent behaviour). So it is that in the West we have witnessed debates about, in the first category: Martin Scorsese's *The Last Temptation of Christ*, *The Satanic Verses* and rap music; and, in the second category: films like *Natural Born Killers*, *Kids* and *Crash*. The politics of popular culture are here understood as its subversive effects on established beliefs and practices. The same thought inspired the Chinese authorities in Liuzhon to ban schoolchildren from video arcades, dance halls and karaoke parlours because they all represented 'unhealthy social practices' (Reuters, 18 April 1996).

Sometimes the desire to control popular culture is, as in China, directly connected to a political ideology. In East Germany, cultural politics were tied to 'the political and ideological offensive of socialism' (Leitner, 1994: 23). In the West, the explicitly political monitoring of popular culture has been associated with the McCarthy witch-hunts in the USA, when films and film-makers (among others) were condemned for promoting communism. Later, the FBI trailed John Lennon across America, recording his songs and his stage announcements, and fighting his request for US citizenship (Orman, 1984: 105–19). And more recently, rap, heavy metal and the photographs of Robert Mapplethorpe have been the target of would-be censors. Censorship of popular culture for political reasons is certainly not consigned to the past. In 1997 in Egypt, the government has cracked down on fans of heavy metal, and in France, local authorities run by the National Front have withdrawn public funding from hiphop bands, theatre companies and artists that do not meet with their approval.

Advocates of censorship see it as a necessary response to the unwelcome politics of popular culture. Critics of censorship, meanwhile, turn their attention on the would-be censors, arguing that these people are responding – albeit vainly – to ideas, values and images that threaten their established interests. Both sides, though, share the view that popular culture is capable of representing ideas that have significant political consequences. Their response to popular culture – by either tolerating or censoring it – is directly linked to a wider set of political values about freedom and choice, and the extent to which forms of popular culture embody either.

The politics of the text

All the previous examples of linkages between politics and popular culture recognize the claim that popular culture can in some way express political ideas and values. This assumption draws attention to the most obvious sense in which popular culture is political: its use as a forum for political propaganda. From the political songs of John Lennon and Bob Dylan to the movies of Oliver Stone and John Sayles, popular culture has used its various media to make political statements. Indeed, popular culture can be viewed as the site of the liveliest and most radical of political exchanges, certainly when compared to the political discussions which are heard in many representative assemblies or which litter daily newspapers. While the form and character of popular culture does not always allow for detailed or lengthy exposition, and while its profundity depends more on rhetoric than on argument, it can still constitute a political forum.

The politics of a text can reveal themselves in a variety of ways. The first, and most obvious, is in the explicit intentions of the artist. A film is produced, a song is composed, a play written to make a political point. The political sympathies may take any form, from a benign humanism (as in, say, Tom Hanks' performance in *Philadelphia*) to a self-conscious class analysis (Sayles' *City of Hope*) or racial conflict (Spike Lee's *Do the Right Thing*); they may identify with any number of causes – AIDS, Bosnia, poverty, rainforests; and they may derive from a variety of ideological perspectives, from the left to the right. But whichever is the case, the politics are an overt part of the package. Yet even where the artist is explicit about his or her purpose, and where everything seems to confirm a single reading, no text escapes counter or multiple other readings. Alan Parker's film *Mississippi Burning* can be read as a liberal exposé of the Ku-Klux-Klan, southern segregation and white corruption. But the film contains another story. Its heroes are two FBI agents (Gene Hackman and Willem Dafoe), and the film portrays them, not the civil rights movement, as the defenders of equality. In short, just as the politics has to be encoded within the cultural form, so it has to be decoded, and in this process other stories may emerge. The obvious implication of this is that we can identify politics in a text that are not those of the artist or of the packaging, or at least not those acknowledged by either. And indeed it is the struggle over rival interpretations that is most revealing of the politics of the text.

Justin Lewis (1991) draws attention to the competing readings of one of America's most popular situation comedies, *The Cosby Show*. The programme is plotted around the experiences of the Huxtables, a middle-class black family. For critics of the show, the Huxtables are used to perpetuate the myth of social mobility and the belief that anyone can succeed. This central idea is reinforced by 'the close identification of Cliff Huxtable and Bill Cosby. Behind the fictional doctor lies a man whose real life is also a success story: fact and fiction coalesce to confirm the "truth" they embody' (Lewis, 1991: 162; his emphasis). Against this critique of *The Cosby Show* is the view that it is a dignified representation of black culture, set within a broadcasting system that is notoriously conservative and traditionally inhospitable to such programming. The show works by acknowledging the limits of its genre, while also subtly introducing political ideas (about South Africa, for instance, by naming the twins Winnie and Nelson). So it is that the show is claimed as 'one of the more progressive forces in popular culture to emerge from the United States in recent years' (Lewis, 1991: 166).

A parallel debate haunts hiphop, where the argument divides between those who see it as providing a legitimacy for homophobia, anti-semitism and misogyny (Samuels, 1991) and those who see it as an honest expression of black experience (Toop, 1984). There are yet others who see rap as containing conflicting and ambiguous political attitudes. Tricia Rose (1994: 103) writes: 'Attempts to delegitimate powerful social discourses are often deeply contradictory, and rap music is no exception. To suggest that rap lyrics, style, music, and social weight are predominantly counter-hegemonic . . . is not to deny the ways in which many aspects of rap music support and affirm aspects of current social power inequalities.' Or as Greg Tate (1992: 125) writes, 'To know Public Enemy is to love the agitprop (and artful noise) and to worry over the whack retarded philosophy they espouse.' As with arguments about *The Cosby Show*, rap provokes a similar range of contrary political readings.

When dealing with the politics of the text – whether revealed in intention or interpretation – the idea is that films, songs or whatever are a version of a political statement, an intervention in a debate or a plea for change or an endorsement of a position. In other words, they form part of well-established patterns of political discourse.

Popular culture as political gesture

Implicit in the use of popular culture as a political forum is an assumption about how the 'text' (the film, song, and so on) links to politics. The most obvious way to make this connection is through the idea that films or songs convey a political 'message', or represent some kind of political statement. Sometimes these messages are explicit parts of the text, as in a protest song or propaganda film. In each case the producers of the item are clear about its political intentions. But to read popular culture as a straightforward – or at least as a typical – political text is to take a very narrow view of its meaning, and hence of its political message(s). As we have noted, the text's meaning will depend on how it is heard and read. Michael Jackson may have intended his 'Earth Song' as an exercise in compassion; others – like Jarvis Cocker – saw it quite differently. One reason why these alternative readings emerge is because of the way the performance of popular culture engages more than a literal text, it deploys gestures and symbols, tones of voice, looks and glances, all of which may tell another story.

To illustrate this, I want to look at the politics of fashion and clothing. The way we dress is perhaps the most obvious way in which the formally inarticulate speaks volumes. From military uniform to punk bondage gear, clothes represent more than the need to keep warm and dry. They set in motion a whole range of ideas and feelings. This is someone recalling life in the early 1960s in Britain: 'I got caned for wearing a duffle-coat. I insisted on buying a duffle-coat and wearing it to school, and it was an offence to wear a duffle-coat, a caneable offence' (Everett, 1986: 41). The problem was not, of course, the coat in itself (an innocent enough woollen item, fastened by toggles); the problem was its association with the Campaign for Nuclear Disarmament and student radicalism. And this is Peter York (1984: 15) writing about Margaret Thatcher: 'She wears career lady suits with lapels and those bows and cravats which are a kind of pretend tie. Her hair is lacquered into Britannia's golden helmet, her voice is stronger, slower, deeper. . . . It all shows she's in control of herself.' This self-control symbolized a wider power: over her Cabinet, over a nation. Other fashions convey other messages. Dave Laing reflects upon the way punks used the safety-pin as a disturbing form of jewellery, piercing their flesh with it. Its use 'was a jolt to conventional ideas of facial appearance, and to the role of the face in interpersonal relations, where it is the first point of reference in making contact. Mutilation with pins, plus the "unnatural" colours of hair and make-up, undermined the possibility of such contact being made' (Laing, 1985: 95). Karel Ann Marling (1994:

170) detected in Elvis Presley's clothes a traversing of racial boundaries:

> Back home they called Elvis Presley the 'Memphis Fash' for the zoot suit drape, the pink sport coat with the black velvet collar, and the pegged pants with darts up the legs that fell open to reveal a pink lining, all bought at Lansky Brothers, where white kids rarely ventured. His taste in clothes suggests a fine disregard for impediments to social movement across lines of class and race.

The use of fashion – whether to sustain or subvert established convention – is not new. Elizabeth Wilson discusses the complicated and contradictory messages that became attached to dandyism in the nineteenth century. As a fashion, it borrowed from eighteenth-century country and sporting wear, evolving tight-fitting breeches and moulded jackets. This style was accompanied by an obsessively polished perfection, and a pose of studied indifference which conveyed a disdain for politics: 'The dandies invented Cool' (Wilson, 1985: 182). But when dandyism was transferred to France, it became imbued with a highly political symbolism. As Wilson (1985: 182) explains: 'Dandyism crossed the English channel, where it was taken up by the *Incroyables*, the avant-garde of French post-revolutionary youth. They transformed it into the counter-uniform of the new republican politics, while the *Merveilleuses*, their female counterparts, pushed Englishwomen's informal, uncorseted muslin dresses towards classical Greek garb: this signalled republican democracy by recalling ancient Athens and Rome.' In a similar vein, Wilson (1985: 162–5) draws atten-tion to the way in which women's wearing of trousers acquired a range of connotations in the early part of this century – as symbolic of immorality, of working-classness, of lesbianism and feminism. Such symbolic meaning lay behind bans on women in trousers at Ascot Races (until the 1970s) and in certain professions.

The idea that fashion 'speaks' for a set of radical or conservative ideas encourages the thought that popular culture furnishes a gestural politics, one in which your appearance, your image, matters in (politically) significant ways. Indeed, such an idea is central to the habit of politicians and their advisers to be most concerned about presentation, about how they *look* and *sound*. This is an issue which is considered further in the next chapter. For the moment, it is sufficient to note the politics to be detected in the gestural language of popular culture, and its use to disrupt or confirm expectations.

The politics of identity

Underlying the way fashion works, and the way it assumes a political significance, is the thought that it helps to constitute an identity. The sounds and styles, the words and images, of popular culture gain their political meaning through the way they form part of an identity which entails a particular view of the world, and which is part of a performance, a way of being. The politics is less a direct product of the text *as text*, but rather one of the interplay of text and context. Identity is a key dimension to contemporary political life, a point made most forcefully by the rise of nationalism, but also deeply implicated in the politics of ethnicity, gender and sexuality. People's sense of themselves has direct consequences for the way they view their interests and their relations with others. And popular culture is often linked to the constitution of identity and its politics. Simon Frith (1996: 272) describes music as creating a form of self-consciousness in the way it brings together 'the sensual, the emotional and the social as performance'. 'Pop tastes', he continues (1996: 276), 'do not just derive from our socially constructed identities; they also help to shape them.' Frith suggests that music is an especially potent medium in the realization of identity, but this is not to rule out other cultural forms. For example, Harry Jenkins (1992: 214–15) writes about how female fans of *Star Trek* use their obsession to tell stories of female experience.

The 'politics' here is often 'personal', in the sense that it seems to be about cultural preferences and tastes, but its implications extend outwards, establishing the ways in which identities are part of an attempt to assert a particular way of being in the world for which alternative readings and role models are crucial. In exploring British black experience, Paul Gilroy (1993: 38) writes about how 'the artefacts of a pop industry premised on the individual act of purchase and consumption are hijacked and taken over into the heart of a collective identity of protest and affirmation which in turn define the boundaries of the interpretative community.' This process of appropriation finds expression in a politics that is

characterized by its antipathy to the institutions of formal politics. Instead, it aspires to a politics of 'autonomy and independence from the system' (Gilroy, 1993: 44).

Crucial to popular culture's ability to provide an alternative
framework and an identity is the way it reorganizes time and
memory. Identities draw upon both: a sense of being in control, a
sense of having a past or a place. Such ideas animate Paul Willis'
(1978) famous account of bike boy culture. The bike boys' love of
rock'n'roll derives from an attempt to 'subvert bourgeois, industrial, capitalist notions of time'. Theirs is an attempt to create a
time-frame that makes possible a different rhythm and way of
life, one that moves at their pace. George Lipsitz (1990) also focuses upon time in his account of popular culture's politics. He
places the emphasis on memory, on the way the past constitutes
present identities. The past and the present are linked through
films, television and music. They are part of a political struggle, a
struggle to remember and retain a populist past against a dominant view which either denies or reinterprets that past. Films can
do this without being 'true': 'We require "true" lies, depictions of
the past and present that are comprehensible to us and that locate
our own private stories within a larger collective narrative' (Lipsitz,
1990: 163). In giving life to memory, popular culture sustains an
explanation of how things are the way they are, and from this
people recover a sense of themselves. This negotiation with history is most apparent in Hollywood epics like *The Last of the
Mohicans* or *Dances with Wolves*, but it also happens elsewhere.
Paul Gilroy (1993: 42) talks of how Britain's black poor live an
expressive culture which contains 'a potent historical memory and
an authoritative analytical and historical account of racial capitalism and its overcoming'.

In these accounts of the collective meaning attributed to popular culture, the politics exists in the creation of a group, a 'community' around which people establish their similarities and
differences (their identities), communities that exist in memory
and in the passage of time.

The politics of production

Up until now, we have located the politics of popular culture in the ways in which it is used, whether by audiences or artists, and the ways it is interpreted, whether by audiences or commentators. And this focus reflects the rough outlines of the 'politics of popular culture' as they are conventionally understood. It is, however, a focus that overlooks an important dimension: the politics of production. Here the politics cannot be read directly off the text or the uses to which it is put or the intentions of the artist, although there may be signs and clues of the politics of production in each. Production involves the organization of cultural industries, broadcasting institutions and the regulations that apply to each, and the politics that emerge in the balance of interests and power, as well as the values and judgements, that go into the creation and distribution of popular culture. The range of identities or political views or uses to be found within political culture is not infinite. Some are more accessible, more available than others. And the limits and constraints that operate are a crucial part of the politics of production.

The politics is located in the views and forms of cultural expression that are marginalized or excluded, whether through direct censorship or through routine practices. Popular culture cannot exist without the industry that produces and distributes it. By the nature of its operation it passes judgement upon a range of cultural possibilities, allowing some to exist and others to be consigned to be ignored. The judgements, insofar as they operate systematically, represent a set of views and/or interests, and promote these to the disadvantage of others. They can be found in the way copyright laws favour certain types of artistic work; or the ways in which broadcasting policy gives air space to some performers and not others; or the ways zoning decisions can discriminate in favour of some kinds of entertainment. They can be found in the way culture is mediated by journalists and broadcasters.

Decisions are made daily about what programmes to make, what films to show, and what musicians to record. These decisions are themselves overlaid by countless others about delivering on these projects, about what resources, division of labour and distribution of power are appropriate. These decisions, and many more like them, are routinized into the common sense of the organizations and individuals who take them. Such systems represent the working out of a political order which has profound implications for popular culture.

The results can be detected in the films that are made (and not made), by the sounds that are heard (and those that are silenced). These, in turn, shape how the world looks and feels, and how we fit within it. Mostly these processes result in a culture which replicates what has gone before, reworking familiar formulae, but sometimes it emerges as the unexpected and the unsettling, when the usual order is disturbed. At this point the politics of production issue in a radical aesthetics. Susan McClary (1991) invests Madonna's music with such politics by focusing on the way that conventional song structures or melodies are refused. Henry Louis Gates (1987: 243) writes of how parody subverts and appropriates the meaning of a song: 'Repetition of a form and then inversion of the same through a process of variation is central to jazz. A stellar example is John Coltrane's rendition of "My Favorite Things" compared to Julie Andrews' vapid original.' Or as the young members of Asian Dub Foundation proclaim: 'You could have a seriously political album with not one word on it. . . . We're challenging people's notion of what Asian music is. . . . The politics, challenging people, is built into the structure of the music, as well as the lyrics' (quoted in Jackson, 1995: 17). The politics of production are a crucial dimension to the politics of popular culture. Later chapters explore the implications of this thought. Here I want merely to draw attention to the fact that in talking about the politics of popular culture, we have drawn – sometimes obviously, sometimes obliquely – upon different understandings of what is meant by *politics* itself.

The politics of politics

'Politics' is often used to describe disagreements about who gets what, when and how. Included in this is the idea that politics refers not only to the process by which such disagreements are settled – how scarce goods are distributed – but also to the values that inform arguments about how such goods *should* be distributed. This account of politics incorporates the constitutions, institutions and ideologies that are the traditional fare of political studies. But the dimensions of politics can be made to extend further. Since political processes involve competing perceptions of what is 'good' – for individuals or for groups – definitions of politics include the ways in which the 'good' is conceptualized, as well as the process by which some versions receive more or less attention than others (see Connolly, 1993: 12–13). How such claims are conceived, recognized and legitimated (or marginalized and denied) depends upon how social groups are organized and how their claims are articulated and represented. The ability to do this is a product not simply of formal political mechanisms, but of the way images and ideas are produced, reproduced and circulated. Such processes affect the way people think of themselves and their interests, and hence the demands they express or fail to express. And in doing this, 'politics' breaches the final traditional barrier, that between the private and the public sphere, allowing for the claim that 'the personal is political'. The struggle to recognize and satisfy interests, to distribute goods and to judge their distribution, is not confined to the formal public arenas of politics, but takes place within the home and in daily routines.

'Politics', therefore, refers to many dimensions of social interaction – from the mediating role of institutions, to the expression of ideals, to the relationship between interests and identities. Politics extends beyond the formal boundaries of the constitution and the political processes as they are conventionally understood. It extends to the ways in which people see themselves and those around them. And it is this broader view of politics that establishes the place in politics occupied by popular culture, making the consumption and production of popular culture a political act. All these dimensions of politics are applied to popular culture. McClary (1994: 34), for example, argues that if the politics of music is 'limited to party politics, then music plays little role except to serve as cheerleader; if it involves specifically economic struggle, then the vehicle of music is available to amplify protest and to consolidate community.' Tricia Rose makes a similar point in her analysis of the politics of rap. She distinguishes between the exposed and the hidden politics in rap, arguing that both are crucial to comprehending the politics of the music. 'Political interpretations of rap's explosive and resistive lyrics', she writes, 'are critical to understanding contemporary black cultural politics, but they reflect only a part of the battle.' The other part, 'rap's hidden politics', exists in the 'struggle over access to public space, community resources, and interpretation of black expression' (Rose, 1994: 145).

The problem with this extended definition of politics is that it can lead to the claim that 'everything is political', which, while it has some rhetorical force in that it exposes the ubiquitous intervention and influence of interests and values, does not help us to distinguish between *types* of political value and *forms* of political interest. It does not recognize that how the public/private split is conceptualized or judged is itself the subject of competing claims (Phillips, 1991). Although making sense of the politics of popular culture means recognizing the permeability or artificiality of the divide between the public and the private, it does not help to conclude, therefore, that all popular culture is political and to use the word 'politics' to refer to anything and everything. Applying the words 'politics' and 'political' to all aspects of popular culture adds very little to our understanding, to our sense of what is changed or can be changed by popular culture, about whose or what interests are involved, and why.

It is not just that describing everything as 'political' thwarts our ability to talk of particular political processes. Applying the word 'political' to all aspects of culture impairs our understanding of culture as well. Janet Wolff argues that not everything can be subsumed within the category of politics, that 'aesthetics' exercises a rival pull, establishes a different field, which must be acknowledged in discussion of culture. As Wolff (1983: 64) explains, culture is inevitably 'political': 'The central point is still that all works of art, being produced in a political–historical moment by particular, located people using established forms of representation cannot fail to be, however implicitly, about politics.' But, she goes on (1983: 65), 'it does not follow that aesthetics and politics are the same thing, nor that art is merely politics represented in symbolic form.' In other words, we need to avoid any crude reductionism in identifying the politics of popular culture; rather, we need to distinguish between types of politics and political process, as well as acknowledging that popular culture is not simply politics conducted by other means.

CHAPTER THREE

Politics as popular culture

Politics today is a minor form of showbiz, governed by the
same shoddy principles. Shame and guilt are left-overs
from fuddyduddyism; all exposure – even if what's exposed is yourself in a borrowed flat committing adultery,
while gamely attired in a Chelsea football shirt – is good.
Peter Conrad on David Mellor MP, 'The Soul of a Disc
Jockey', *Independent on Sunday*, 21 April 1996

A market research company reported recently on popular perception of British political parties. It discovered that:

> When voters think of the Tories, they smell pipe tobacco and old
> churches. . . . They taste cream teas, feel leather armchairs and hear
> retired colonels snoring. When they think of Labour, they hear brass
> bands and northern accents, taste chips and pints of bitter, feel bro-
> ken glass and smell men sweating. The Liberal Democrats put the
> electorate in mind of the sound of doves' wings, the smell of sand-
> wich spread, the feel of Crimplene and the taste of muesli. (*Daily
> Telegraph*, 29 November 1996)

These findings were produced by techniques traditionally applied
to consumer goods of various kinds. This was the first time they
had been applied to political parties. But though it may seem a
bizarre development, there is a coherent logic to it. Parties and
politicians are increasingly marketing and packaging themselves
to attract voters, using the same devices as advertisers deploy for

perfumes and cars. Much political time is taken up in garnering the right image, in acquiring the right odour. (Labour, it appears, is working on ousting the smell of sweat and replacing it with that of lime.) Popular culture is a crucial intermediary in this ambition.

In 1996, Tony Blair, leader of the Labour Party, gave a speech of fulsome tribute. It was not to celebrate some great event or tradition in the labour movement's history, nor was it to announce plans for export-led growth or indeed for any other worthy political initiative. He was speaking at a music industry awards ceremony, and he was there to praise David Bowie. What was a leading politician, someone tipped to be the next Prime Minister, doing taking on the role normally fulfilled by fading rock stars like Michael Hutchence or Bob Geldof? The answer was, of course, quite straightforward. He was working on his image; he was soliciting votes; he was using popular culture as part of his political armoury. It is a familiar sight these days, politicians cuddling up to the icons of popular culture. Bill Clinton has become famous for the White House's star-studded guest list (from Robin Williams to Michael Jordan). The Republicans have a different take on the use of stars. When George Bush was President, the Chairman of the Republican National Committee, Lee Atwater, brought together some of the key figures in the history of American black music. The event, though, was not about winning votes. According to Greg Tate (1992: 101), 'The show was Atwater's way of paying homage to his beloved rhythm and blues, and a way of educating his fellow Republicans about the African-American musical tradition.'

It is not surprising, of course, that these gestures, whatever their intention, are interpreted as cynical exercises in opportunism. Giles Smith (1996: 269) observes slyly:

> Shortly after he succeeded the late John Smith as leader of the Labour Party, Tony Blair was asked in an interview what kind of pop music he liked. . . . Mr Blair came up with REM, Seal and Annie Lennox. I'm prepared to believe he fired these names off the top of his head, that these are indeed the three acts whose tapes are in ceaseless rotation on Mr Blair's in-car stereo. Yet if the party had commissioned an expensive advertising agency to spend seven months in collaboration with a public-relations firm researching this declaration, it's hard to believe they would have come up with anything so beautifully poised. REM, Seal and Annie Lennox: an American rock group and two British singers, one black male, one

white female, with fingers in pop, soul and dance, an ample musical spread, economically achieved.

It is, though, always possible to read a politician's behaviour in this light, whatever he or she gets up to. And indeed such a view is reinforced by the stars with whom they are allied. Rather than a match made in heaven, the relationship of popular culture and politicians often resembles a marriage of convenience. The musician Paul Weller reflected witheringly upon his experience of Red Wedge, an attempt to promote the Labour Party with the aid of pop music: 'They were a bunch of wankers, looking back on it. The Labour Party people as well. It wasn't me at all, I'm not into meetings and being part of somebody's club. . . . We'd meet MP's around the country and they were more showbiz than the groups' (du Noyer, 1995: 86). Politicians can be equally wary. John Redwood – one-time Cabinet minister and rival to John Major as leader of the Conservative Party – once wrote: 'I don't sing Oasis hits in the bath, nor do you catch me humming Supergrass behind the Speaker's chair. . . . Let me declare firmly my lack of credentials. I do not admire middle-aged trendies who pretend to a second teenage by strenuously enjoying modern stars.' (*The Guardian*, 23 March 1996). But whatever the mutual mistrust, politicians continue to make use of popular culture, a use that has a considerable history.

British politicians have made every effort to link themselves to the success of the Beatles. Labour's Harold Wilson awarded them medals; his opponent Edward Heath praised them for their contribution to the British fashion industry; and John Major gave Paul McCartney a knighthood. In the United States, presidential candidates have depended on rock musicians and film stars to raise money for their campaigns and to enhance their image. The desire of some politicians for publicity seems to know few limits – for the TV cameras, British politicians have been prepared to don a bear costume for an interview, or to sketch maps of their constituency on the naked stomach of a young woman (although they draw the line at dressing up as an eight-foot penis) (*The Guardian*, 14 February 1996). These tasks were set by a TV show hosted by the comedian Mark Thomas. The satirizing of politicians' craving for publicity was taken a stage further by Chris Morris', *Brass Eye*, a parody of current affairs broadcasting, in which politicians were duped into commenting on non-existent social evils. For example, Morris invented a new illegal drug called 'cake', and the deluded politicians issued dire warnings about its dangers. So it has continued, with the connection between the worlds of popular culture and politics becoming ever more intimate.

The relationship takes three forms. First, politicians have simply tried to associate themselves with popular culture and its icons, in the hope that some of the popularity will rub off. They have, therefore, made themselves available to popular culture; hence Bill Clinton played the saxophone on MTV, and Blair's predecessor, Neil Kinnock, appeared in pop videos and on children's TV shows. Margaret Thatcher graced chat shows and discussed her taste in clothes. In the same spirit, the 1996 US presidential contender, Bob Dole, borrowed Gary Glitter's 'Rock and Roll (Part 2)' for his rallies, as before him George Bush used country star Randy Travis (Freedland, 1996). Meanwhile in Russia, Viktor Chernomyrdin availed himself of MC Hammer.

The second form in which politicians have embraced popular culture has been in the blending of commercial and political interests. This is most dramatically symbolized by the rise to power of Silvio Berlusconi, the Italian media tycoon, whose political career was orchestrated by his television stations. Here popular culture has provided the basis for political success. Less blatantly, other politicians have recognized the commercial importance of popular culture, and have seen it necessary to both fête and favour it. They have, in particular, acted to protect its source of revenue through the promise of tape levies, or trade barriers, or copyright reform.

The third and final form of the relationship between popular culture and conventional politics is witnessed in the way politicians have come to rely upon the techniques and methods of popular culture in the performance of their political role. The most familiar example of this is the career of Ronald Reagan, which took him from Hollywood to the White House. Most politicians aspire to less grand models than film stars (even B-movie ones), and draw instead upon the chat-show host as the embodiment of trust and of easy communication. Staged events in which they are required to interact with 'ordinary' voters are often designed to resemble the familiar formats of TV shows (Kavanagh, 1995). As Alan Schroeder (1996: 64) has noted: 'Televangelist, talk show host, news anchor, pundit, commercial pitchman – all are roles Bill Clinton has mastered and used to his advantage.' They paid off in

1992 because Clinton's populist 'New Television approach' tapped into contemporary viewing conventions in a way that Bush's 'Old Television – television from the mountain top' did not (Schroeder, 1996: 63). When Bob Dole lost to Clinton in the battle for the presidency in 1996, it was said that Dole's failure was partly a consequence of long, rambling speeches, which were short on soundbites. They just were not 'television friendly'.

In developing these techniques and approaches, politicians have come increasingly to call upon the skills and advice of those who practise the art of chat-show hosting or news reading. Party campaign teams are staffed by advertising executives and television producers. These people are not just giving guidance in the handling of publicity or providing copy for the adverts. Advertising professionals give lessons on posture and dress, on speech and mannerisms. They design telegenic conference sets and write speeches. When he was working for the Saatchi & Saatchi advertising company, Tim Bell tried in 1983 to create the right 'tone' for the Conservative Party, one that was 'warm, confident, non-divisive and exciting'. Political analysis and ad-speak became one language. But these advisers are not just helping to package politics, they are also helping to *make policy*. Writing about the role played by Peter Mandelson (then a television producer) and Philip Gould (an advertising executive) in transforming the Labour Party, Hughes and Wintour (1990: 183) say: 'they forged between themselves an approach to political strategy which has never before been seen – certainly in the Labour Party, and arguably, ever in British politics. They welded policy, politics and image-creation into one weapon.' Advertising techniques – like the 'focus group' – are used in assessing policy proposals, and indeed in developing them in the first instance. Market research now features explicitly in the strategy of parties. The talk is of 'directional research' and 'target areas'. This approach has been institutionalized within shifting party structures, assigning real power and responsibility to these advisers. And in the same way the 'common sense' of politics has adapted too. Politicians have developed the skills of persuasion and of advertising; Reagan even put a Hollywood gagman on the White House staff to provide a supply of suitable jokes (Maarek, 1995: 20). And if we seek further evidence of the trend, then we need look no further than the money invested in it. Advertising alone accounts for between a half and two-thirds of British parties' electoral budgets, with much of the rest being devoted to market research (Scammell, 1995: 144).

Together these three dimensions of the relationship between politicians and popular culture constitute a change in political practice. But to observe this change is not to tell us much about its significance or its effects. Does the use of popular culture merely indicate change in the instruments of politicians and parties, a change in means but not ends? Or does it indicate a transformation in politics as it has been traditionally practised?

These questions tend to be addressed under the general umbrella of the 'packaging of politics'. On both sides of the Atlantic, researchers have been charting the rise of media consultants and image makers; they have been monitoring the role of spin doctors and ad agencies in the changing styles and techniques of parties and politicians; they have observed the rise of campaign budgets and the spending on advertising; they have witnessed the increasing 'razzmatazz' of politics; and they have been arguing about the consequences for democracy. Thirty years on from Joe McGinniss' *The Selling of a President* (1969), we are no longer talking of the marketing of a single actor, but about the transformation of politics itself. The discussion is now of 'packaging politics' (Franklin, 1994) or 'designer politics' (Scammell, 1995), of the emergence of 'the electronic commonwealth' (Abramson, Arterton and Orren, 1988) and of 'mediated political realities' (Nimmo and Combs, 1990).

But while there is agreement about these general trends, there is much less consensus over their significance. There are those who argue that the use of such techniques has always been part of politics, and that, in any case, they improve the quality of political life (Scammell, 1995). Others (Abramson, Arterton and Orren, 1988; Kavanagh, 1995) take a more neutral stance. They contend that the new techniques are merely means to the same old ends – politicians have always used whatever techniques are available to communicate with voters and win them over. There are others who view the changes as malign, as threatening the quality of democratic life. Todd Gitlin (1991: 129), for instance, writes that while 'American politics has been raucous, deceptive, giddy, shallow, sloganeering and demagogic for most of its history', there are signs that it is getting worse. This, he says, is the result of the 'fascination with speed, quick cuts, ten-second bites, one-second "scenes" and out of context images [which] suggest less tolerance of the rigours of serious arguments and the tedium of organized political life' (Gitlin, 1991: 133). In a similar vein, Michael Billig and his colleagues (1993) argue that modern elections are characterized by the dominance of the image over the word, and that this is devaluing politics and consolidating the authority of the powerful.

For the critics, the increasing use of advertisers and their ilk has diminished seriously the quality of political life. They look upon recent developments with dismay. They see the intrusion of the values of popular culture and the techniques of marketing as vulgarizing political life. They do not always see popular culture as the *cause* of this degeneration, but as a powerful symbol of a larger shift in the quality and character of politics. Advertising provides the discourse which now links politicians to citizens. The relationship between leaders and led is essentially a commercial relation. As Nicholas Garnham (1986: 47–8) argues: 'Politicians relate to potential voters not as rational beings concerned for the public good, but in the mode of advertising, as creatures of passing and largely irrational appetite, to whose self-interest they must appeal.' Although Garnham is drawing attention to the larger process by which commercial interests are eroding public space, his argument depends upon claims about the diminished character of communications that are couched in the language of advertising.

In this chapter, I want to take issue with such criticisms, and I want to suggest that politics has always depended upon popular culture and that this relationship does not automatically diminish the quality of political discourse. However, it is not my view that politics is necessarily the beneficiary. Rather, we need, in fact, to develop a way of discriminating between forms of the relationship, to appreciate the different qualities of the connection and to judge it accordingly.

Politics is primarily a matter of 'performance' – it is about giving life and relevance to ideas, about evoking trust and claiming representativeness. This creates obvious affinities with popular culture. And just as there are bad performances in popular culture (where 'bad' can refer to any number of aspects, both technical and ethical), so there are bad political performances. In order to develop this case, I want first to examine the assertions of those who see politics being sullied by its association with the 'packaging' process. The voice of the critics, warning of the drowning of democracy under the combined weight of spin doctors, advertising agencies and the rest, has tended to dominate the debate, setting the agenda for those who wish to disagree. I will look first, therefore, at the particular claims of those who see politics as being damaged by being 'packaged'. My focus is on one recent example of this genre, Bob Franklin's *Packaging Politics* (1994).

Packaging politics

Franklin's book is a systematic attempt to chart the changing habits of politicians and their agents as they try to deploy the mass media and popular culture to their advantage. This relationship has, of course, been documented elsewhere, most obviously in America (for example, Jamieson, 1992). What distinguishes *Packaging Politics* is not its British focus, because there are precedents for that too (for example, Cockerell, 1988; Crewe and Harrop, 1986, and 1989), but its synthesis of the different trends and processes at play in the complex relationships between politics and the media.

Franklin is concerned not just to document the changes, but also to assess them. He is clearly disenchanted with what he sees as media manipulation, and is fearful of its consequences for democracy. This is most evident in the book's title, which draws on the idea that to package politics (in the same way that products are packaged) involves some diminution in quality, marked in part by the tendency to prioritize form over content. More strongly, 'packaging' suggests that, rather than the genuine item, we get an artificial or inauthentic product. The book's epigraph makes explicit its key theme. It is taken from J. S. Mill's essay on 'Civilization', written in 1836 (Mill, 1977). Mill bemoans the way in which success is judged by appearance rather than substance, 'mere marketable qualities become the object instead of substantial ones, and a man's labour and capital are expended less in doing anything than in persuading other people that he has done it. Our own age seems to have brought this evil to its consummation.' Mill's anxiety is translated by Franklin into the modern practice of 'packaging' politics. 'Packaging' is linked to 'marketing', and both carry the suggestion that they describe lesser or debased activities. 'Packaging' entails the implication that appearance counts for more than reality, that form subsumes content.

In expounding upon his main concerns – the increasing presence of the media and media-related techniques in politics –
Franklin draws attention to recent developments in the political
economy of the press and broadcasting in Britain. The political
trends are a consequence of commercial developments which forge
an even closer bond between politicians and media empires. Politicians have both the incentive and the opportunity to use the
media to advance their own particular interests. Franklin (1994:
49) writes:

> The growing number of newspaper monopolies, the enthusiasm of
> some politicians for statutory press controls, the increased use of
> censorship and central government's use of the Lobby for news
> management, the growth of free newspapers with their editorial
> reliance on non-journalistic sources of news and their financial re-
> liance on advertisers, the continuing influence for owners over edi-
> torial content and the expansion of local newspapers published by
> politicians, all signal a growing possibility for politicians to influ-
> ence the way in which political news is reported.

In these circumstances, there is a strong further incentive for the
'skilled and highly paid marketing and communications professionals' to become part of the political entourage (Franklin, 1994:
13). The merging of political ambition and marketing skill is forged,
finally, in the fact that 'image' has become, according to Franklin
(1994: 13), the key determinant of popular political choice: 'the
attractiveness of the marketed image of politicians and policies
has become at least as influential in winning public support as an
understanding of the policy itself.' Similarly, politicians are also
seen as creatures of the television age, people who, in the words
of Ken Livingstone, 'think in soundbites' (quoted in Franklin, 1994:
5). The same applies to central government, with its increasing
tendency to 'sell' policies by advertising. These developments are
seen by Franklin as damaging to democracy: parties should be
judged by their policies, not by their image; politicians should argue a case, not deliver a slogan; and governments need to persuade people of their good intention; instead people are subject to
mass management and manipulation.

For Franklin, the consequence of all these various uses of the
media – whether by politicians, parties or governments – is the
'packaging of politics'. But why is this idea so upsetting? The key,
I think, lies in the use of words like 'packaging' and 'marketing'

and 'designer'. These convey – in some minds, at least – a pejorative judgement. Packaging, in particular, is used to denote some form of deception: it is a device for distracting attention from the content, of presenting things in a way that fails to reflect their true character. The package is a trivial or superficial disguise. Packaging also suggests the devaluation of something that was once 'genuine' or 'authentic'; packaging is the mark of standardization.

The critics of packaging are appalled when they see ministers who are more concerned with the presentation of policy than with its principles. They see parties drawing up political agendas on the basis of what voters will 'buy' rather than what principle requires. They see politicians whose only real concern is their image. They see politicians who think and speak in catch-phrases like comedians and DJs. They see party bureaucrats whose only concern is how the party *looks* on the nightly news broadcasts.

For these critics, packaging produces a political system in which cynical politicians and their party managers seduce and delude the voters. The electorate are sold policies and parties just as they are sold film stars and the National Lottery. Politics is no longer a matter of democracy but a branch of marketing – and this is to be deplored. It is a world in which Mary Spillane of the image consultants Colour Me Beautiful delivers a lecture called 'Get Real – How to Turn the Voters On' to forty aspiring Conservative candidates.

Repackaging politics

But should we share Franklin's bleak view of the state of politics? Is 'packaging' politics to be regarded as a damaging process? There are four issues I want to raise in connection with Franklin's general argument: the cultural context of media–politics relations; the incentives for (and effects of) packaging; the possibility of separating form and content; and the political economy of mass media and popular culture. Each, I want to suggest, provides a better comprehension of what is going on in contemporary electoral politics and of its relationship with the packaging business.

First, the argument about the media's relationship with politics needs to be set within a broader cultural context. This can best be illustrated by reference to Franklin's fear of the soundbite. Rather than seeing it as a substitute for thought, the soundbite can be regarded as just another means by which politicians try to accommodate themselves to the medium in which they operate. This is, in one sense, no different from the way in which we all tailor our language to our audience or our setting. And, it might be added, politicians have always operated like this. Adapting to your audience and your medium is, as Scammell (1995: 17 and 272) suggests, an essential part of 'rational electioneering'. The soundbite is one in a long line of techniques that have been adopted by politicians. The current antipathy is just a reaction to change, and makes no more sense than arguing that we should renounce the microphone and return to the bullhorn.

But even if the soundbite marks a qualitative change (rather than a purely technical change), it has to be understood as part of a wider cultural shift. Ken Livingstone 'thinks in soundbites' because this is the form of address that his generation of politicians has learnt. Previous generations regarded the media with suspicion, as a dangerous beast to be treated warily. But for subsequent generations television and its language were part of the political furniture. Television provided a particular language for speaking to people, it supplied the conditions for a new form of populism (McGinniss, 1969; Nimmo and Combs, 1990: 52–71; Scammell, 1995: 50–1). In the sixties, mainstream mass communication was given a further political twist by its engagement with the counterculture, which also used symbols and gestures, images and signs, to convey its messages. The soundbite is, in this sense, just another version of the slogan, and like the slogans of the sixties – drop out, turn on – it is tailored to the medium, linked to techniques of marketing and cultural expression. This is not necessarily to excuse or celebrate it, but rather to see it as part of a larger cultural trend from which politics is not immune.

But even if this connection with sixties cultural politics is denied, or if the adoption of it is seen as a failing of particular politicians, there are still other reasons for looking less harshly upon the packaging of politics. This is the second issue I want to raise: there are strong incentives for packaging. These have less to do with the politicians and more to do with citizens. The lesson of the economic theorists of democracy, or public choice theorists generally, is that there are strong incentives for people to remain ignorant or uninterested in what their prospective representatives have to offer. These (dis)incentives derive from the costs of information. Detailed political information is costly to research and these costs are not counterbalanced by some clear return on the investment. It is necessary, therefore, for parties and politicians to present information in a 'cheap' form and for citizens to limit their 'expenditure'. The net effect of this can be 'packaged politics'. Parties emphasize, in Downs' (1957) argument, 'brand images' – slogans, logos, photo-opportunities, and so on; and citizens survey the paraphernalia, making judgements on the basis of personality and style, as they do in their viewing habits generally (Morley, 1992). As Scammell (1995: 18) writes: 'the marketing concept may possess intrinsic virtue precisely because, in principle, it makes politics more democratic.' Schroeder (1996: 59) points out that presidential debates 'make good television because they are personality driven, just as other programming genres are personality driven – from soap operas to newscasts to talk shows. For viewers, presidential candidates function as glorified television characters, regulars in long-running series.' And just as people pass judgement on the characters in soaps, so they judge political candidates.

This brings me to a third issue: the impossibility of separating form and content. For Franklin, citizens who act on the basis of images and soundbites are allowing form to get the better of content, to let the medium dominate the message. But such claims rest upon the possibility of distinguishing form and content, medium and message. And here too, I think there are reasons for scepticism. Style and image are, it might be argued, rich in meanings and messages. It is sometimes suggested that *seeing* John F. Kennedy argue with Richard Nixon during the 1960 presidential election campaign unfairly favoured the good-looking man over his perspiring rival, and the evidence for this is that radio listeners formed a different judgement. But can it really be claimed that radio is somehow 'more objective', allowing a 'truer' picture of the candidates? Surely it is the case that the two media provide *different* means of perceiving the candidates. In listening to an argument, we are hearing not just the words, but also the tones of voice, the silences and stutters; just as when we are watching, we take note of the movement of eyes and hands, the facial expressions and body language. The same is true of political communication. Schroeder (1996: 67) tells of the occasion when, due to a technical hitch, the Ford–Carter debate had to halt for twenty-seven minutes. The two candidates 'remained rooted to the spot, staring straight ahead'. Their behaviour raised real, and legitimate, questions about how either would cope in a crisis. Political messages are not simply products of the words being uttered; they are contained in gestures and in silences.

Finally, in reassessing the packaging of politics, we need to acknowledge the commercial context in which the process takes place. Early in his book, Franklin draws attention to the changing economics of newspapers and television, and in these remarks he hints at the consequences of economic change for politics. He does not, though, pursue this line of inquiry as fully as he might. The packaging of politics is a consequence of the 'packaging' of mass media. As Franklin acknowledges, the emphasis on style and image is partly a product of changing news values, themselves a product of the competitive and commercial pressure on broadcasters and newspapers. Those same pressures have prompted the decline in the direct coverage of politics, and its replacement by political commentators, people who write about politics as soap opera. The pressure to 'entertain' requires a shift in the way politics is covered and reported (Curran and Seaton, 1991). The point is to recognize the packaging of politics as part of a larger process which affects media generally, and which shifts the explanation for the new devices away from the parties and politicians and onto the media and the culture industry.

In raising these four issues about the packaging argument, I have been trying to make a general point about how the debate needs to be conducted and developed. The worries of those who see politics as being packaged, and the attempts at rebuttal, all point to a connection between political coverage and popular culture. In drawing attention to the wider context, it is apparent that understanding political communication means understanding popular forms of communication generally. Political communication cannot be separated from popular culture; it is not just about conveying information or about persuading people through the force of argument. It is about capturing the popular imagination, about giving acts and ideas symbolic importance. This means drawing on the techniques of those who are practised in these arts: advertisers and television producers; it also means borrowing from the rhetoric and practices of the populism that popular culture embodies.

This connection with popular culture emerges from the

points I have already made about Franklin's argument. First, there is the thought that techniques of political communication derive from the cultural context and assumptions of their practitioners; these are drawn in part from popular culture. Secondly, the creation of 'cheap information' is precisely what popular culture offers. Thirdly, the study of popular culture has revealed the ways in which style and imagery convey messages of political and cultural importance (Hebdige, 1979). And finally, the commercial pressure to produce image-conscious politics is the same pressure that is pushing news and entertainment into ever closer contact.

Making politics a branch of popular culture is, of course, what Franklin is committed to avoiding. It is possible to read *Packaging Politics* as part of a general critique of the debasement of culture. Franklin's tone and complaints echo those who – from the left and the right – have worried about the impact of popular culture. And anyone persuaded by these critiques of popular culture is unlikely to be very sanguine about the connection between popular culture and politics.

However, even if one is generally concerned about the effect and character of popular culture, this does not remove the need to study it in making sense of contemporary political communication. The newspapers and programmes that carry political information are themselves part of popular culture. So to establish whether or not the 'packaging' of politics is in fact deleterious to the quality of political life, we need to engage with arguments about the politics of popular culture generally. This means that even those who see the marketing of politics as having benign effects cannot see, as Scammell (1995) tends to, 'designer politics' as traditional politics conducted by other means. Politicians and parties are not simply using new techniques in an instrumental way, they are also being changed – in their language and their priorities, and in the way they are 'read' by their citizens.

Performing politics

There are certain things that follow from the preceding argument. All politics is packaged, and the point is not to distinguish between the 'authentic' and the 'inauthentic', the 'contrived' and the 'genuine'. What needs to be done instead is to work at discriminating between *types of packaging*, to make judgements and assessments of the packages. Just as there is good and bad popular culture, so there are good and bad forms of packaging. The implication of this is that we need to look at the way audiences can be addressed and constituted, to see how different forms of political involvement can be created by the format and style of interviews, by the codes and genres of the media's political discourse (Corner, 1995). Simply, the 'packaging' of politics is determined in part by the 'packaging' of television programmes. And in making sense of this, we also need to heed the context within which it is happening: the commercial and other interests which organize our papers and our broadcasting system.

We may, in the end, conclude that politics is being packaged in ways that harm our democracy. But this is a conclusion that can only be reached once we have looked more closely at the character and quality of the packaging process, at the meanings it supplies and the responses it elicits. To do this, we need to recognize the way political communication borrows from, and cohabits with, popular culture.

Political discourse is rarely, if ever, the disinterested examinations of political values and ideas. And the language of such discussion is itself part of the political debate: political discourse is a form of *performance* in which ideas and values are represented, in which speakers try to present themselves as 'trustworthy' or 'compassionate' or 'concerned'. The way we understand particular words or images is shaped by the way they are conveyed. What were the trials of O. J. Simpson if not elaborate performances, however real and tragic the circumstances to which they referred? Following the trial of mass-murderer Rosemary West, witnesses re-enacted their evidence for the newspapers. In doing so they gave a performance; they acted out their role in the plot. When the Princess of Wales was interviewed on the current affairs programme *Panorama* she too performed – in the way she chose and uttered her words, in the way she averted her eyes. Each of these performances worked within a set of conventions or rules that enable certain sounds and images to take on meaning. And one key source of these rules and conventions is popular culture. Politicians use the model of the chat-show host precisely because the latter evokes a sense of trustworthy authority.

Conclusion

In judging politics' use of marketing devices, we should not simply react with blanket dismissal. Rather we need to discriminate
in the same way that we discriminate in popular culture. We need
to judge the quality of the performance. We do not need to be
committed to any crude, populist measure of 'success'. Just as sales
or audience figures are not themselves proof of the quality of culture, so the number of votes cast are not an automatic indicator of
political quality (this would make all demagogues into great politicians). Equally, judgement of culture is not a matter of pure
aesthetics; there are moral and political values also entailed.
Furthermore, judgement does not issue directly from clearly established criteria or traditional canons; they, like the performances
being judged, are the product of the moment, of the concatenation
of many diverse features of the event and its witnesses. Performances within politics have a similar character and need. Some politicians 'work' their audiences better, have a more effective rapport
with 'the folks'. Their ability to do this is not just a matter of what
interests and ideologies they represent, but how they convey and
symbolize those interests and ideologies. Politics, like popular
culture, is about creating an 'audience', a 'people' who will laugh
at their jokes, understand their fears and share their hopes. Both
the popular media and politicians are engaged in creating works
of popular fiction which portray credible worlds that resonate with
people's experiences. To this extent, therefore, political performance has to be understood in similar terms to those applied to
popular culture.

But in appreciating these similarities in their discourses and techniques, we also need to understand their context; that is, the changing political economy of mass media and popular culture. The
uses to which popular culture is put, and the incentives which
underlie them, are produced by the changing structures and practices within the culture industries. The relationship between politics and popular culture is framed by these, and any attempt to
make sense of it must refer to this larger context. This is the concern of the next three chapters; I return to the question of judgement later in the book.

PART TWO

Governing Global
Culture

CHAPTER FOUR

All around the world:
the global politics of
popular culture

Charlie Chaplin, Big Bird, and Marcel Proust may have
little else in common, but they are all figures in a cosmo-
politan culture that, for the first time in history, embraces
the globe.
          Ithiel de Sola Pool, *Technologies Without Borders*

It is easy to think of the politics of popular culture as simply the
product of its economics; and to think of its economics as the result of the market strategies of global corporations. Popular culture has, after all, often been used to symbolize globalization. It is
pointed out that its icons can be found throughout the world. Mel
Gibson or Madonna are as well known in Brazil as in Belgium;
Guns'n'Roses or *Jurassic Park* draw huge audiences in Tokyo and
in Toronto. The pervasiveness of popular culture, its apparently
universal appeal, stands for the existence of a global culture, one
that transcends or transforms national cultures. Seen like this,
popular culture might seem to be denuded of politics. The machinery of political administration is presumed to play no part in
the character or content of popular culture. It is not just nations
that are transcended by global industries; politics is too.

This, though, is a highly misleading impression. We need only
to recall the wrangling in the last round of the GATT (General
Agreement on Tariffs and Trade) negotiations over whether the
film industry should be included in free trade agreements (and
the final decision that it be exempted) to illustrate that politics is

an inextricable part of any global order and that things are often less global, and more parochial, than they appear. None the less, there is an important truth in the notion of globalization. Much contemporary popular culture does emanate from corporations which span the world, and whose power and products can be detected everywhere. If we are to understand the relationship between politics and popular culture, then we cannot afford to overlook the industry, and we must not let the economics obscure our sight of the politics.

It is easy to see why the political dimension has been ignored, especially in relation to popular culture. The thought that popular culture and its market have been universalized – that the same artists, films or television programmes are consumed in London, New York and Paris, and that they are marketed by the same group of transnational corporations – leads to the view that politics is irrelevant. There are two elements to this claim. The first is that there are no effective political controls or institutions at the global level, only the corporations with their purely commercial interests. The second is that at the level at which political controls do exist, at the national or sub-national level, the responsible organizations are powerless. Attempts to resist the intrusion of transnational corporations, in the name of local culture or economic autonomy, inevitably fail. For some this is a fact to be celebrated, for others a source of profound regret. Ithiel de Sola Pool, for example, argued that attempts to resist globalization are bound to fail, and indeed deserve to fail. 'Restrictions', he wrote (1990: 148), 'are likely to be only delaying factors'; they just slow progress towards 'a new freedom'. By contrast, Herbert Schiller (1996: 116– 18) talks gloomily of the 'flattening out' of public debate and growing inequality as a result of new communication systems. Both de Sola Pool and Schiller agree about the shift in power; they disagree in their reaction to it.

The point of this chapter (and the two that follow it) is to reassert the importance of politics in the development and dissemination of popular culture. My focus here is on the idea of globalization, not because I think it is necessarily the most accurate characterization of the locus of power in popular culture, but because it directs attention to a key debate in the discussion of the political economy of popular culture – that is, the claim that we are witnessing the homogenization of national cultures and the erosion of local differences. This chapter assesses these claims and asks whether changes in popular culture occur despite, or because of, political processes.

My analysis begins from the assumption that the production and distribution of popular culture is of fundamental importance to the experience of consuming it. Nice though it might be to adopt the populist line that culture is what we – as fans, as consumers – make of it, that we can refashion it to suit our purposes through what Paul Willis (1990) describes as 'symbolic creativity', the reality is rather different. Or rather the ability to use culture in this way depends on many prior conditions. This is to adopt an argument most boldly stated by Simon Frith (1988a: 6–7) when he writes:

> My starting point is that what is possible for us as consumers – what is available to us, what we can do with it – is a result of decisions made in production, made by musicians, entrepreneurs and corporate bureaucrats, made according to governments' and lawyers' rulings, in response to technological opportunities. The key to 'creative consumption' remains an understanding of those decisions, the constraints under which they are made and the ideologies that account for them.

In examining claims based around 'globalization', we need to look at the conditions under which culture is produced, distributed and consumed, and particularly at their political dynamics. I want to draw attention to what is too often omitted from accounts of popular culture: that political institutions are involved at a variety of levels in its organization, and that, as a consequence, glib talk of globalization should be heavily qualified. We need to begin, though, by looking carefully at what is being claimed in the name of globalization.

Globalization

Marjorie Ferguson (1992: 71) defines globalization as 'a more visible and powerful supernational order, a "world system" . . . , that shifts many former national concerns to the world geopolitical stage.' John Thompson (1996: 150) identifies three particular implications of this process: '(a) activities take place in an arena which is global or nearly so (rather than regional, for example); (b) activities are organized, planned or coordinated on a global scale; and (c) activities involve some degree of reciprocity and interdependency, such that localized activities situated in different parts of the world are shaped by one another.' In other words, globalization describes a shift in the location of power and an increase in interdependence. These definitions do not make the nation state redundant, but they do indicate a new context within which it must be viewed. It is important to note, however, that to see globalization as a shift in the location of power does not automatically assume an accompanying process of cultural unification and standardization. As Mike Featherstone explains, there is no inscribed logic which requires an inexorable movement towards 'cultural homogeneity and integration'. Indeed he is sceptical of any approach to culture that views it as either homogenizing or fragmenting, preferring instead to see such possibilities as 'frames of reference for comprehending culture' (Featherstone, 1990: 1–2). Part of the reason why we need to be wary of the possible misreadings of globalization is that the term itself has been borrowed by the rhetoricians of the political right who seek to represent the world in a particular way: as being driven by market forces, as signifying the end of the state. Globalization may describe an ideal rather than a real predicament (Scott, 1997). 'Globalization' has, therefore, to be viewed with a certain caution, and its existence or its form should not be assumed. It contains many competing ideas and processes, and the extent to which it transcends politics, or can be made subject to it, depends upon a more detailed analysis of the phenomenon.

Such an analysis needs to recognize the different dimensions of globalization. One dimension is that of production, the means by which cultural artefacts are manufactured or made. Another dimension is the product itself. It is, after all, possible to have control over the methods of production and distribution without making that product universally available and accessible. Transnational corporations are often responsible for selling national or local culture back to the nation or the locality. French films shown in France sometimes have American distributors; African popular music is marketed in Africa by European conglomerates like EMI or BMG. If, on the other hand, the definition of global culture focuses on the product, then globalization would be defined as the distribution of a single product across the globe. A third dimension of globalization can be found in consumer taste and practices. The fact that the same product is made available everywhere is no guarantee that it achieves the same success or popularity (let alone acquires the same significance or meaning). In short, globalization can apply to production, distribution or consumption – and within each dimension, politics will assume a different guise and will have different consequences for the character of popular culture.

Global production

The popular culture industry has changed dramatically in the last decade. One measure of this change is the way in which 'globalization' has become part of the industry's rhetoric. Keith Negus (1992: 5) reports how, for example, Time Warner sees itself as 'feeding the [global] appetite for information and entertainment'; and how, in the company's own words, 'Sony is global.' Taking the record industry as one instance of this trend, we can see how consumers across the world are spending large sums on the purchase of records. In 1992, world sales of records netted $28.7 billion, of which the USA contributed 31 per cent, the EU 32 per cent and Japan 15 per cent. According to the British Phonographic Industry (1993: 55–6), 'the major areas of growth over the next ten years or so will be in the Far Eastern Markets and Pacific basin territories.' In 1982, sales of music in Singapore generated $6.5 million; in 1988, they were worth $31.3 million (IFPI, 1990: 85). Sales in South Korea in 1992 were worth $471 million and in Taiwan $326 million (BPI, 1993: 55). And the products upon which this money was being lavished were manufactured by a group of five corporations who together have rights in 70 per cent of all music bought (Negus, 1992: 1).

These corporations are part of larger conglomerates with interests in many other forms of popular culture. Rupert Murdoch's News Corporation has stakes in satellite and terrestrial television, films, books and newspapers in the USA, the UK, Australia and Hong Kong. The Sony Corporation, owners of Columbia Records, Tri-Star and Columbia Pictures, is perhaps the most telling example of this phenomenon. With its operating headquarters in Japan and the USA, Sony not only has the rights over a vast range of sound recordings and films, it also has major interests in the production of music and films. These are linked so that Sony soundtracks accompany their cinema releases. But this is not the end of the story. Sony is a major player in the market for the hardware that reproduces these products (CD players, video machines, and so on). Similarly integrated marketing characterizes the Disney Corporation's endeavours. *The Lion King*, for example, tied together Burger King, Toys R Us and Kodak, and produced endless spin-offs (books, records, meals, games, and so on) (Schiller, 1996: 114). National industries inevitably feel the pressure from these global players. Paul Rutten (1991: 295) describes the predicament of the Dutch recording industry: 'the recording and marketing of local artists has, throughout that industry's development, been only one of its activities. At present, the principal activity of Dutch recording firms – both majors and independents – is that of distributing and marketing foreign, mainly American products.' It seems, therefore, that the international production of popular culture is part of a transnational corporate system (see Tunstall and Palmer, 1991).

Global distribution

But the appearance of globalization does not end with the manufacturing of products. It extends into distribution. The networks that make the product available – the retailers, the cinemas, the television channels – are also part of another (often the same) transnational network. This is especially true of television, a crucial carrier of popular culture. As Annabelle Sreberny-Mohammadi (1991: 125) observed, 'Ted Turner's Cable News Network is received by the Kremlin and the Islamic Republics, and *Dallas* enjoys an international audience in over 90 countries.' CNN is now part of the Time Warner conglomerate, and Turner is its Vice-President.

As more television is transmitted by satellite, less significance attaches to national borders and the presumption of national control. The technologies of cultural distribution seem to enhance the new global order. National governments appear to be almost powerless to determine what their citizens view. Even totalitarian states seem to be thwarted. In the old Eastern bloc, pictures and images of Western life (and then the political uprisings in their own countries) were available to the citizens of these regimes, despite attempts by their governments to deny access. The same problem was encountered in the West, where the British government could present only a token barrier to pornographic channels such as Red Hot Television, T.V. Exotica and Rendez Vous. National governments are also engaged in a rearguard action to defend national culture and sports against the effects of powerful broadcasting and entertainment interests. They have attempted to impose quotas on 'foreign' culture and to prevent certain sporting events from being granted exclusively to pay-to-view and non-public service broadcasters, but it appears that control of the distribution of popular culture is slipping from the grasp of national governments. Certainly, this seems to be Canada's experience, where efforts to protect a national popular culture have been met with limited success (Berland, 1991; Grenier, 1993; Straw, 1993).

Global consumption

Time Warner once adopted the slogan 'The World is Our Audience'. There are two ways of viewing this aspiration to global consumption. The first is to talk of a single, common culture; the second is to talk of a global multiculturalism, where consumers pick and choose from an array of cultural forms and styles. As we have seen, it does not follow automatically that, because the carriers of popular culture are controlled by one set of interests or by a small cartel, they propagate an identical culture. The same corporation can own channels in Japan and the USA, but there is no necessary presumption that they will show the same programmes. There is, however, some evidence for both versions of global consumption.

The first can be seen in the apparently universal success of certain products or artists. Performers like Julia Roberts or Whitney Houston, or film-makers like Steven Spielberg, are launched onto a global stage. U2 and Bruce Springsteen set out on *world* tours. Meanwhile, MTV's declared ambition is 'One Planet, One Music'. The corollary of this picture of global consumption is the decline of regional or national tastes. Record companies, film-makers and publishers are less interested in works that they see as being aimed at a single market. For British writers or artists, this often means appealing to a US audience. The domestic market, the argument runs, is not sufficient to generate a profit. For people in other European countries, it means deciding which language to use, and to feel the pressure to communicate in English.

Against this picture of global uniformity, there is evidence for an alternative version of global consumption, one in which a multicultural array of products is on offer. It is now possible, after all, to see and experience the cultures of many different groups and societies. The spread of tourism or the fashion for 'world music' are both illustrations of this. Travel agents advertise trips to ever more 'exotic' locations. Record shops sell the music of Memphis and Mali. This diversity feeds into the making of culture, into the way artists draw upon other cultures to create a new hybrid. This practice is apparent in the music made by Peter Gabriel, Youssou N'Dour, David Byrne, Paul Simon and Sting. This is not, of course, a new phenomenon. Almost all cultural forms are the product of cross-fertilization (Mitchell, 1996: 52). 'Rock'n'roll', for example, fused sounds that came from Africa, Ireland, Scotland, France and America. But while the notion of 'global culture' can be represented in different ways, and while it has familiar roots, it is assumed to identify a new world of cultural consumption.

In each dimension – production, distribution and consumption – it is possible to see evidence for the emergence of a global culture with an attendant political economy. It may take different forms, but it has the same essential features. It is not controlled by any one nation, nor is its access or content peculiar to any one region. It seems that, under this regime, nation states become increasingly marginal players, unable to protect local culture or to control the production and distribution of the culture their citizens consume. But is this picture an accurate one?

The myth of globalization?

There are many critiques offered of globalization. My own concern is with the way in which the rhetoric of global culture has become detached from the material and institutional conditions that underlie its appearance.

The term 'global culture' itself suggests, as we have seen, two visions of the product. Either it refers to a multiplicity of forms of expression, values and experiences, deriving from across the world, with no one combination taking precedence over the others. Or it refers to a single culture which is specific to no one group – an interpretation of the Live Aid vision that 'We are the World', in which 'we' refers to everyone who inhabits the planet. Both these pictures of the global culture are attacked by critics who argue that, in fact, there is a single, particular dominant culture (see Featherstone, 1990; McGrew and Lewis, 1992; Murphy, 1983). The culture being touted across the globe often emerges from specific parts of the world (America and Europe), and is manufactured and marketed by corporations based in the USA, Europe and Japan. This commercial order is symbolized by Sony's decision to pay $1 billion for the right to market Michael Jackson. It is represented too in Hollywood's domination of the film industry. And although some of these products are modified to appeal to their international audience, the product itself still retains the hallmarks of its cultural origins. There may be concessions, ways of 'tailoring' an original design, to suit certain markets, but these are small compromises within the main framework. It is not just that English is the language of much popular culture; it is also that the images and concerns of America are most prevalent. The film *Black Rain* may have been shot in Japan and used Japanese actors to star alongside the American Michael Douglas, but it was fear of Japanese economic success that fuelled the plot. At the same time, the Far East represents the major new market for Western and Japanese companies. Which is why, as Schiller notes (1996: 112), Star Television (part of the Murdoch empire), which broadcasts to Asia and the Middle East, carries advertisements for 'Audi, Canon, Coca-Cola, Hennessy, Levi Strauss, MasterCard, Mobil, Motorola, NEC, Nike, Panasonic, Pepsi-Cola, Reebok, Sony, Sharp, Shell and Toshiba'.

A similar criticism can be directed at 'global multiculturalism'. Access to the global pathways is not granted to everyone everywhere. Western artists can draw more easily on non-Western cultures; the reverse is less easy. Tour operators choose their resorts because of what their wealthy (Western) clients expect. 'World music' is defined by Anglo-American record companies according to marketing strategies that particular audiences represent or require (Frith, 1989; Redhead and Street, 1989).

So the first challenge to the notion of the global culture is that no such culture exists, in either its unitary or its multicultural form. This is not to deny that the world is increasingly connected up, that there is greater interaction between cultures, only that the net effect is not a plurality of equal cultures, or a harmonious synthesis of them in one global culture. Cultures form part of a struggle for power, in which resources (both cultural and financial) are not evenly distributed (Jayaweera, 1987), and which makes some countries 'defenseless against the maneuvers of the world business system' (Schiller, 1996: 119).

Another line of criticism is less concerned with the product itself, and more with the use to which it is put, the way it is interpreted. Even if there is a global culture, it would be wrong to see it as meaning the same to everyone. This is amply demonstrated by the way jazz was used and abused in the Soviet Union. At one time it was banned as a product of capitalist decadence; at another it was fêted as the authentic voice of an oppressed people (Starr, 1983). It is also evident in the wild array of reactions that Elvis Presley provoked – for some, he was the embodiment of free America, to others the devil incarnate. Culture does not simply impose itself upon peoples. While, as Ferguson (1992: 81) notes, Canada imports 90 per cent of its anglophone TV drama, 'there is considerable evidence that Canada continues to maintain a value system and way of life distinctive from the US.' In Japan too, Western culture may be available, but it is not automatically accepted. Guy de Launey (1995: 204) observes how in Japan: 'Record shops are full of material by Japanese acts, with separate, smaller sections for western artists. Japanese artists dominate the charts and feature strongly on television. Perhaps most tellingly of all, ask any high school student who their favourite artist is and the likelihood is they will give the name of a Japanese artist.' Writers about Britain also warn of the danger of seeing American culture as a synonym for 'Americanization' – American culture does not deliver a single message, but many different ones, and the point is to see what (and why) some get selected and others ignored (Strinati, 1992; Webster, 1988). In other words, the thought that there is a global culture may also be vulnerable to the argument that there is not a global process of cultural interpretation. The same artefact does not elicit the same response wherever it is seen or heard. In popular culture, context is vital. 'We may all hear each other's sounds these days,' writes Frith (1991a: 281), 'but we still read them differently.' John Thompson (1996: 174) makes a similar point when he argues: 'The globalization of communication has not eliminated the localized character of appropriation but rather has created a new symbolic axis in the modern world, what I shall describe as the axis of globalized diffusion and localized appropriation.' This is not just a theoretical point about how culture is understood, it is one about the *organization* of culture and about relations of power; it suggests that a process of globalization may define distribution, while not defining consumption (or vice versa). In the late 1980s, Chinese children developed a craze for the Transformer toy range. On the surface, this looked to be a classic case of Americanization, but as Bin Zhao and Graham Murdoch (1996: 214) explain, the craze owed much more to the process of 'transformation in contemporary China, from marxism to "late arriving" modernity'. The toys were part of the business of coping with change.

If the 'global culture' is actually the culture of particular parts of the globe and if there is no single form of reception, then we may be suspicious of the claim that we are now dealing with global industries. Rather, we are dealing with multinational corporations who need to expand their market or their product base. This means discovering, or organizing, new audiences; it also means finding 'new' products. The phenomenon of 'global' companies can, in fact, be a mistaken description of 'corporate transnationalization at a higher level of magnitude' (Ferguson, 1992: 75). The appearance of global companies may disguise a reality in which what is actually happening is that corporate structures are being forced to adapt to new markets or technologies.

Furthermore, the picture of a global industry operating unconstrained also misses out the possibility of national and local mediating interests. The actual delivery of popular culture depends on processes which are peculiar to particular national (and subnational) structures. This process is most apparent in the organization of broadcasting, and is clearly exemplified in the contrast between Britain and the USA. The degree of regulation both of the airwaves and of the organizations allowed to inhabit them has an impact upon what can be heard and seen (McQuail and Siune, 1986; Malm and Wallis, 1993). Decisions about the distribution of broadcasting frequencies and the regulations applying to their use have a profound influence upon the culture people make and consume. As Stephen Kline (1993: 317) notes of US TV: 'Television could have been institutionalized in other ways that might have given emphasis to alternative social purposes and cultural forms, such as news, documentaries, state propaganda, education or religion.' As it was, the emphasis was on commerce. By way of contrast, the sound of British pop can be read as the product of the BBC and public service broadcasting, just as the sound of US pop owed much to US radio and commercial broadcasting (Frith, 1988a). Put another way: that broadcast culture is the same in any two countries is not necessarily evidence of some transcendent globalizing logic, but rather of the adoption of policies within each country that have a similar effect. That everyone is subject to the same sounds may owe more to national-level policy than to any grander process of globalization. Indeed the appearance of this kind of globalization can be traced to the dominance of a particular political ideology. The key organizing ideology of the 1980s in the West was that of market liberalism. This held that culture was best managed by the market – that culture was in fact, or ought in principle to be, free from political interference. Such claims actually disguised the reality that, rather than being free of political interference, culture was subject to particular forms of political scrutiny and control. All systems of communication are subject to censorship and regulation which affect profoundly the character of the culture that is heard, seen and read (Reporters Sans Frontières, 1993).

'Global culture' is also subject to the effects of other agencies besides the broadcasters. Government – at various levels – can have an impact on what is available and what access is allowed to it. Writing of the interaction of government and the music industry, Malm and Wallis (1993: 26) observe: 'Laws can be made, taxes can be introduced and exempted, cultural and media policies can be formulated, subsidies can be constructed aimed at increasing the music industry's activities with national and local music (as opposed to international imports).' It does not follow from this, of course, that national governments succeed in their ambitions. It is a long path from policy intent to policy implementation. None the less, the way nation states organize culture involves a process of negotiation and struggle. And what Malm and Wallis reveal, with a series of detailed case studies, is that there are many different results to these relationships, results that can be measured by the music making and consuming that any one country enjoys. Much too may depend on the structure of interests within a nation state. Governments may be able to regulate some aspects of broadcasting better than others. In Tanzania, the radio carries a high proportion of nationally produced music. Television cannot match this because there is no national film industry to supply videos. Thus, the TV stations make use of imported videos, courtesy of MTV. In other words, there is no unitary process of globalization, and the extent of outside influence is dependent upon political structures and forces which are specific to national and local states.

It is not just that states differ between themselves in the ways in which they try to manage popular culture. Within each state, the form of infrastructure has an effect upon what is being consumed and how. Though there is a pervasive impression that the world has been 'wired up', it is not altogether accurate. While it is true that in Britain and America there is a high penetration of radio and television (in 1989, 98 per cent of households had at least one TV set [PSI, 1993: 2]), other nations have much lower levels of access. And in Britain, the cable network developed much more slowly than in other European countries (Dyson and Humphreys, 1986). Furthermore, the access and use of communications technology is not uniformly spread. British Asians and Afro-Caribbeans are more likely to have a satellite dish than other groups; they also show a greater willingness to subscribe to cable (PSI, 1993: 3, and 19). In short, we have to be wary of accounts of the political economy of popular culture that assume a monolithic structure set upon a single course.

Conclusion

This chapter began with the claim that popular culture had been 'globalized' and with the evidence used to support such claims. From here, the focus shifted to the counter-claims, and to the 'myth' of globalization. What I want to suggest is that while we need to be wary of particular readings of globalization, we cannot treat it as a pure myth. It contains much that is important to an understanding of the dynamics of popular culture. It draws attention to the shifting location of commercial and cultural power, and hence to the context in which political processes operate. It is evident that there are ways in which political processes and distributions of power shape the tendency towards globalization.

For the most part, though, this chapter has dwelt upon the nega-

CHAPTER FIVE

Ruling the waves:
the state and popular
culture

'Music' includes sounds wholly or predominantly charac-
terised by the emission of a succession of repetitive beats.
Criminal Justice and Public Order Act (1994),
Section 63, 1(b)

Think of state control over popular culture, and the mind con-
jures up visions of a totalitarian censor poring over some new
artefact and deliberating as to its political soundness. Or perhaps
thoughts turn to the propaganda, thinly disguised as art or entertainment, that seemed to typify fascist and communist states. State
involvement in popular culture, it might seem, is a peculiarity of
authoritarian regimes. The corollary of this is that (Western liberal) democracy is characterized by a world in which the state
plays little or no part in popular culture. Indeed, it is almost an
article of liberal faith that this is how it should be. First, cultural
taste is part of the private world that should be protected from
public intervention; secondly, artistic creativity depends upon freedom of expression, to which state interference is antithetical.

But such lines of demarcation, and the assumptions that underpin them, are wholly inadequate. They miss, for example, the (ad-
mittedly rare) appointment of Bruno Lion as France's ministerial
delegate for rock music in 1989. Lion, a former concert promoter,
was expected to help export French rock and to develop an infrastructure to improve employment prospects and talent among

inner-city youth (Toop, 1993). They also miss the ways in which France, like many other countries, use official quotas and subsidies to protect and promote its film and its music industry. Western states, just like totalitarian ones, can have a profound impact on popular culture. What I want to do in this chapter is to look more closely at what the central state does to popular culture.

This discussion is set against the background of the globalizing tendencies described in chapter 4, and it focuses primarily (but not exclusively) on music, because, as Malm and Wallis (1993: 7) observe, 'the music industry is . . . at the forefront of a move towards global standardization of cultural products.' This observation, however, is an acknowledgement not of an inevitable global trend, but rather of the conditions in which the industries exist, and under which they and the state operate. As Deanna Robinson and her colleagues (1991: 4) conclude: 'even though information-age economic forces are building an international consumership for centrally produced and distributed popular music, other factors are pulling in the opposite direction.' A complex political process stands between global intentions and global effects, provided by an array of institutions and the policies generated within them.

This chapter examines the ways in which this political mediation is managed. I concentrate, in the second half, on particular examples of this role and the effect they have. Each provides an insight into the state's power over popular culture. But before this, I want to say more about the institutions and structures from which such policies emerge. This is a topic that has received rather less attention than it deserves. There are, of course, exceptions to this rule. One of these is *Media Policy and Music Activity* by Malm and Wallis (1993). It represents an attempt to map the way in which state policy shapes cultural practice. The authors' focus, as with their previous work *Big Sounds from Small Peoples* (Wallis and Malm, 1984), is upon countries outside the Anglo-American mainstream. Their sample includes Jamaica, Trinidad, Kenya, Tanzania, Wales and Sweden. Though each country operates under very different circumstances, they all are engaged on a similar project: managing the making, distribution and consumption of music. In their survey, Malm and Wallis emphasize that there is a policy process that organizes and influences popular culture. Music does not just leap from the artist's imagination into the audience's heart. While policy may tend to lag behind technological and economic change, coping rather than leading it, this does not detract from the fact that policy shapes the final outcome (Malm and Wallis, 1993: 197). For example, local radio stations may operate in a state of relative autonomy, or they may simply use programmes bought from satellite suppliers, adding only a minimal amount of genuinely local material – weather, traffic, news reports (Malm and Wallis, 1993: 202). Which approach is chosen depends on the country's media policy, itself a consequence of principle, pragmatism and power. The effect of any policy can be felt directly in the range of music available. Following the granting of a commercial TV franchise, Malm and Wallis (1993: 206) observe that 'Swedish media policymakers virtually abdicated any ability or duty to force operators to observe obligations regarding music activity in the output of a national commercial TV channel.' Decisions to deregulate broadcasting can lead to greater similarity in content, not greater diversity – which adds further weight to the argument of chapter 4 that it is not *globalization* that is the cause of change, but the introduction of a policy of *deregulation by individual states*.

What is disappointing about the work done by Malm and Wallis, however, is that while they are good at describing the processes, and at identifying particular arrangements and their consequences, their analysis remains largely untheorized. We are left unclear as to how, say, the local and national interact, or why particular agencies adopt one policy rather than another. These concerns are the traditional fare of political science, rather than cultural or communications studies. Not that political science has had much to say about cultural policy in particular; it has, though, said a great deal about policy-making in general.

It is true, of course, that many Western countries do not actually have a single, explicit cultural policy. They have many policies which effect the form of culture, but no specific strategy. This is certainly true of Britain and the USA (Crane, 1992); it is less true of France (Rigby, 1991; Wachtel, 1987). To acknowledge this is not to close off analysis. It is instead to require that we think of cultural policy as a variety of practices, which stand in many different relationships to global, national and local power.

I want to draw attention to three dimensions that seem essential to any coherent account of the character – and hence the impact – of cultural policy. These are *institutional practices, the policy process* and *ideology*. In considering each, I want also to draw comparisons between British and French cultural policy. The contrast is a stark one. In 1985, France spent 1,450 million ECUs (0.98 per cent of the state budget) on cultural activities; while Britain spent only 201 million ECUs (0.2 per cent of the state budget) (Commission of the European Communities, 1987). This difference in spending does not just reflect differences of priority; it also marks differences of political structure, practice and ideology.

Making cultural policy

The institutions of cultural policy

The institutions which organize cultural policy have their own established patterns of behaviour, and their own specific characteristics; their remit and their policy instruments are crucial to determining the outcome. It might seem trivially inconsequential, but it mattered considerably to British arts funding that, in 1964, responsibility was transferred from the Treasury to the Department of Education and Science. With its own Minister (Jennie Lee) and its own budget, the arts gained real political leverage. In a White Paper issued in 1965, there was talk of the need to bridge the gap between the ' "higher" forms of entertainment and the traditional sources – the brass band, the amateur concert party, the entertainer, the music hall and pop group' (Hewison, 1988: 58). In 1967, jazz was funded for the first time, and arts policy became less London-centred and more focused on the regions (Laing, 1992: 81).

Such moments need to be understood in their larger context. They built upon a history of arts policy that begins with the Arts Council. In its links with the government, the Arts Council has played a crucial part in, among other things, defining 'culture' in largely elitist and consumerist terms. But while this policy may be the result of a particular set of circumstances and particular key actors, it is also a result of the Arts Council's origins in the Council for the Encouragement of Music and the Arts (CEMA), established during World War II. Its brief and approach were created out of the division between CEMA and the 'light entertainment' supplied by the Entertainment National Service Association (ENSA). These origins both established a status outside direct government control (as a 'quango') and also perpetuated the split between 'high' and 'low' culture (Gray, 1993: 4). The fact that cultural policy was, in the early 1990s, assigned to a *heritage* ministry gives a further clue as to the kind of institutional interests being established. The Ministry was to protect the past rather than promote the future. When there was public concern about the prospect that a painting by Lucian Freud would be exported, the Heritage Ministry declined to get involved because the work of art was too recent – that is, it was painted in the last twenty years. Such limits to political intervention on behalf of culture make it very difficult to resist globalizing tendencies.

In France, by comparison, cultural policy is accorded much greater political status, but as such it is more vulnerable to changes in the governing elite. The 1960s – and especially the events of 1968 – marked the fragmentation of the Gaullist institutions of culture. The particular targets were the *Maisons de la Culture*, established after de Gaulle's accession to power in 1959. Their role had been to supply the best of international and national culture, providing culture *for* the regions, not *from* the regions (Rigby, 1991). The system, like the British one, facilitated globalization. After 1968, however, the institutional structure altered under the guise of *action culturelle*. Now the rhetoric was decentralization and democratization. In fact, the distribution of power remained at the centre, but what changed was its allocation within the core. The Ministry of Culture began to emerge as a key actor in the political system, a process that was to reach its peak with Jacques Lang in the 1980s. Under Lang, the Ministry of Culture struggled ideologically and practically to protect French culture from globalizing forces (Hayward, 1993).

Culture and the policy-process

The practices and predispositions of the key institutions are, however, only part of the story. It matters how these institutions relate to each other, and how, as a consequence, cultural policy is made. There is, of course, a formal political account which explains how these institutions represent some sort of constitutional or legitimate process – leaders are democratically elected, their actions are open to public scrutiny. This, though, paints only a partial picture. An equally partial picture emerges if one concentrates exclusively upon the plethora of groups around cultural policy and draws the conclusion that an informal pluralism operates. Both presumptions have to be qualified. Clive Gray (1993: 9–10) argues that British cultural policy is 'characterised by the twin features of organisational diversity and value limitation, which lead to an institutional pluralism but a behavioural elitism.' This arrangement is maintained by the existence of an 'issue network' (Rhodes, 1988), which is typified by an unstable coalition of a large number of groups acting with limited autonomy. In other words, cultural policy-making in Britain resembles that which operates elsewhere in the system. The appearance of democratic competition is belied by a reality in which the outcome is imposed or engineered from above, and implemented by a network of agencies and through the market.

This combination of devolved control, market mechanisms and elitist leadership is apparent in the recent history of government policy on the British film industry, where gestures of support have, in fact, led to the gradual erosion of state subsidy through the removal of levies and other devices (Hill, 1993). It is also evident in the trend towards broadcasting deregulation and towards the liberalization of cross-media ownership in Britain. Here the policy process was driven by the particular symbiosis of Thatcherite practices and the business interests of Rupert Murdoch's News Corporation. The consequence of changes in film and broadcasting policy was to make Britain more vulnerable to global forces, by weakening the film industry's competitiveness and increasing opportunities for private media ownership. Once again, this makes globalization seem less an inevitable process and more a political project.

This point is reinforced by the French experience. It is noticeable how France's cultural policies, particularly in relation to its film industry, have been directed at resisting aspects of globalization, and have been formulated within a much more deliberative, politicized policy system. France was a leading (and successful) campaigner against a free trade in film under the 1993 GATT agreement. These efforts were not simply the product of individual political will. They were the result of a policy process which is much less permeable to the pressures to which Britain succumbed. The post-1968 cultural policy network in France was, according to Wachtel (1987: 23), formed by a powerful alliance of middle-class interests in the cultural realm. These interests captured the key institutions within the elite policy process, and under the guise of decentralization were able to establish a powerful political presence for culture. This bore fruit in the period 1981–6 when Lang focused cultural policy on 'three principles: education, creation and research' (Wachtel, 1987: 45). Lang was able to control and coordinate cultural policy, sustaining local and national cultures and fighting off globalization (Hayward, 1993).

Ideology and cultural policy

Cultural policy cannot be understood simply as the result of institutional practices and policy processes. Allowance has to be made for the role of ideology (Gray, 1993: 16). Even the view that cultural choice and provision should be left to the market – ostensibly to allow for the free interplay of preferences, unconstrained by ideological diktat – is itself informed by a set of value judgements and political assumptions. More subtly, these are realized in the way the 'public' and the public sphere are regarded: whether culture is a matter for private consumption or public expression. Culture can be treated as a form of private indulgence, or as a key aspect of the education and environment of a society. No country subscribes exclusively to either of these extremes, but these alternatives frame the range of possibilities within which states are located.

At the simplest level, the conventional range of ideologies – liberalism, conservatism, socialism – can be applied to the development of cultural policy. In France in the 1980s, just as in Italy in the 1970s, socialism was linked directly to culture: the development and deployment of cultural resources were integral to the creation of an alternative social order. In Britain, Thatcherism introduced a New Right liberalism which had the effect of privatizing culture. It was this era that saw the rise of commercial sponsorship of the arts. By contrast, the British Labour Party has failed to propound a consistent socialist perspective on culture, although it is linked to a tradition of municipal cultural provision (see Waters, 1990). Tony Crosland's vision, outlined in *The Future of Socialism* (1956), is a notable exception. Recalling the example of William Morris, he argues that cultural provision was crucial to socialism (Crosland, 1956: 527). He imagines a world in which 'we need not only higher exports and old-age pensions, but more open-air cafés, brighter and gayer streets at night, later closing-hours for public houses, more local repertory theatres . . . more pictures and murals in public places, better designs for furniture and pottery and women's clothes . . .' (Crosland, 1956: 521–2)

New Right arguments tend to mix pragmatism and principle in their attitudes towards the arts. These are forged in the tension between a general distrust of public subsidy and a desire to promote a particular vision of 'Great Britain'. This was very apparent in attempts to find private funding for millennium events. The Conservative government was forced to intervene directly after the private sector failed to provide the necessary support and leadership. But such compromises should not deflect from the fact that ideology still plays an important part in cultural policy. As one commentator observed, 'Thatcher espoused a right-liberal populism whose New Right ideology regarded art as a commodity to be bought in the market place by customers' (Beck, 1993: 12). In the 1980s, this led to a reordering of the issue network around cultural policy, in favour of business sponsorship and the tax breaks needed to encourage it; it also led to attacks upon perceived 'elitism' within the arts establishment and an emphasis on art as heritage – art as consumption of the past, not as production for the future (Beck, 1993). The suspicion of bureaucracy, characteristic of New Right ideology, gave further impetus to a desire to reduce arts administration and to limit its ability to promote new activities (Beck, 1993: 19). The auctioning of ITV franchises as part of the 1990 Broadcasting Act epitomized this approach. The right to broadcast was assigned to the company or consortium who offered to pay the most for the privilege. Initially, the legislation made no reference to the quality of the service offered by the prospective franchise-holder; it was only after vehement lobbying that a 'quality threshold' was introduced. Even with this modification, the bidding system introduced a new incentive into the broadcasting system (most obviously, the need to recoup the cost of the bid), with consequences for the type of culture on offer – more game shows, fewer documentaries; more imports, less expensive dramas.

Ideology is not exclusive to New Right cultural policy. In Britain in the early 1980s, the Greater London Council tied its socialism to a version of 'culture' and to policy instruments intended to sustain it. Socialist administrations in France and Italy also operated with cultural policies that were marked by their ideologies (Bianchini and Parkinson, 1993). In France, the Socialist Party's policy of *action culturelle* was an attempt to animate popular participation in the conduct of community life (Wachtel, 1987).

But to appreciate the full impact of ideology on cultural policy, it is important to move beyond the conventional political categories. This means refining and separating out the categories within the traditional camps and introducing new ones. Ian Henry (1993), for example, distinguishes between versions of the left's approach to culture. Put simply, there are those on the left who see culture as part of the problem, as reproducing existing social norms and inequalities; and there are those who see it as part of the solution, as a weapon with which to challenge the dominant elite. Nicholas Garnham adds a further twist to left thinking on culture by noting variations in the conceptualization of culture. Some views of culture give 'special and central status . . . to the "creative artists" whose aspirations and values [are] seen as stemming from some unfathomable and unquestionable source of genius, inspiration or talent' (Garnham, 1990: 154). This perspective inevitably places the artists at the centre of cultural policy, and sees the key question as being how audiences might be delivered to the creator. By contrast, others on the left focus on the audience, and pose a different policy question: what kind of art or artists should be supplied or supported? The first approach favours a policy of cultural elitism, the latter one of cultural populism. In 1965, the Chairman of the Arts Council, a major source of income for culture in Britain, allied himself with the first option when he said: 'I speak for the Arts; I do not speak for amateur theatricals' (quoted in Laing, 1992: 82).

Summary

In summary it is clear that the making of cultural policy is the product of a number of different elements – of institutions, policy processes and ideologies. Each of these shapes the form and character of that policy, and in their various combinations, they allow different sets of interests to be decisive in fashioning culture, in determining, among other things, its resistance or vulnerability to global tendencies.

By separating institutional practices, policy processes and ideologies, I do not mean to give the impression of discrete elements interacting within confined limits. Policy is the result of constantly shifting alliances and patterns of interaction. This is not just a product of the changing environment in which policy has to operate;

nor is it simply a result of shifts in political relations and ideas; it is a consequence of the interaction of these and other factors. To give a clearer sense of how these links operate, I want to consider a number of examples of state involvement in popular culture, to draw attention both to the way in which the state influences popular culture, and to the political processes that organize this influence. My examples are censorship, broadcasting, education and industrial policy.

Implementing cultural policy

Censorship and popular culture

There are many instances of state censorship of popular culture. Typically, these are associated with the practices of authoritarian regimes. Under apartheid, the South African government banned countless books, plays, songs and films. The Nazis took particular exception to 'swing youth', a group of young bourgeois who chose 'to dance to the "decadent Jewish" and "degenerate" prohibited music of Benny Goodman, Tommy Dorsey, Duke Ellington, Louis Armstrong, and other giants of the age of jazz' (Burleigh and Wippermann, 1991: 220). A similar view was taken within the Eastern bloc, albeit with different values attached. The communist states banned many national and foreign examples of popular culture – including the Beatles, Cliff Richard and the musicals of Andrew Lloyd Webber (Starr, 1983).

But such practices are not the exclusive preserve of totalitarianism. In the West, the censorship may have been less systematic; it could, though, be detected in the decisions of broadcasters to refuse airtime to certain 'offensive' pop songs (Cloonan, 1996; Street, 1986). The West's desire to censor may have been less explicitly political in its motivation, although during the McCarthy era in the United States censorship was inspired directly by fear of communism (Denisoff, 1971), and in the UK there is a long history of censorship of art – especially on television – connected with Northern Ireland (Curtis and Jempson, 1993). But if politics, conventionally defined, has not been a common object of censorship, the portrayal of sex and violence has been a constant target of various political interests. In Britain, government ministers have spoken of the deleterious effect of soap operas like *Brookside*, and the police and courts were used in an unsuccessful attempt to prosecute Island records for releasing an album by rappers NWA (Niggaz With Attitude). In the USA, the Parents Music Resource Center, a coalition of concerned parents (including Tipper Gore, wife of Bill Clinton's Vice-President, Al Gore), led a campaign against 'obscene' rock lyrics. The FBI busied themselves deciphering the words to rap records, and complained about the expression of anti-police sentiments (Marsh and Pollack, 1989). Also in the USA, there have been attempts to ban the exhibition of photographs by Robert Mapplethorpe. This was part of a more general campaign by right-wing senators to curtail all public funding for the arts.

I return to the issue of censorship in a later chapter; here I want just to make a few brief points about its politics. While it is evident that state censorship is not the sole preserve of authoritarian regimes, it is too easy to assume that all states censor in the same way. First, there are clear differences in the incentives and motives for censorship between political regimes. This is not just true of the comparison between communism and capitalism; it also applies *within* each type of system. The former Yugoslavia was less censorious, for example, than the USSR; and Singapore censors more than the United States. If we compare liberal democracies, it is evident that North European states – like Sweden or the Netherlands – are less prone to censor than, say, the UK. It is also evident that the objects of censorship vary between and within types of political system. The film *Crash* was held back by British censors while it was being shown elsewhere in Europe and in the United States. This suggests that in understanding the state's role as censor we need to look at the political institutions that organize censorship.

Institutional variation needs to be supplemented by two other dimensions. The first is ideology. The need to censor, and the objects of censorship, are themselves a product of particular worldviews. They reflect ideas about how thought and action are influenced, about standards of acceptable behaviour, and about the role and responsibility of the government in distinguishing between, and regulating, public and private space. An account of the ideological disposition of censors has, finally, to be combined with an account of the opportunity to give effect to the ideology. The success and failure of censors depends upon a network of other political conditions and interests. The attack on rap in the

USA, for instance, owes something to the rise of the 'moral majority'; but it is also inseparable from issues of racism (the acts most
commonly targeted are African-American); and of commercial
interest (the music industry depends upon the government's willingness to police copyright). In the same way, film censorship in
the UK has depended upon the collaboration of distributors and
studios. In short, understanding state censorship means understanding a complex political process which links institutions, interests and ideology. Together, they create the conditions which
allow the state to determine what can be heard, seen or read. Censorship, though, represents a negative political power, the power
to prevent. Power can also be used to facilitate, to make things
happen, and it is important to see how the state can play this positive role in relation to popular culture. The most obvious mechanism is broadcasting policy.

Broadcasting and popular culture

A country's broadcasting system owes something to the technology it uses, but a great deal more to the political interests and
ideas which organize it. Every government, whatever its structure or ideology, has to regulate the airwaves. The broadcast spectrum is not an infinite resource (although digital technology will
greatly expand it); it can be used up. Governments diverge in the
way they manage this scarce resource. Compare the ways in which
broadcasting is run in different countries. The USA, for example,
produced a commercially driven, privately owned radio network
in the early twentieth century, while Britain, using essentially the
same technical knowledge, developed a government-financed,
public service system. The reasons for the differences, according
to Lewis and Booth (1989), lie with a number of key political factors. In the USA, for example, the Constitution requires freedom
of expression, and this is interpreted as the absence of government interference – hence the presumption in favour of allowing
people to broadcast. By contrast, the UK is not bound by such
constitutional obligations. Instead, the emphasis is on official se-
crecy, and the authorities' natural disposition has been to limit
the spread of information systems. This tendency was reinforced
by the historical links between military defence and radio. The
incentive to develop and deploy radio came from a military need

to coordinate military campaigns (Lewis and Booth, 1989). Commercial interests were also to play a part in shaping the evolution of broadcasting. The distribution of patents, the ownership of rights and broadcasting hardware, created different policy networks in each country. In the States, these were able to establish the principle that the airwaves were there to be filled; in the UK, they were to be rationed and monitored by the government. In order to carry out these duties, the British deployed (for a further set of political reasons) the public corporation model of control, which created a relatively autonomous, publicly financed organization, with an appointed board which answered to the government. By contrast, the USA produced the much less interventionist regulatory system, fronted by the Federal Communications Commission.

With the British decision to introduce a centralized broadcasting system, it became necessary to decide what the service should provide. It was, by definition and formation, a public service, but what did this mean? Judgements had to be made about who 'the public' was or were; was it a single, unified group, or a plurality of interests? These questions found their answers in the way the public was addressed and the range and style of programmes it was offered. Under John Reith, the first Director General of the BBC, a particular set of answers evolved, and became enshrined in the public service ethos 'to inform, educate and entertain'. Contained in this were many ambiguities and competing interpretations, but the important point remains that broadcasting was hedged around by a set of expectations, and these in turn were premised upon a particular set of political principles and interests, which only began to change with the emergence of commercial TV in the 1950s. Even then, broadcasting was still in some important aspects bound by the public service ethos (and much more tightly regulated than the press). This continued in the 1960s, when in 1967 the British government outlawed the so-called pirate radio stations, dotted around the coast. They were replaced by the BBC's pop channel, Radio 1. Indeed, it was not until the 1980s, and the changing political and technological landscape, that the public service ethos in popular culture began to crack.

The crucial question is, therefore, what effect does the structure of broadcasting have upon the content and form of popular culture? The fact that a system has a limited number of channels does not mean that it necessarily produces less cultural diversity than a multi-channel system. Those different channels can all provide the same kind of programming. Much depends on the pressures, incentives and regulations that organize the available air space. It is possible for the airwaves to be monopolized by a particular sound or style, such that other forms will be lost to view. This does not just mark a loss of choice, it also marks a narrowing of perspective and cramping of experience. It is such thoughts, after all, which inspire various governments (in Sweden, France, Canada) to impose quotas to protect local culture.

When in the early 1990s the British government sought to broaden the range of radio stations, it created the Radio Authority to allocate the franchises and to determine the kind of stations to operate. Clause 84(2) of the 1990 Broadcasting Bill specified that there should be three new national, independent (that is, non-BBC) radio stations. The legislation required that one of the three should consist 'wholly or mainly . . . of music other than pop music'. The Radio Authority and politicians then had to interpret this requirement. It produced, for example, an earnest debate in the House of Lords about how – or whether – pop and rock should be differentiated. It also led to decisions being made (as they were also made for TV franchises) about the financial and programming proposals of the rival bidders. These decisions were further overlaid by judgements about which part of the radio spectrum should be occupied by which station. Winners of the rock franchise, Virgin Radio, were upset to be allocated the AM waveband which provided poorer quality reception than FM. In short, the government and other agencies of the state played a direct role in determining the kind of culture that could be heard on the radio. The political influence does not, however, end with these general conditions.

Several writers have charted the way in which the BBC's public service ethos shaped the form and content of entertainment. Simon Frith, for example, draws attention to the ways in which Reith set his face against 'mass culture', defined largely through its association with the USA: 'BBC culture was, first of all, a response to the fear of Americanization' (Frith, 1988a: 25). In place of the American variant, the BBC evolved its own particular version, 'light entertainment', which was a way of reworking popular culture into a 'middle-brow' form. This meant creating a format that encouraged audiences to discriminate actively, rather than to be entertained passively. The aim was to improve people's tastes, but it was not to deny them their pleasures; the BBC was to entertain without succumbing to pure populism (Frith, 1988a: 27–8).

Pleasure was to be firmly located in the family home, a discreet, well-ordered middle-class home. The family were not to be unduly perturbed as they relaxed after their day at work and at school. They were to be given music that was not too demanding and that did not need to be taken too seriously. The BBC established the distinction between what was serious and what was relaxing, and between what was good and bad taste. It was a process that came to map 'the distinction between commercial and non-commercial "light" music, between "real jazz" and pop' (Frith, 1988a: 38). These judgements were framed by the way the audience were implicated in them, the way their intimacy with the voices and sounds was established and re-enforced through tone, content and format. Performers projected a kind of 'ordinariness', says Frith (1998a: 42), which both confirmed and flattered the 'ordinariness' of the listener. By this means, the 'people' were created in the image of the BBC.

The BBC's power as purveyor and sculptor of popular music was to cause changes in the music industry, reshaping the notion of 'popularity' in terms of 'radio suitability' and 'record sales', and marginalizing live performance (Frith, 1988a: 39). This way of organizing popular culture also shaped the style and skills of the performers. Its most dramatic effect was to create the conditions out of which were to emerge – most famously – the Beatles: 'Rather than simply imitating the style of American Top 40 Radio, British youth club shows such as *Saturday Club* promoted local enterprise. Skiffle is a case in point. They also gave groups such as the Beatles a chance to develop a relationship with their radio audience that was not just a sales pitch' (Frith, 1988a: 3). The Beatles, like the 'people', were also a product of the BBC's broadcasting practices.

The thought that the format, and the incentives that shape it, affect the nature of popular culture takes on a clear political dimension when we consider proposals to change broadcasting policy. The key issue here is 'deregulation', and the leading advocates of it have been the New Right, who see it as a device for removing the BBC's paternalist control, replacing it with populist consumer choice, and releasing radio's commercial potential (Veljanovski, 1989). For the New Right, Radio 1's large audience figures and its exclusive commitment to commercial popular music seem to make it an anachronistic institution within public service broadcasting.

Opponents of this argument, however, contend that there is still an important role for the public service approach within the commercial arts. Their case is embodied in the figure of the disc-jockey John Peel. In a broadcasting career lasting thirty years, Peel is the only broadcaster who has remained from the station's foundation in 1967. His longevity, though, is not the only measure of his importance. He symbolizes public service popular culture, a role belatedly recognized in the award of an Honorary Degree (from the University of East Anglia) and acclaim as National Broadcaster of the Year in 1993. *The Guardian* (3 May 1993) headlined a profile of him, 'The Lord Reith of Rock'n'Roll', and quoted fellow DJ David Jensen as saying, 'he has always subscribed to the BBC as first and foremost a public service. . . . There is something about the BBC in him which is kind of at odds with him as this rebel music leader. He actually is very Reithian . . .' As Stephen Barnard (1989: 156) explains, Peel embodies 'the Reithian principles of encouraging audiences to discriminate in their listening and of bringing the more difficult and demanding to their attention'. Peel has, in other words, done more than fill in the gaps between records. He has used his various shows to encourage new talent and to expand popular taste: the first by providing, through the BBC, the opportunity for inexperienced groups to record one of the 'Peel Sessions'; the second, by compiling his show from music that fails to achieve success through the crude populist criteria of the charts. Were it not for him, the Smiths would not have enjoyed their brief but immensely influential career. He has acted, with others, as the nurturer of talent, as someone who creates audiences rather than crudely representing them.

The argument here is that the public service ethos, as enacted by John Peel, creates the conditions for a broader and better popular culture than would exist under a more populist or commercial format. How, though, does this connect with the role of the state and the relationship between politics and popular culture? In the first instance, it is state policy which plays a decisive role in the allocation of public funds to broadcasting and in deciding how the broadcaster is to be regulated. Secondly, the character of these decisions is determined, in part, by ideology, so that different political dispositions generate different accounts of 'quality' in culture and of the relationship between audience and broadcaster. And thirdly, the outcome of the policies and ideologies is experienced in the character of cultural life. The 'politics' of this last dimension may not be immediately clear – why should the range of music we hear or perform matter politically? That it does will become clearer if we turn to the third dimension of state policy: education.

Education and popular culture

Governments are responsible for educating their citizens. This generalization, however, admits of many qualifications, and appeals to many underlying justifications. The point is that governments recognize that they have an interest in equipping young people with certain skills and facilities, of developing certain attributes and conveying certain knowledge. One question that all governments have to resolve, therefore, is what control should be exercised over the curriculum and what it should contain. For many governments, for example, the skills of performing or consuming popular culture can – and should – be taught and learnt. There are, of course, within this general view, arguments about which aspects of popular culture are appropriate for such treatment, how the skills should be disseminated and which system best serves this process. The motives may be very different. For some, it may constitute a way of competing in the world market; for others, it may be driven by the desire to preserve local cultural traditions. For Lenin, education was necessary to political participation: 'An illiterate person stands outside. He must first be taught the ABC. Without this, there can be no politics; without this, there are only rumours, gossip, tales, prejudices, but not politics' (quoted in Donald, 1992: 150). But whatever the goal, the implication is that the state should, in some way or other, provide the facilities or the conditions for this education to occur. How the details are added to this general disposition will have profound consequences for popular culture.

During 1992, an earnest debate was fought out in the British Parliament, in the columns of the serious broadsheets and on the very exclusive airwaves of Radio 3. The contributors to the argument were exercised over the place of music in the National Curriculum, the state prescription for education in British schools. Just as furious rows had broken out about English and history, so too music prompted heated exchanges over what should be included and how it should be taught. All the arguments ran along parallel lines, falling into the two camps of the traditionalists, who wanted old methods of teaching to be allied to facts and to a conservative account of a classical tradition, and the liberals, who favoured more student-oriented forms of teaching, drawing on personal experience and on a more diverse range of sources. In the argument over music, this debate ranged over the competing claims of performance and appreciation, and the rival values of classical and popular forms.

The row focused on a report issued by the National Curriculum Council (NCC) in 1991. Its working party had recommended that pupils should receive a broad musical education, which took in pop and non-Western music as well as the 'classical' canon. Students were to learn African drum patterns, pop chord changes, Scottish fiddle music, together with the rules of Indian and other musics. The working party responsible for advising on this policy contained two representatives of the pop industry, composer Mike Batt and the manager of the Stranglers, Colin Johnson. When word of this advice leaked out, the traditionalists voiced their discontent. Anthony O'Hear, a professor of philosophy, said: 'I personally object to the teaching of rock music. It is barbaric and degrading. Music education has a close connection with moral attitudes. Pop encourages the notion of the "quick fix" to every problem, emotional, political, cultural' (*The Observer*, 20 January 1992). Faced with this outcry, the NCC capitulated. Rejecting its working party's recommendation, it suggested that children of seven years old should listen to Haydn, Mozart and Stravinsky, while eleven-year-olds were to encounter Bach, Beethoven and Wagner. It did allow that children should also encounter jazz, blues, calypso and rock, but the emphasis was to be on the 'special' classical tradition. The *Independent on Sunday* (19 January 1992) editorialized in favour of the NCC's revised position: 'It is because the experience of classical music is so rare – and because a full understanding of it requires patience – that it is all the more important for schools to give children of all classes an early opportunity to appreciate it.' Besides, the editorial went on, there was no desirable alternative, only 'commercialised mass entertainment'. It was these traditionalist arguments that were to win the debate over the National Curriculum.

The effect of this victory is not just to be measured in the opportunity for the young to hear and discuss pop and to be exposed to different musical traditions; it is also to be felt in the chance young people have to acquire the skills needed to perform them, and in the sense that they have of the value of these skills. The idea that pop is 'meaningless', or that it can be easily appreciated, automatically designates it as 'low culture', and this, in turn, is to pass judgement on those who practise or study it. It is a judgement that operates too in higher education where the study of 'low' popular culture is typically assigned fewer resources than the study of high culture. These judgements are exercised daily in what counts as literature, and indeed in the assumption that written texts should take precedence over visual ones. In setting its rules, the National Curriculum does more than establish a canon or draw boundaries between the high and low in culture, it also creates a political community: 'the literate or educated public was to be identified in terms of the cultural *content* of the curriculum. To qualify for membership is to be at home with *this* form of language, *this* selection of books, *this* Christianity, *this* heritage' (Donald, 1992: 165; his emphasis).

In its influence over the organization of education, the state can, therefore, play a part in determining the access to, together with the status and shape of, popular culture, and, in doing so, it can forge a particular political order. There is, of course, no simple or determinate relationship involved, no neat connection between political interests or ideological disposition. But insofar as the state is able to control education policy, it is also influencing the standing of popular culture and determining what kinds of knowledge and skills, what kinds of people and activities, are to be valued. It is helping to define citizenship, and the place of popular culture within it.

Industrial policy and popular culture

In the West, it is widely supposed that popular culture is a legitimate source of private profit. This assumption does not, however, stand for a universal truth. First, the ownership and control of popular culture is, in some countries, not assigned to the private market but held to be a public responsibility of the state. This was, for instance, true of the former Eastern bloc. But even in the West the state plays a more prominent role than is often recognized. The capacity to make money from popular culture depends on the regulations and rights that constrain and facilitate market relations. Whatever the New Right pretend, markets are not entirely spontaneous forms of human interaction, able to exist independently of the initiatives of government and other agencies. Government's role may be limited (whether out of choice or necessity) but it has one none the less.

This can be illustrated by seeing how government industrial and economic policy can affect the production and consumption of popular culture. We can begin with the most obvious of government devices – legislation, which can either apply specifically to the popular culture industry or include it in a range of other industries. In the first category falls the use of subsidies. Governments differ greatly in the extent to which they encourage or support the film industry, either through the use of direct financial contributions or through forms of tax relief. They can also play a crucial and direct part by supplying the infrastructure (or by licensing its introduction) through which popular culture can be consumed. In a similar vein, some states have introduced levies on blank tapes, as a way of raising revenue and of limiting the abuse of copyright. By the mid-1980s, six European countries (Austria, Finland, France, Germany, Iceland and Portugal) operated a levy, albeit set at very different levels (Laing, 1987). These states differed among themselves also in the way in which the levy was raised, some using a royalty system, others a tax system. A further issue for those who intervene is how the levy is to be used. There is no guarantee that it will be fed back into the industry that produced it. The French government required that 25 per cent of the levy should be used to promote new artists and new cultures, the rest was to go back to existing industry interests (musicians, composers, and so on).

State policies also regulate the activities of entire corporations. Monopolies and mergers or anti-trust legislation can have a direct effect upon the power of cultural industries, represented in, among other things, market share. Rules imposed on cross-media ownership can also affect the structure of the cultural industries and the extent to which they can be used to sustain or support particular products. Co-ownership of press, film and TV interests can allow a corporation to lock consumers into a network which severely limits choice and competition. States differ considerably in the degree to which such legislation is enacted and implemented.

Copyright legislation can vary in a similar way. The assignment of rights, the legal framework of ownership, is vital to determining how profits from a work of art can be made and distributed.

Frith (1988b, 1994) notes how, for example, Britain has long recognized the performing rights in records (that is, the public playing of them), whereas France and the USA do not recognize these rights. Many other issues spring from the organization of copyrighting, particularly with the development of sampling technology and the question of 'ownership' it generates (Negus, 1992). Again, however arcane these issues may seem, they are not simply legal niceties. They are matters which have a direct impact upon how popular culture is created and consumed.

Conclusion

This chapter has journeyed through various aspects of the state's involvement with popular culture. Against the backdrop of globalizing tendencies, we have seen how states vary in the way they seek to manage popular culture. This process of management is organized through the interaction of institutions, policy processes and ideologies. Variations in each make a difference to the degree of control available to the state. In the latter part of the chapter, we have looked at the products of cultural policy-making, exploring the ways in which state decisions (themselves the product of ideologies, institutions and interests) influence the character of popular culture. One important theme here was the way in which the content of popular culture was 'political'. The thought is that the quality of cultural life is important to the quality of political life. This parallels a general argument about the relationship between democracy and the system of broadcasting.

The deregulation of broadcasting, and the concomitant proliferation of channels, makes the notion of 'the public' less and less coherent. Instead, the trend is towards an erosion of public space and the privatization of information, and in turn, says Garnham (1983: 20), towards a world in which the citizen becomes a consumer in a 'social structure within which isolated individuals only relate to each other statistically'. Underlying this judgement, though, is an acceptance not of a technologically led inevitability, but of a set of political decisions. Garnham's analysis is informed by a view of what the state *could* have done. It could give radio franchises to more democratic, alternative stations; it could also have established better mechanisms for assessing the services of the franchise winners. The fact that such things were not done threatens the public sphere and the operation of a democratic politics (Garnham, 1986). If states acquiesce in the creation of a communication system that encourages broadcasters to target specific, narrowly defined audiences, then the notion of a 'public service' disappears, and with it the hope of a politics based on anything other than the aggregate of discrete interests.

At stake also are the opportunities for informed choice. This depends on the provision of alternative cultural visions and methods for understanding and developing the skills entailed in producing them. It is here that a state's educational and industrial policy can shape the possibilities available to its citizens. It can also go some way to defining that citizenry, by including or excluding cultural traditions or values. In short, the state is a key – if often neglected – agent in the structuring of the production and consumption of popular culture, and thereby affecting political life. But this kind of intervention in popular culture is not confined to the national and transnational system; it happens at the local level too.

CHAPTER SIX

The local politics of popular culture

1. Right hand of gentleman must not be placed below the waist nor over the shoulder nor around the lady's neck, nor lady's left arm around gentleman's neck. Lady's right hand and gentleman's left hand clasped and extended at least six inches from the body, and must not be folded and lay across the chest of dancers.
2. Heads of dancers must not touch.

Rules and Regulations for Public Dance Halls,
Chief of Police, Lansing, Michigan, *c.*1920

In the rhetoric of rock writing, origins matter; and in the business of making music, places matter. So the pop press talks of 'the Manic Street Preachers . . . the band from Blackwood South Wales' and of 'Derby's Bivouac' or 'Pavement from Stockton, California'; Prince is forever linked with Minneapolis, the Grateful Dead with San Francisco, Bruce Springsteen with New Jersey, and Nirvana with Seattle. This is *Melody Maker* on Collapsed Lung, a group of English rappers: 'Imagine four kids brought up on the gangsta groove of Ice-T on the council estates of Essex (oh, but it's a hard cold land down there).' The unstated assumption of this rhetoric is that we cannot understand the music unless we know where – physically – it is coming from. This is not always true – nobody seems to trouble much about the home towns of Madonna and Michael Jackson, but when it does apply, it suggests that culture is, in some important way, linked to place. This connection seems

obvious in the loyalty given to local sports teams or in the celebration of place in popular song ('Galveston', 'Spanish Harlem',
'Cypress Avenue', 'On Broadway'), but there is more to it than
this. The connection is not just a matter of rhetoric. It actually describes a key feature of the way popular culture is both created
and enjoyed. Local networks, and the opportunities they create,
help shape the culture that is produced. And local politics, like
national politics, plays its part in this process, by the regulations
imposed and the support given.

This chapter examines the extent to which the locality, and especially local politics, influence the production, distribution and
consumption of popular culture. How do they affect what is seen
and heard, what is composed and created? How do local political
ideas and values, local institutions and interests, interact to shape
popular culture? Such questions are important because of the implications they have for the role of government in the quality and
character of cultural life, and for the role of cultural life in politics.
This chapter focuses in particular upon the ways in which local
politics and the local state shape popular music, but my approach
and my argument apply equally to other forms of popular culture. I want to continue to challenge those assumptions associated with 'globalization': first, that it has led to the homogenization
or elimination of local and regional variations; and, secondly, that
popular culture is simply a commercial product, controlled and
distributed by large multinational corporations through the
market. Local politics provides one reason for doubting both
assumptions.

If popular culture is thought to be the product of a global industry and market, it is easy to see how local markets and industries come to be viewed as being of little or no significance. It is
easy also to see how such thoughts fuel the fear that national and
regional musical cultures are under threat from the new global
order (Robinson, Buck and Cuthbert, 1991; Wallis and Malm, 1984).
After all, even in those countries that seem to dominate the world
market in popular culture (the USA and UK, for example), there
is little evidence of local tastes and cultures. What is a hit in Salford
is also one in Norwich – sales across the country are very similar
(BPI, 1991); the same films, records, TV programmes, are available everywhere. There seems, therefore, little *prima facie* case for
supposing that 'the local' makes much difference.

In challenging this thought, I want to look first at the ways in which local political decisions can indeed have a profound impact upon the cultural life of the locality. I want then to explain why local authorities come to be involved in the organization of popular culture. The answer does not lie simply with political will and the personal whims of local politicians; it lies both with wider political pressures and with the changing political economy of popular culture. And finally, I want to ask what *difference* local initiatives can and do make to popular culture. Mavis Bayton once told me that in Oxford there were roughly a thousand rock musicians, only thirty of whom were women; but in a small village not far from the city, there were three all-women rock bands. The reason for the difference, she said, was that in the village there was a (state-funded) youth worker who actively encouraged girls to learn to play and perform. My questions are about, therefore, how and why different political structures and different political decisions actually affect the kind of cultural opportunities, the kind of cultural life, available to people. Does it really make sense to link sounds to places (whether Seattle or Manchester), and to make local politics and practices the engine of such connections?

Forms of local state involvement

Despite the assumption that the local and the political are marginal to the fate of popular culture, there is evidence for a quite different conclusion. Work by Sara Cohen (1991) and Ruth Finnegan (1989) in the UK, by Will Straw (1991) in Canada, and by Barry Shank (1994) in the USA has highlighted the local dimension to both the making and consuming of popular music. They show how music depends upon a complex set of arrangements which allow people to perform or hear music, whether involving church choirs or amateur orchestras or folk groups or dance clubs. Music does not simply 'happen'; there have to be arrangements which enable it to exist. These arrangements can be viewed as the product of a local network or 'scene'. Where no such arrangements or connections exist, there will be silence. What is more, the shape of the local network – where it leads, whom it connects – will affect the type of music being heard and played. What this means is that when people talk of the 'Manchester sound' or the 'Seattle scene', they are not evoking some mystical connection between place and aesthetics – it is not something in the air, or in the 'nature' of the people. It is, in fact, the consequence of particular arrangements which allow music to be made in one way rather than another and which encourage one set of aesthetic judgements to take precedence over another. In this sense, the locality is crucial in structuring the business of making and enjoying music. But what is not clear from this literature on the role of the locality is the extent to which the *local state* is a significant actor within local scenes and networks.

Local states are not involved in the making of copyright laws or tariff policy. The scope of their powers is much more limited – or at least, their powers are different from those of the nation state. They can, none the less, make an important difference. Consider the policy instruments available at the city level. City authorities can, through such devices as zoning or licensing, shape the cultural opportunities available to their citizens. They can decide what counts as a residential area and what a commercial area, and what activities are appropriate to either. So it is that 'Boston has used zoning to restrict much of its pornography and prostitution to a single area, the "control zone"; Los Angeles is using zoning to keep bondage sex clubs out of specific neighbourhoods' (Logan and Molotch, 1987: 158–9). These strategies matter to the way people experience the world. Ken Worpole (1992: 105–6) talks of how involvement in community arts leads to civic commitment, how 'the use of festivals, carnivals and special events' can 'reclaim public space'. To the extent that cities can be 'designed' in this way, then city authorities can profoundly influence the cultural geography of the urban landscape and the world view of those who inhabit it. To illustrate the complex politics of city cultural policy, I want to focus on the case of New York.

The story of legal wrangling over New York's cabaret regulations may not seem the most appetizing of subjects, but Paul Chevigny's study *Gigs* (1991) proves otherwise. Chevigny is a lawyer and jazz fan who found himself embroiled in a campaign to reform the laws governing public performances in the city. These laws were not petty inconveniences. 'The cabaret laws', writes Chevigny (1991: 4), 'branded popular, especially jazz, music as deviant with great precision and for a very long time.' They did so through city zoning, which designated some areas as suitable for public performances and others as not. These general constraints were then overlaid by licensing regulations which affected the *type* of performance that could be given. Cabaret licensing, for example, 'forbade percussion as well as typical jazz frontline instruments such as horns, [and] restricted the number of musicians to three' (Chevigny, 1991: 15).

These arcane rules were introduced during Prohibition, as part of the battle against alcohol, but they remained in force long afterwards. Their survival owed much to a failure of political organization: the musicians' union was slow to defend the interests of freelance live performers (and only began to do so when union membership started to fall). The rules remained in force also because of a larger set of political interests. Until the mid-1960s, the police had control over the cards that allowed musicians to perform, and they used this power to refuse cards to people they deemed 'low-lifers', a category that often included jazz musicians (Chevigny, 1991: 61). It was only with a change of political administration, and hence of police practice, that this regime was liberalized. The election of Mayor Lindsay in 1966 saw the abolition of the card system.

The zoning system remained, however, and music continued to be forced into particular parts of the city. The function assigned to different districts reflected judgements about the 'dangers' which music brought with it and about what defined a residential area (and the quality/character of life to be associated with it). These decisions were themselves overlaid with a wider set of values, most obviously expressed in the tension between the desire to create some kind of urban cultural diversity and the desire to provide a controlled and protected community.

The challenge to these rules and decisions, mounted by Chevigny and those he represented, was intended to expose the *politics* behind them. The case focused on the claim that the regulations restricted freedom of expression. Implicit in this claim was the idea that freedom of expression was not just about the ability to say or write certain ideas; it was also entailed in the right to make certain sounds in certain ways. Freedom of expression was restricted, the argument ran, where constraints were placed on 'the style and instrumentation of music'. The regulations affected the 'special musical ideas which plaintiffs want to express through their instruments, as well as against the range of expression that is available through the sounds, voicings and peculiarities of varied combinations of instruments' (Chevigny, 1991: 112). The court agreed, and ruled that the regulations were indeed a restriction

on freedom of expression. It thereby confirmed the formal connection between political values and musical practice, and the
mediating role by local political institutions. What the court could
not do, however, was to make the change that its ruling implied.
This depended on political will. And as before, this required the
election of a new Mayor (David Dinkins) in 1989.

The New York case is an example of the local state acting first to
restrict popular culture and then to deregulate it. In the UK, similar forms of political intervention can also be observed. The local
state regulates local cultural life through the use of licences. Decisions are made as to who is allowed to run a club, about the hours
it can be open, or about when/whether alcohol is available. They
all have an impact on the kind of place and the kind of activity
that the club represents. Thus, judgements made by the local police, fire services and magistrates shape the organization of popular culture. In the same way, planning decisions also determine
the form and character of popular culture. These can extend from
proposals for new buildings (cinema multiplexes, for example) to
altering existing ones – turning churches into music venues or cinema clubs. And connected to these are decisions about the rent or
rates charged to those who wish to run such venues. These regulatory devices are, however, only a sample of the policy instruments available to local authorities. The local state can take on a
more pro-active role by directly subsidizing and sponsoring cultural activity.

Since 1980, a substantial number of UK local authorities have
been responsible for the provision of recording studios, live venues, concert promotion and music training schemes, all of which
have been directed towards the production of pop music. (A survey conducted in 1989 found twenty-four such initiatives [Street
and Stanley, 1989]; there are now several more.) These ventures
have involved considerable sums (nearly £1 million on the creation of a venue alone [Street, 1993]) and have represented shifts in
political agendas and policy processes – other projects have fallen
by the wayside, other facilities have been underfunded.

In places like Cambridge, Norwich and Newcastle, the local state
has funded venues – the Junction, the Waterfront and the River-
side. Each has brought new sounds and styles to its respective
city, connecting local audiences to national and transnational cultures. Sheffield City Council helped to fund Red Tape, a recording and rehearsal complex that enabled musicians to develop skills

and to create networks which allow music-making to happen. Many other local authorities have traditionally funded cultural events (from brass band competitions to literary festivals). Cambridge City Council has, for example, run a major annual folk festival for over thirty years. These same authorities are also responsible for supporting arts centres, cinemas and community workshops.

The point of these examples is to illustrate some of the ways in which the local state may engage with popular culture. At stake in such involvement are different possible relationships to globalizing trends. In their surveys of cultural policy around the world, Malm and Wallis (1993; Wallis and Malm, 1984) reveal that local sources of power can sometimes be used to protect local cultures from external cultural forms, at other times to expose them to it. Robinson and her colleagues (1991) point out that local arrangements affect the kind of culture that is available to people in particular localities. To observe these practices is not, however, to understand them. We need to look more closely at the forces which lead to local state involvement and at the ideas informing it – to recognize that local involvement is inspired sometimes by protectionism, sometimes by the desire for integration into the global economy. In order to explore in detail the rationale behind local state involvement, I am going to concentrate on the case of support for popular music venues in the UK.

Reasons for local state involvement

It might be supposed that no explanation is needed, or rather the reasons for local state involvement are to be found in history and tradition; it is what they have always done. Certainly there is a well-established pattern of local support for the arts. As the English Association of District Councils (1989: 7) explained: 'Although district councils do not have a statutory duty to make provision for arts activities, they have a long and distinguished track record in building and supporting theatres, museums and art galleries, concert halls and arts centres, and in promoting a wide variety of arts events.' This support cost 330 local authorities £93 million in 1987–8. Theatres, halls and arts centres received £45 million; museums and art galleries benefited by £38 million (ADC, 1989: 8). But even if this support is part of a long tradition, we would still need to explain that tradition, and in doing this to explain why, for instance, it has not typically included pop and rock music. The answer lies, in part, in the fact that such music is seen as a 'commercial' form which is sustained by the market rather than by the state (Mulgan and Worpole, 1986). It has not been subject to the kind of market failures that legitimate other locally subsidized ventures. Local authorities have made an implicit distinction contrast between 'entertainment', serving the leisure market, and 'creative art', aspiring to some truth about the human condition. This distinction has legitimated the decision to support some cultural activities and to ignore others. So why has this separation been breached in recent years, and why have local authorities become actively involved in 'commercial' popular culture? It is not enough to claim, as the Association of District Councils does, that the support is simply the result of recognizing 'the creative energy expended by young people in this field'. Instead, we need to consider the different incentives at work.

The first, and perhaps obvious, reason for supporting popular culture is that it makes economic sense. As Mayor David Dinkins' deputy, Barbara Fife, explained when New York City implemented the court's ruling on the cabaret laws, their action was driven by hard-nosed material considerations: 'The city needs a reasonable number of jobs for musicians. This is part of our general commitment to a new economic development. . . . We need new kinds of economic life – more diverse jobs for young people, in more diverse neighbourhoods. This decision was part of that' (quoted in Chevigny, 1991: 153). Similar thoughts inspired Sheffield City Council's support for Red Tape. In the 1980s, Sheffield bands – like the Human League – were receiving national acclaim, but this success had a very limited impact on the local economy. The money went to London instead, where the studios and the record companies were based. Creating a local recording infrastructure would help to establish a rival pull. This strategy was underpinned by recognition of the commercial importance of entertainment, especially during a period of de-industrialization. As Patrick Seyd (1990: 344) observes of Sheffield's cultural policy strategy: 'Consumerism and leisure are regarded as the two activities primarily capable of stimulating economic growth.'

The connection between economic growth and culture is a common feature of the modern city. In their study of cities in the USA, Logan and Molotch treat urban economic development as the product of a 'growth machine which avidly supports whatever cultural institutions can play a role in building the locality', so that 'museums, theatres, expositions' are viewed as 'auxiliary players' (Logan and Molotch, 1987: 61–2, and 76–9). The cultural sector acts to improve 'the quality of life' in the city and to form part of a strategy for encouraging inward investment. In short, there are strong economic incentives for investing in popular culture.

Political incentives run parallel with the economic ones. At one level, the provision of popular local resources enables politicians to endear themselves to their constituents and to win votes. Equally, control over the distribution of cultural resources can be used to thwart political opponents. Logan and Molotch (1987: 61–2), for instance, found that key actors were 'always ready to oppose cultural and political developments contrary to their interests (for example, black nationalism or communal cults)'. The institutions of popular culture are part of a mechanism of political or social control, and they can be used to achieve certain effects. We have already seen this in the use of zoning and licensing decisions, but they can also be deployed in more positive ways. One local authority, worried about increasing levels of violence and vandalism on a particular train, installed a juke-box and turned a carriage into a club. The vandalism ceased. It is perhaps no coincidence that a number of the British music venues were launched in the aftermath of the city riots of the summer of 1985. Venues were seen as a way of distracting alienated and bored young people.

The idea that cultural provision can work as a form of social control is itself premised on a set of assumptions about the role played by culture. Creating venues is not just a matter of providing somewhere to go; it is about giving effect to a particular way of life. As the case of New York's regulations made clear, the organization of culture can represent and express certain values, so that restricting or supporting cultural activity means promoting or marginalizing particular values. The idea of 'freedom of expression' can be realized in the hearing or playing of sounds. In the same way, support for popular culture can make available different kinds of cultural experience, thereby extending not only people's freedom of choice but their sensitivity to others. This thinking lay behind the Greater London Council's use of music in their commitment to multiculturalism. It is true that the GLC promoted conventional rock concerts, either as part of their commitment to recreation policy or to their various political causes, but these conventional events were part of a more ambitious policy to develop the skills and resources of its citizens, and to promote cultural industries in London. Support for popular music was treated as part of general desire to provide job training and to boost the local economy, as well as serving its commitment to multiculturalism (Biachini, 1987). Summarizing their strategy, the GLC's Michael Ward and Peter Pitt (1985: 5) wrote of their desire to provide 'a resource which can enable far more people to take part in creating their own culture and their own meaning'. Insofar as culture gives expression to political values, and insofar as local authorities are committed to those values, here is a further incentive to support popular culture.

What we have looked at so far are the incentives for local state support, but in themselves these do not explain the decision to act. For that, we need to look at the political process that brought these policies and resources into existence. There is, of course, no single explanation for why and how the local state becomes involved in popular culture, so what I consider here are the kinds of explanations that might be advanced.

Making local state policy

Policy-making is part of a process of social learning, which makes previous examples crucial to present practices. The general trend in local authority provision in the UK stems in part from the initiative taken by the Greater London Council in the early 1980s, before it was abolished by the Thatcher government in 1985. The GLC's sponsorship of both the production and consumption of popular culture, its support for the culture industry as well as for one-off events, created an important precedent. Its legacy can be detected in the development of such Sheffield projects as the Leadmill venue and Red Tape; and these, in turn, were to provide the inspiration for the Norwich Venue Campaign, which was itself to act as a model for similar campaigns in Ipswich and Cambridge.

To talk of this chain of influences is to assume the existence of a crucial precondition: the ability to communicate these examples. This depends on the existence of a network that allows people to discover what is going on. In Holland, there are well-established networks designed to keep people informed; in the UK, they are less well developed (Frith, 1993). But, in any case, information alone is not enough, nor is the fact of the precedent. It is not just a matter of knowing what others have done; it is also a matter of wanting to intimate them. For this, there has to be a recognition of the benefits of the precedent; people have to ally their interests to the change.

One possible explanation for political interest in popular music is the politicians themselves. It is, the argument runs, the product of individual enthusiasts. The idea is that the policies only emerge where there are advocates – product champions – to endorse them, and that such endorsement is largely inspired by personal interest. In thinking about policies designed to promote popular culture, the temptation might be to associate such policies with a younger generation of politicians who, by virtue of their age, have a particular commitment to music. But while members of the GLC's Labour group were younger than their colleagues elsewhere in the country, the age difference was not great (Gyford, Leach and Game, 1989). In any case, given the ever increasing age range for popular music, it does not make sense to talk of pop as the exclusive preserve of youth. The important question is, therefore, not who likes pop/rock music, but who thinks it is politically significant. This, I would argue, is a function more of cultural experience than of age alone.

The idea that popular culture constitutes a site for political engagement, that it is part of a legitimate agenda, cannot be assumed. For the most part, politicians of all political parties have been – at best – uninterested in popular music, except as an instrument of self-advancement (see chapter 3). A poll of British MPs in 1996 revealed that few took any interest in pop music, although one or two admitted to buying the latest George Michael album *Older* (*The Guardian*, 29 July 1996). What the GLC, and its imitators, embodied was the view that popular music was culturally, politically and economically important, a view that owed something to the experience and rhetoric of 1960s flower power and late 1970s punk. It was these moments that forged the political connection with popular culture. But while this experience may explain the politicians' willingness to allocate resources to popular music, it does not provide an interest for doing so. For this, there has to be some identifiable (party) political gain.

Individual dispositions may help to explain an inclination to support a popular music venue, a sympathy for a music policy, but the key actors are not individual politicians. The more important element is the political party. Without the backing of the party, individual initiative counts for relatively little. The question is, therefore: what party interests were entwined in support for popular music?

Almost all the councils involved in building and sponsoring studios and venues were Labour ones, committed to one brand or other of social democracy. There is, though, a danger of reading too much into this. The correlation may owe more to the fact that the initiatives were linked to city/town centres, rather than to Labour strongholds. In other words, the policies were the product of the political economy of urban areas, and not of ideology alone. There are two reasons for taking this position. The first is provided by the fact that, on the one hand, some non-Labour councils were responsible for such initiatives, and, on the other, a number of Labour councils resisted local pressure for venues (Street, 1995). Secondly, Labour nationally had no tradition of, or ideological commitment to, commercial popular culture. Its cultural associations had been primarily with folk music, and then mainly as a soundtrack to its other concerns. Red Wedge was the exception rather than the rule (Street, 1988). And on this one occasion when the Labour Party might have demonstrated a genuine concern in the political economy of popular culture, and might have promised new policy initiatives, it did not do so. Red Wedge was treated as an exercise in image-enhancement and vote-winning, not cultural policy-making. If the Labour Party saw pop music primarily as a useful means of winning the youth vote, and if it tended to marginalize the cultural and industrial aspects of commercial music, then national party politics do little to explain the commitment to venues and studios. Besides, given that such policy developments entailed taking substantial economic and political risks, there has to be more behind them than a cynical electoral calculation. If party politics are significant, then it may be that it is their local form that matters most.

Although the national Labour Party was under no very intense pressure to expand its commitment to popular music provision, local parties found themselves being targeted by campaigns for venues. This lobby was not felt by the national party because national provision was not something over which the party had control, or for which there were obvious sources of pressure (the Musicians' Union's relative weakness compounded this). At the local level, however, musicians and fans did come to articulate a demand for improved facilities. In Norwich, Cambridge and Ipswich, for example, local campaigns were organized around the demand for venues. Both the Norwich and Cambridge lobbies were ultimately successful (Stanley, 1990; Street, 1993).

However, pressure alone is not sufficient explanation, if only because pressure in itself, whatever its intensity, does not produce results. Outside pressure needs internal collaborators ('advocacy coalitions'). For this to happen, there needs to be a degree of sympathy between lobbyists and politicians, a sense of a shared culture. It is significant, for example, that two of the key activists in the Norwich campaign had gained political experience through Youth CND and a local cooperative. This enabled them to tailor and target their campaign in ways that prompted a response among councillors, especially when these same councillors were being lobbied by local residents who were fearful of the proposed venue. But such explanations need to be supplemented by some account of why the lobby itself formed and why its particular agenda was adopted by local politicians (given the infinite range of alternative projects – leisure centres, swimming pools, and so on – that could have been taken up).

One way to think about this is to consider an example where lobbying failed. While the local campaigns organized in Norwich and Cambridge succeeded, a similar lobby in Ipswich was rejected. Despite the existence of a venue campaign and of sympathetic councillors (one of whom managed a local record store), no effective advocacy coalition formed. Some of the other councillors were unimpressed by, or even hostile to, the GLC example, and the more sympathetic politicians could not themselves find reasons for subsidizing rock music in preference to the local theatre. Perhaps crucially, the council committee (Recreation and Amenities) responsible for the decision defined its brief in such a way that 'leisure' was linked more to 'sport' than 'entertainment'. In other words, the success or failure of venue campaigns depends upon the micro- and bureaucratic politics of the local state. However, these details of the local policy process need to be placed within a wider institutional and ideological context. The decisions being taken in city halls are not isolated ones, but are part of a larger structure of relations and ideas.

The period in which local authorities invested in popular music coincided with a major shift in the relationship between central government and local government. The change had been experienced as a shrinkage in local budgets and a restriction in the range of policy options available. The combined effect of this state of affairs was to push local authorities into a different mode of policy-making and to cause a revision of their political agendas (Young, 1991). These trends forced councils to be more receptive to new ventures, especially ones that would promote local economic development.

While market forces can generate a supply of cinemas for Hollywood films, at least in towns over a particular size, the market cannot bear the costs of supplying non-mainstream cinema or music. For this reason, national, regional and local political actors are required to fill the gap left by the market. There is support to be had from regional arts funding, most notably that provided through the Arts Council, but this money is directed to cinema and fine art, rather than popular music. The supply of venues for music has had to depend on *ad hoc* subsidy or more established subsidy (through local colleges and universities). For local councils to intervene on a systematic basis there had to be a powerful set of incentives.

One of these was provided by a growing awareness among councils of the need to attract investment to their region. Investors have to be persuaded of the desirability of the locality. One measure of 'attractiveness' is the arts and leisure facilities, the cultural environment. Many councils put money into leisure and arts for just this reason. Norwich's Waterfront was sited near an area intended for the city's future development. Similarly, Ipswich Borough Council supported the creation of a European Visual Arts Centre, arguing that 'the most exciting possibilities were in the development of a new, purpose-designed building on the waterfront in the Ipswich Wet Dock, as an integral part of the impending redevelopment of large parts of that important area' (DGIMT, 1988). This process has been described as the 'marketing' of cities, the selling of investment locations within a global economy (Bianchini and Parkinson, 1993).

The second dominant incentive was the need to provide employment and training within the realm of responsibility. This pressure is most sharply focused in the desire to help inner-city regeneration. As the Association of District Councils (1989: 37) observed: 'It has increasingly been recognized that the arts are an important *industry* employing large numbers of people, generating a lot of income, attracting many tourists, earning foreign currency, and that it is quite wrong to see them only as a burden on the taxpayer and rate payer, a minority, elitist activity of marginal relevance to the mainstream of the economy and society' (its emphasis). What is true of the arts in general is particularly true of popular culture.

These pressures pushing local authorities towards spending on pop music ventures were reinforced by developments within cultural policy and the cultural industries. The expansion and proliferation of the entertainment industry have served to emphasize its cultural and economic importance. Popular music, especially since Live Aid in 1985, can no longer be viewed as the exclusive province of the young, nor can it be described as part of a dissident sub- or counter-culture. The pop music industry is, as we have seen, now part of a global network, marked by increasing centralization and cross-media connections. Because corporations such as Sony and Polygram have developed dominant, interlinked entertainment interests, they have been able to integrate pop into many aspects of everyday life so that it now forms part of the cultural mainstream. To this extent, local authority cultural provision has to take account of this new order. At the same time, the pop industry still remains dependent on the regions, both as a source of talent and as a way of constructing the cultural significance attached to its production and consumption. For the local authorities, these twin needs – to both supply and be supplied by the dominant culture – lie behind their political involvement with popular culture. There is a political and cultural desire to mark the region as 'special', but this difference has to be achieved within a national and transnational industry. A similar logic applied to those lobbyists who acted to pressure local authorities to build venues. They wanted to be able to hear *national* bands in *their* town.

Conclusion

This chapter began with a straightforward aim: to demonstrate the local state's involvement in popular culture. This involved challenging two assumptions which have dominated the study of popular culture – that it is an exclusively global/national phenomenon and that it is largely unaffected by the state. This marginalization of the local and the political was, I suggested, misplaced. The local state has, in fact, become involved in the sponsorship of popular culture. The important question then becomes why this involvement has occurred. The commitment of resources to popular music has been the result of local, national and global factors, in which political and economic interests have been linked with more general patterns in the development of culture and the culture industries. More precisely, the incentive to solve the market failure represented by an absence of venues has come from, on the one hand, the political ideologies and interests of political activists and local campaigners, and, on the other, shifts in the character of local government, measured by a revision in its agenda, and driven by its exposure to new economic goals and political demands.

There is one final issue that has to be addressed: what is actually achieved by the local state's involvement? After all, if we look at the legitimating rhetoric, these ventures carry a considerable burden. Local authorities and their lobbyists, in justifying the commitment of funds to venues and studios, have used the rhetoric of 'empowerment' and 'democracy'. In a similar way, Chevigny talked of freedom of expression in challenging the regulations that operated within New York. Such language indicates that 'culture' is not simply about leisure and economics, but that it has considerable political importance too. The suggestion is that culture – whether in the form of 'art' or 'entertainment' – is a means by which political interests are registered and realized. Cultural policy, therefore, may not just be a product of the political process but an element within it.

The rhetoric of 'empowerment' implies that local resources enable people to control their lives and to establish their identity. One way in which this happens is through some notion of local distinctiveness, of cultural specificity – hence the idea that places have their own sound, that there is something special about the city or town. As Tony Mitchell (1996: 264) observes in his survey of local musics around the world, local practices and musical idiosyncrasies are increasingly important to the way people identify themselves. When the Waterfront was threatened with closure, this plaintive letter appeared in the local newspaper:

Having grown up and gone to school in Norwich, it always struck
me as sad that many of my friends in their late teens felt the need to
leave Norwich for other cities, often in the hope of finding greater
excitement. . . . I tried hard to argue that this [Norwich] wasn't the
provincial backwater that some people made it out to be. . . . The
Waterfront became central to my arguments. . . . The fact that the
venue had been created by Norwich people, and was so popular,
was proof that Norwich was indeed looking forward. . . . (*Eastern
Evening News*, 5 May 1993)

What this letter reveals is, on the one hand, a thought that Norwich is special, while it also shares something in common with
other 'great' cities in the larger national and international scene.
It is not that Norwich is unique, or the birthplace of an exclusive
local culture, but rather that it is able to take part in the key cultural networks. As Frith (1993: 23) argues, the modern notion of
local distinctiveness emerges through participation in a global
order: 'the local is now equated with the different not by reference to local histories or traditions but in terms of a position in
the global market place.' The identity deriving from place is
defined not endogenously, without reference to an outside
world, but rather by both locating the place in that outside world
and, at the same time, by establishing a sense of difference
from other similar communities within it. Or as George Lipsitz
(1994: 180) argues: 'space and place still matter; the global processes that shape us have very different inflections in different
places. Cognitive mapping in the future will require both local
and global knowledge, demanding that we blend rootedness in
specific cultures and traditions with competence at mobility and
mixing.'

The Waterfront served to put Norwich 'on the map'. That is, it
provided an entrance into the dominant cultural network. This
was most apparent when it was announced in January 1992 that
the Waterfront was to host a week of live broadcasts for BBC Radio 1. The Waterfront became part of the national scene, and in
the process – paradoxically – the importance of the locality was
confirmed. This, though, did not mark the incorporation of the
Waterfront into the national processes. The existence of a local
live venue – where the bands come to Norwich – gave local fans a
focus for their own sense of difference, and this sense of 'difference' fuels a sense of political identity (Frith and Horne, 1987;
Grossberg, 1992a). Local authority provision is part of a wider

PART THREE

Political Theory/
Cultural Theory

CHAPTER SEVEN

Cultural theories of politics

The ignorant child listens with curiosity to the tales, which flow into his mind like his mother's milk, like choice wine of his father, and form its nutrient. They seem to him to explain what he has seen: to the youth they account for the way of his tribe, and stamp the renown of his ancestors; to the man they introduce the employment suited to his nation and climate, and thus they become inseparable from his whole life.

Johann Gottfried Herder, *Reflections on the Philosophy of the History of Mankind*

The relationship between politics and popular culture has taken many guises in this book. In recent chapters, we have seen popular culture as the product of the policy process: either as an object of censorship and regulation, or as a beneficiary of state resources and institutions. Before that, we saw how politicians, actors, musicians and others have all used popular culture to advance political causes. We have seen too how political importance has been claimed for popular culture – as a weapon in political struggles, as an expression of political ideas. But despite the many links made between politics and popular culture, it does not follow that there is any necessary logic or coherence to the connection. Films may be censored for political reasons, politicians may consort with media stars, and rock artists may promote worthy charities, but this does not mean that any of it makes any difference. They may all rest upon a delusion – that censorship prevents the spread of certain thoughts, that politicians look better in showbiz company, and so on. The politicians' use of advertising and their reliance on the stars of popular culture may reveal something about contemporary political practices, but have no relevance beyond this. It may tell us nothing about the effect of popular culture on political discourse and political action. In the same way, media performers may like to *think* they can make a political difference through popular culture, but we should not assume that their efforts will yield their intended effects.

We need to have good reason for believing that popular culture does indeed matter to the way political thoughts and actions are formed. After all, popular culture may merely be holding a mirror (a distorting one, at that) up to the world. It may be perfectly reasonable to claim that if we really want to understand political life, the way actors and institutions operate, then studying popular culture tells us little. What we actually need to know about, according to this view, are the forces which determine the roles or interests of political actors. It is only if popular culture actually contributes to the character of these roles and identities that we can attribute political importance to it. The mere fact that politicians target popular culture, or stars pronounce on politics, should not be taken as evidence for the idea that popular culture makes a political difference.

This chapter attempts to establish whether, in fact, it does make sense to refer to popular culture in explaining political action. Does popular culture do more than mimic or reflect political change, is it more than an instrument of politics? And if so, what exactly does it do? How might the pleasures of popular music or football or dancing or soap operas be related to the way people think or act politically? Such questions are central to any account of the 'politics of popular culture'. My argument is that popular culture does indeed matter to the way we understand politics, but to say this is to not to claim some crude causal relationship. Watching *Die Hard* is not going to turn anyone into a Republican voter, any more than listening to Bruce Springsteen will make them a Democrat.

To give a hint of how popular culture may, however, be embedded in political action, let me offer the example of punk rock (1976–8), or rather the way its history has been written. In books like Jon Savage's *England's Dreaming* (1991) and Greil Marcus' *Lipstick Traces* (1989a), the music is not a mirror upon a 'real' world, its sounds and sentiments are not simply reflections of changing social conditions. Equally, punk does not make people behave in particular ways; it did not make them anti-social or rebels. Rather, according to Savage, engagement with punk was engagement with politics. Punk was a way of experiencing and articulating political feelings, a way of making sense. For Marcus, punk was part of a conversation in which certain ideas, ones that are denied formal recognition, are given currency. Punk was part of a secret history of dissent, in which 'common sense' was being challenged and disrupted. Both Savage and Marcus, therefore, see punk as part of the way the world, and the sense we make of it, is constituted. Both writers refuse the boundaries that typically divide 'politics' from other forms of life (like 'entertainment'), and in blurring these boundaries, the authors embrace an account of human action that places popular culture at its centre. It was not just that popular culture was touched by the politics of economic and social change, nor that popular culture commented on these changes. Popular culture *was* politics. To make this sort of argument is to make two related claims. The first is that popular culture is a form of political activity, that it involves the expression of political ideas and the inspiration of political actions. The other claim is that in understanding 'politics', we have to allow for the role played by cultural activity, and, in particular, popular cultural activity. The first claim is the subject of the next chapter. Here I want to examine how 'culture' might be incorporated into an account of politics, how the boundaries get blurred. I want to begin by looking at the way, traditionally, the study of politics has treated the part played by culture.

Arguments about cultural explanations

There are those who deny that culture can play any useful explanatory role. For them, culture is part of the background (at best), adding perhaps a little local colour to the main action but not contributing in a significant or profound way. The intellectual roots of this attitude can be found in marxism and functionalism. Both treat culture as subservient to material forces or systemic requirements. Such positions do not necessarily deny all relevance to the ideas and values which constitute a culture, but they do limit severely its role in explaining political activity. And even those who, like Brian Barry (1978), belong to neither methodological camp believe that there are usually more parsimonious explanations for political action than that provided by culture. Accounts of national decline which focus on 'laziness' or 'the collapse of family values' are essentially cultural explanations, in which unflattering comparisons are made with other nations which are economically successful and have an ethos of hard work and a reverence for the family. Apart from the problem of actually measuring concepts like 'laziness' or 'hard work' or 'family values' (especially in different times and contexts), there is also the difficulty of identifying them as the *cause* (rather than the symbol) of decline. Explanations which address the historical and economic conditions of decline are regarded as more convincing.

Other thinkers, however, make culture a core idea. Early in the second volume of *Democracy in America*, de Tocqueville (1988: 434) writes:

> ... for society to exist and, even more, for society to prosper, it is essential that all the minds of the citizens should always be rallied and held together by some leading ideas; and that could never happen unless each of them sometimes came to draw his opinions from the same source and was ready to accept some belief ready made.

Political thought is not the product of original reflection upon new circumstances, it is the result of pre-packaged thinking; it is the product of a culture. Furthermore, such thinking is essential to social existence. As de Tocqueville (1988: 434) explains:

> If a man had to prove for himself all the truths of which he makes use every day, he would never come to an end of it. He would wear himself out proving preliminary points and make no progress. Since life is too short for such a course and human facilities too limited, man has to accept as certain a whole heap of facts and opinions which he has neither leisure nor power to examine and verify for himself, things which cleverer men than he have discovered and which the crowd accepts. On that foundation he builds the house of his own thoughts. He does not act so for any conscious choice, for the inflexible laws of his existence compel him to behave like that.

This view is an echo of arguments advanced by Johann Gottfried Herder a century earlier, and quoted at the beginning of this chapter. Herder (1968) believed that society was founded upon shared ideas. Both de Tocqueville and Herder make culture – the ideas and values of a society – central to their account of society and behaviour within it. A contemporary version of these views can be detected in Michael Walzer's (1992: 66) argument for the crucial role played by symbolism in politics: 'Politics is an art of unification; from many, it makes one. And symbolic activity is perhaps our most important means of bringing things together, both intellectually and emotionally, thus overcoming isolation and even individuality.' For Walzer, like de Tocqueville and Herder, the cultural realm creates the terms through which people live; it makes possible political action.

This broad suggestion, that political life is the product of culture, is the inspiration behind Cultural Theory, a view most actively promoted by the late Aaron Wildavsky. Addressing a major conference of US political scientists, Wildavsky (1987) announced that it was culture which generated people's preferences, and that these, in turn, drive the political process itself. Wildavsky drew upon the anthropology of Mary Douglas (1992) for his argument, but a similar line can be detected within postmodern theorizing. In its mistrust of grand narratives and first causes, postmodernism has placed increasing weight on cultural accounts of human action (Rorty, 1989). It is hard not to hear the whispered echo of Herder and de Tocqueville in Jon Simons' (1995: 696) recent pronouncement on the nature of contemporary political life: 'the circulation of signs, images and ideas holds society together and legitimates the system . . . postmodern social systems do not need to be legitimated by political theory because communicative technologies legitimate the system as image.' Receptivity to such arguments has been encouraged by the rise of nationalism, which is seen by some as a cultural phenomenon. The political importance of culture is also claimed in the debate about the effect of mass communications on behaviour. Video games and violent films, tabloid papers and television soaps, have all been blamed for our social ills and our political practices. But to observe these trends is not, of course, to establish their authority; we should not mistake them for an incontrovertible case for the reinstatement of culture as part of an account of political action. They do, however, suggest that there is a serious argument to be examined.

If culture has a useful role, though, it must do more than simply fill out the details of political action; it must actually shape (or even determine) the character and intention of that action. A cultural theory must account for action more persuasively than do, say, materialist or rational choice theories. Or more weakly, it must be able to demonstrate that culture is an indispensable and decisive factor in such accounts. If either is the case, then culture acquires an important explanatory role. I want to begin this inquiry into cultural explanations of politics by considering a classic, if flawed, attempt to provide systematic evidence for such an account: *The Civic Culture* by Gabriel Almond and Sidney Verba (1963).

The Civic Culture

The Civic Culture did much to revive the notion that culture (or, more particularly, 'political culture') was crucial to the operation of any political system. Its impact owed a great deal to the fact that it was a cross-national comparison which supplied hard data on the views of citizens in different political systems. And on the basis of this data, the authors claimed to find a correlation between the attitudes of citizens and the performance of their political system.

Citizens' attitudes, according to Almond and Verba, are the elements which create a 'political culture'. These attitudes are to be understood as psychological dispositions of individuals: 'attitudes towards the political system and its various parts, and attitudes towards the role of the self in the system' (Almond and Verba, 1963: 13). They are composed of three orientations: (i) cognitive, (ii) affective and (iii) evaluative, which refer, respectively, to individuals' knowledge of the system, their feelings towards it and their judgement of it (Almond and Verba, 1963: 15). What Almond and Verba wanted to know was: how did these dispositions differ within and between countries, and how did the differences between them affect political stability? By studying 'the concepts of political culture', they aimed to reveal 'the relationship between the attitudes and motivations of the discrete individuals who make up political systems and the character and performance of political systems' (Almond and Verba, 1963: 33). Note, though, that they assume some such connection exists. 'One must assume', they write (Almond and Verba, 1963: 74), 'that the attitudes we report have

some significant relationship to the way the political system operates – to its stability, effectiveness and so forth.' Such an assumption allowed them to claim, for example, that Britain's balance of
'diversity and consensualism, rationalism and traditionalism'
made possible the development of British democracy (Almond
and Verba, 1963: 8). This relationship between attitudes and performance is conceived in terms of 'congruence'. It is not that attitudes create systems, or systems attitudes. Instead, the two exist
independently, and the point is to observe the 'fit'. If attitudes
and system gel together, if they are congruent, then we have stability. Where they are incompatible, there is instability. There is a
final nuance to this argument. For Almond and Verba, there are
types of culture, and only one – the civic culture – works effectively in a democracy: 'the civic culture is a participant political
culture in which the political culture and political structure are
congruent' (Almond and Verba, 1963: 31, also 21, and 50).

Implicit in these claims about the congruence of political structures and political attitudes is the thought that individual attitudes
make a difference to, among other things, political stability. This
connection between individual attitude and aggregate performance is provided by political culture, which links 'micro politics
and macro politics', and which builds a bridge 'between the behaviour of individuals and the behaviour of systems' (Almond
and Verba, 1963: 32). What is interesting about Almond and Verba's argument is that the attitudes need not be explicitly political,
but may be composed of the 'nonpolitical attitudes and nonpolitical
affiliations' of civil society (Almond and Verba, 1963: 300). Ordinary daily, apparently apolitical attitudes can take on political significance. Almond and Verba's five-nation comparative data were
used to put the flesh on these theoretical bones and to confirm the
idea that political stability was a product of particular attitudes.

Almond and Verba's analysis has been subjected to considerable criticism. Some critics, for example, argued that despite all
the detailed information that was recorded, the results were more
impressionistic than systematic (Lijphart, 1989: 41). As Barry (1978:
51–2) commented: 'although it provides a wealth of fascinating
survey data on political attitudes, there is very little attempt made
to provide evidence about the relation between these attitudes and
the working of a country's actual political system.' For Welch, this
problem stems from a fundamental tension within *The Civic Culture*. It wants both to provide a comparative analysis of political

cultures *across* countries, for which some level of generalization is necessary, and to provide a sociological account of political cultures *within* each country, for which specific local detail is required. Welch argues convincingly that the two cannot be reconciled, and further that the explanatory power of political culture is under constant threat: 'The more fully cultural differences are specified, the less easy it is to separate them from their putative effect' (Welch, 1993: 71). The culture becomes part of a complex web of connections which make it impossible to identify a discrete role for culture.

Other critics argued that political culture could best be seen as the result, not the cause, of political processes; it is the oil that smooths the operation of the political machine. Thus, Barry suggests that 'political culture' is merely composed of 'reasonable expectations founded on common experience' of the existing system. 'Obviously, if this interpretation is correct,' he continues (1978: 51–2), 'there are no grounds for saying that the correlation arises from the conduciveness of the "civic culture" to "democracy", but rather for the unexciting conclusion that "democracy" produces the "civic culture".'

A similar scepticism has been voiced by materialists for whom culture is little more than the outward sign of an inner reality. Thus, Jerzy Wiatr's (1989: 114) marxist critique argues that Almond and Verba neglected 'the relationship between socio-economic reality and political institutions, on the one hand, and the impact this relationship has on political culture on the other'. Or as Pateman (1989: 84) put it, their 'argument completely neglects the association between class and participation and implies that so-cial status is irrelevant to which side of the balance a citizen occupies, or to the citizen's view of the rationality of action or inaction.' There are, in short, two linked lines of attack on political culture's explanatory usefulness: first, it may be an effect rather than a cause of political processes; and secondly, insofar as it has a significant role, it is to serve pre-existing social and political interests.

Lijphart has attempted to defend Almond and Verba from these criticisms by clarifying the explanatory role attributed to culture. He argues that the question of political culture's explanatory power has been wrongly posed. For Lijphart, it is a mistake to think in terms of either/or – either structure or culture. The two are in fact interlinked so that 'the performance of political structures is there-fore both a cause and an effect of the political culture' (Lijphart,

1989: 32). But if Lijphart wants to make this claim for culture, then he (and Almond and Verba) has to develop a much fuller picture of what culture involves. It cannot be seen simply as the 'dispositions' described in *The Civic Culture*.

The idea of culture

Almond and Verba operate with a very narrow notion of culture, one that derives primarily from their behaviourist assumptions. Political culture is seen as the sum of individual psychological states, themselves the product of a process of 'socialization'. Such a view conceives of human thought and action as part of a stimuli–response system. Attitudes are inculcated and then become the cause of particular perceptions and actions. For Richard Topf (1989), Almond and Verba's 'pattern of orientations' inevitably gives rise to an instrumentalist account of action in which political attitudes are exclusively concerned with attempts to change government policy. Apart from the rather crude psychology and the mechanistic politics, their approach used a very basic notion of culture. Culture is merely the aggregate of individual dispositions, which means it has no separate, collective form – it is precisely the sum of its parts; nor can it be the subject of interpretation – its meaning and significance are limited to the behaviour it produces.

Against such views of culture are those which invest it with an expressive role and a structure, rather than treating it as instrumental and an attribute of individuals. This view of culture derives, according to Raymond Williams (1981), from two different ideas. One of these defines culture as a form of self- or collective expression, seeing it as some branch of the arts (whether 'high' or 'folk'). The other notion of culture is most closely associated with anthropology. According to this definition, culture is constituted as a general set of background thoughts and assumptions, 'ways of life' and 'habits of mind'. For Williams, these two versions of culture are intimately linked. He finds a common ground between a view of culture (a) as an 'informing spirit' which manifests 'the central interests and values of a "people"' and (b) as the establishing of 'a general social order' through a particular way of life. For Williams (1981:10–14), the two are inseparable. Culture is a form both of expression and of social order, and as such it cannot be reduced to a set of individual dispositions. It becomes instead a kind of public language through which individuals communicate. This broader definition was to be acknowledged in the rediscovery of political culture in the 1980s.

While *The Civic Culture* generated much discussion, it stimulated little emulation (one notable exception was Marsh, 1977). This was partly a result of the daunting empirical task which such study required, but it also reflected changes in the paradigms of political science and social science generally. The rise of a marxist and marxist-influenced agenda marginalized political culture (Brown, 1979: 3–7), an effect that was to be reinforced by another, very different paradigm: rational choice theory. For many marxists, culture was an epiphenomenon of the material conditions which determined the conditions of class existence. Culture was primarily a reflection of imbalances of power, whose main effect was to reproduce class inequalities. It had no independent effect. A similar conclusion is reached via rational choice theory. All action is to be understood in terms of individual games played by rational individuals. A culture may emerge as a result of these interactions, but it serves simply as a coordinating device. The culture can take any form, since it should be understood only in terms of its role within games played within any given setting (Elster, 1989: 248–9). However, growing disillusionment with these purely materialist or individualist accounts of politics has allowed political culture to re-emerge as an important topic in political science. On the one hand, culture was acknowledged as enjoying some relative autonomy from the material base, and in this autonomy, it could have political effects which help to change those material conditions. Equally, rational individuals could not, in themselves, generate the conditions necessary for their successful interaction: markets need a culture of reciprocity to sustain themselves. Both trends led to a re-examination of the role of culture.

The revival in interest in political culture brought with it a richer notion of culture, one derived from developments in other disciplines – notably sociology, literature and history – in which culture was treated as a powerful active agent. This new version of political culture incorporated a far wider range of human responses and a broader portrait of the 'political' than was envisaged by Almond and Verba. David Robertson (1985: 263), for example, defines political culture not just as 'the totality of ideas and attitudes towards authority' but also as the ideas and attitudes towards 'discipline, governmental responsibilities and entitlements'. In other words, political culture represented a set of moral or ideological judgements. In a similar vein, Richard Rose (1980: 116–17) writes of the 'values, beliefs and emotions' which, while being 'taken for granted', 'constitute' the culture and 'give meaning to politics'. These definitions portray political culture not as a set of dispositions or pre-ordained attitudes, but rather as, in Topf's words (1989: 53), 'the form of the moral order'. Political culture is something *lived*. Topf (1989: 67) argues that political attitudes should be viewed as 'expressions of "values", or better, of positions in the moral order, constitutive of the political culture'. In a similar vein, Brian Girvin (1989) attributes to political culture the task of defining a country's political ideals and identity. Thus, political culture does not describe a pre-given set of psychological states, but becomes part of the language of politics, and as such constitutes political experience.

In his comparison of political culture in North America and Britain, Richard Merelman (1991: 45–56) deploys the revised version of political culture; that is, one in which the focus is on ideas (rather than attitudes) and upon the collective construction of (rather than individual disposition towards) concepts like liberty. These ideas are seen to shape political activity, determining people's views about whether the system delivers 'individual freedom'. As Merelman (1991: 55) writes: 'culture consists of collective representations which eventually influence people's subjective dispositions towards conflictive democratic participation.' For Merelman, culture consists of symbols which motivate action, and different cultures will produce different political responses. Of particular significance here is that, in this broadened account of culture as 'collective representations', Merelman is inviting the inclusion of popular culture as a form of political culture. Merelman's approach echoes Walzer's in that it emphasizes the importance of the symbolic in politics. Culture provides the terms in which politics is conducted. Take the key notion within democratic politics: 'the people'. Walzer (1992: 66–7) argues that the 'people' 'can only be symbolized' because they have 'no palpable shape or substance'. Indeed, for Walzer, 'the image [of the people] provides a starting point for politics.' If this is the case, the source and character of those images take on considerable political importance.

Underpinning such claims is an argument that links culture to social and political action. The crucial element in this connection is that of 'the symbol' – the way in which images and artefacts can evoke a range of political attitudes and experiences. What is lacking in Merelman and Walzer is, however, any account of how symbols perform their role. This issue is addressed, however, by John Thompson in his study of the connection between culture and ideology. He too grants a key role to symbols. Thompson (1990: 58) views them as *constitutive* of social relations: 'Symbolic forms are not merely representations which serve to articulate or observe social relations or interests which are constituted fundamentally and essentially at a pre-symbolic level: rather, symbolic forms are continuously and creatively implicated in the constitution of social relations as such.' The same kind of thought is to be found in the work of Pierre Bourdieu, who writes (1986: 253; my emphasis): 'The reality of the social world is in fact partly determined by the struggles between agents over *the representation of their position in the social world* and, consequently, of that world.' This approach, which treats culture as an integral component of social action, makes explicit the shift from a narrowly defined political culture to a more general cultural theory of political action, itself derived from cultural studies.

Emerging from the work of people like Raymond Williams and Richard Hoggart, who sought to meld the worlds of social science and literature, and borrowing from Gramsci and from the Frankfurt School, cultural studies came to view 'culture' as a place in which imagination and lived experience coalesced. In his essay 'Culture is Ordinary', Williams (1989: 4) wrote: 'Every human society has its own shape, its own purposes, its own meanings. Every human society expresses these, in institutions, and in arts and learning. The making of a society is the finding of common meanings and directions, and its growth is an active debate and amendment under pressures of experience, contact, and discovery, writing themselves into the land.' This argument is realized in the idea of 'symbolic creativity' and the thought that people use existing cultural resources to engage in 'the formation and reproduction of collective and individual identities' (Willis, 1990: 6). Such an approach automatically places considerable weight upon the role of symbols and upon the dynamic part played by them in human thought and action. The cultural studies view of culture sees it both as being actively created out of the available resources and as constitutive of political relations; it is neither the product of a behavioural disposition nor a functional necessity.

These approaches to culture inevitably blur any neat line between it and politics. By defining culture as a 'moral order', by seeing it as expressive and constitutive rather than instrumental, and by treating it as interpreted or created, the suggestion is of a much more complex relationship between culture and political action, in which to talk of 'congruence' or 'fit' is to miss the point. On the one hand, culture consists of the judgements citizens pass on political behaviour. On the other hand, those attitudes are also constitutive of politics, in the sense that they help to create the language through which politics is conducted. I want now to draw out the implication of this approach more fully, to see how these general accounts of culture are linked to political thought and action.

The case of nationalism

In order to explain what is at stake in competing claims about the role of culture in politics, I want to look briefly at the case of nationalism. It is, after all, a political phenomenon which is often represented in cultural terms, through the language and images which define the nation and its members. This cultural identity is then interpreted as the basis of decisions to protest, fight, secede or whatever. But can such political activity be attributed to the power of culture? Do the symbols of nationhood provide reasons for taking up arms? We can certainly find writers who make the first move in this argument, who treat national identity as cultural.

Anthony Smith (1991: 91–2), for example, argues that the idea of the nation, of the boundaries of a political identity, is culturally formed: 'More than a style and doctrine of politics, nationalism is a *form of culture* – an ideology, a language, mythology, symbolism and consciousness – that has achieved global resonance, and the nation is a type of identity whose meaning and priority is presupposed by this form of culture' (his emphasis). In a similar vein, Benedict Anderson (1983: 15; his emphasis), like Walzer, sees the nation as something that exists in the imagination; the nation

exists as an 'imagined political community. . . . It is *imagined* because the members of even the smallest nation will never know
most of their fellow members, meet them, or even hear of them,
yet in the minds of each lives the image of their communion.' David
Miller (1988: 648, and 657), who sees nationality as 'the shared
beliefs of a set of people', argues that these beliefs are constituted
by the stories which are told about the past. These stories may not
be 'true', they may be myths, but as David Archard (1995: 477–8)
notes, this does not alter their political impact: 'They [the myths]
are deeply rooted in popular culture, and insofar as they do serve
important practical purposes they will continue to be accepted as
true.' Tied into these myths about the nation are myths about other
nations. As Linda Colley (1992: 5–6) suggests, a nation is constructed around ideas of the Other, of who does not belong. The
point is that the idea of the nation is dependent on cultural representations.

Culturally sustained boundaries and identities then become the
subject of political conflict. In Northern Ireland, for example, the
Ulster Young Unionist Council announced:

> The political relevance of culture today can be clearly seen when
> one examines the way our enemies especially in Sinn Fein have
> hijacked the so-called 'Gaelic culture' of Ireland. They have made
> street names and schools into political issues which they exploit
> and by reason of the fact that we reject this so-called Irish culture,
> they claim that we are not Irishmen; and therefore have no right to
> claim this country as our own. (Quoted in McAuley, 1991: 68)

But there is a danger of slipping too easily from seeing cultural
representations as symbolic of political divides into seeing them
as the source of those divides. As Bourdieu (1991: 222) observes:
'The frontier, that product of a legal act of delimitation, produces
cultural difference as much as it is produced by it.' The rest of this
chapter takes up the issue that Bourdieu addresses: the extent to
which culture is implicated in political action, whether it merely
reflects underlying divisions or whether it actually constitutes
them. What follows is an examination of four different answers,
each one the result of a competing set of assumptions and ways of
comprehending political action. The four are categorized as follows: materialist, idealist, individualist and interpretative. They
represent views in which culture plays a central role, and views
where it is of marginal significance, and between them they cap-

ture the main theoretical disputes, as identified by Martin Hollis (1994), within the social sciences.

Culture and explanation

Materialist explanations

According to this approach, culture has an important role in politics, but only as an intermediary. The key divisions and interests derive from elsewhere. In *Acts of Union*, Desmond Bell (1990) maps the construction of sectarian identity in Northern Ireland, in an attempt to establish its place in political action. Drawing on both interviews with, and observations of, Loyalist youth, Bell explains how, through rituals and symbols, a sense of political identity is created and fuelled. Working with the extended notion of political culture, Bell traces the construction of ethnic division, the process by which 'ethnic identities emerge and become defined in response to political developments' (Bell, 1990: 11). He draws directly upon Anderson's notion of the 'imagined community', and he argues that Loyalist identity is 'dependent on the rehearsed myths, ritualized practices, and confrontations of the marching season'. These 'symbolic practices are the specific means by which an exclusive Protestant identity is represented and renewed in the Loyalist mind' (Bell, 1990: 20). In other words, what it is to be a Loyalist can only be understood by reference to an individual's active engagement with a range of special rituals and symbols which in turn give form to her or his preferences. But forming preferences, argues Bell, is not the same as determining interests.

While *Acts of Union* dwells on the rituals of Orange parades and other aspects of Protestant culture, Bell treats these as secondary to the material factors which ultimately drive action. Protestant youth tries to resolve, 'at the level of the imaginary, *the real material contradictions* confronting the Protestant working-class in contemporary Northern Ireland' (Bell, 1990: 23; my emphasis). Thus, although *Acts of Union* gives a rich picture of the world of Loyalist youth, it remains wedded to the view that material interests play the key role, even when some place is allowed for interpretation and 'symbolic creativity'. A similar position is apparent in other accounts of Northern Ireland's politics. Ruane and Todd (1991:

28), for example, want to explain conflict and instability in terms of underlying interests: 'The overt signs of conflict – bigotry and intransigence – arise because the communities' fundamental interests are incompatible within Northern Ireland as it is presently structured.' The implication is, therefore, that 'community relations within Northern Ireland developed according to the logic of the situation' (Ruane and Todd, 1991: 34). The 'logic' is a result of the pre-existing interests and is not attributable to their cultural representation. With this kind of approach, the myths and symbols of the actors' lives are held to inform the identity of actors, but this identity is itself the consequence of a set of underlying interests; the cultural realm clothes them but does not create them. The imaginary life of participants, therefore, has a relatively marginal effect upon their actions.

There are problems with this account. Even if the underlying material or political conditions are determinant, the culture to which they give rise cannot, in fact, simply 'mirror' those conditions. They cannot be represented directly, they have to be mediated through metaphors and myths, and these automatically loosen the determinist link between the conditions and the culture. The representation of the conditions is dependent upon the process of comprehending the images and metaphors that describe those conditions. The symbols have to be 'decoded'; they have to *mean* something. This does not just require them to be 'understood'; they have to be part of the thoughts that inform action. The suggestion is not that symbols determine action, any more than do material conditions, but rather that there is a constant process of interpretation and reinterpretation. There can be no straightforward mechanical link between conditions and culture. Furthermore, the view that culture is subservient would have to assume that it is possible to draw a clear dividing line between what is cultural and what is 'fundamental'. It is in the rejection of this dichotomy that the idealist position emerges.

Idealist explanations

The idealist alternative places culture at the head of the explanation. The traditional way of representing such claims is through accounts of behaviour which refer to the values and ideas of a society. An example of this approach is Martin Wiener's *English*

Culture and the Decline of the Industrial Spirit 1850–1980 (1981). It contends that 'English culture', and the values it represented, thwarted the advance of industrialism. 'The dominant collective self-image in English culture', writes Wiener (1981: 158), 'became less and less that of the world's workshop. Instead, this image was challenged by the counterimage of an ancient, little disturbed "green and pleasant land".' Two assumptions inhabit such descriptions. The first is that it is possible to talk of 'English culture', and to define it in a particular way (that is as an anti-urban, rural idyll). The problem with this assumption is that it is far from clear there is (or was) a single English culture, and to the extent that such a thing existed, whether it should be described in one way rather than another, as rural rather than urban. The second assumption is about the relationship between the culture and political action. Wiener's argument rests upon a claim about how the culture produces the observed effects (that is national decline). Answers to such questions need a fuller account of how culture is integrated into action, and particularly how it affects people's interests and their perception of them. Wiener does not provide this; and indeed few have done so. One exception is provided by Aaron Wildavsky (1987) and the 'Cultural Theory' school (see Coyle and Ellis, 1994; Douglas and Wildavsky, 1982; Thompson, Ellis and Wildavsky, 1990).

Cultural Theory argues 'that issues, opinions, and institutions are not isolated phenomena but rather intimately connected with basic choices about how we wish to live, choices that are constrained by our cultural context' (Coyle and Ellis, 1994: 1). Hence, Wildavsky (1987: 3) argues that one of the 'major subjects of political science' is 'the formation of political preferences', and, therefore, it is necessary to ask: how do 'people figure out what their interests are?' To do this, Wildavsky calls upon culture and Cultural Theory.

Wildavsky defines culture as 'the shared values legitimating social practices', and he argues that the particular character of culture determines the kind of preferences people will develop. People's interests are established culturally; their thoughts and actions are the consequence of their cultural location. These locations divide themselves into four basic types, defined along two dimensions: grid and group. 'Group' is a measure of the extent to which a person's predicament is shared with others – whether he or she lives as an isolated individual or as part of

	Low Group	High Group
High Grid	*fatalism*	*hierarchy*
Low Grid	*individualism*	*egalitarianism*

| **Low Group** | **High Group** |

(Fig. 1)

some collectivity. 'Grid' refers to the degree to which a person's life is constrained by external forces – whether he or she is locked into a hierarchy or is relatively autonomous. Where people fall in these two dimensions establishes their general disposition, the way they think and feel about the world. Four general dispositions are discerned: fatalism, hierarchy, individualism and egalitarianism (see Figure 1). These world-views are the logical consequence of the institutional form of each location and of the values which uphold them. They create a bias through which people assess their own prospects and preferences (Douglas, 1992). Wildavsky (1987: 4) offers this analogy: 'Preference formation is much more like ordering *prix fixe* [than *à la carte*] from a number of set dinners or voting a party ticket. Only those combinations that are socially viable, that can cohere because people are able to give them their allegiance, to share their meanings, may be lived.' Preferences are, therefore, extensions of people's cultural habitat, itself defined by the type of social institutions (grid–group) that organize that culture. People exist within one of the limited range of cultural forms, and from within these they adopt the preferences appropriate to their culture.

The attraction of Wildavsky's thesis lies with its desire to address a core political question: how and why do people perceive their interests in one way rather than another? It also supplies an answer: perception of preferences and interests is a product of culture. But despite its initial appeal, Wildavsky's thesis is flawed. Critics have pointed to the parochial and ahistorical nature of the four cultural forms. The four categories are so abstract as to defy application to any recognizable context. As Jeffrey Friedman (1991: 334) writes, they use the cultural forms as 'an implausible means of universalizing . . . cultural insights to all times and places'. Beyond this, though, is the awkward mixture of voluntarism and determinism that pervades the thesis and which makes individuals both authors of their culture and victims of it. Once inside a particular cultural formation, actors have their responses patterned for them. Friedman (1991: 347–9) accuses Wildavsky of making individuals 'the passive recipients of socially functional preferences', while simultaneously making 'culture' serve only as a method by which people 'coordinate their movements'. Culture seems to act both as constitutive, giving people a sense of themselves, and as regulative, coordinating the preferences they already have. It clearly cannot be both. Culture cannot both pattern preferences and serve as a device for coordinating individual aspirations.

Faced with this tension, the obvious temptation is to commit to one side or the other. Either to see the culture or the individual actor as the key determinant. The latter route clearly marginalizes the role of culture, giving it a relatively subservient role. But could we generate an account of preferences by this means? Is culture just a regulatory device for organizing individual preferences? This answer is suggested by the rational choice explanations, with their emphasis on the individual.

Individualist explanations

In *The Cement of Society*, Jon Elster, a leading and sophisticated proponent of the rational choice approach, writes of culture as being constituted by the belief systems and religions which inhabit society. Culture, for Elster (1989: 250), refers to a set of local bonds, operating below the national/state level, which establish 'norms, altruism, envy and other social motivations'. Culture, though, acts to expedite the underlying interactions; it does not create them, it dresses them in a wardrobe appropriate to their social purpose. In this sense, the role given to culture seems similar to that accorded to it by the materialist approach. Elster, though, does not expand at great length on culture's role. But someone who does, and who also works within the rational choice paradigm, is Patrick Dunleavy.

Dunleavy uses rational choice theory to ask why people engage in political activity, and, in particular, why they join interest groups. This is a variation on Wildavsky's question about how people acquire interests. Dunleavy assumes that people have given interests, the point is why they *act* on them. This has always been an awkward problem for the rational choice theorist (see Olson, 1965). For any individual calculating the personal costs and benefits of an act, the costs of participation will tend to outweigh the benefits. No individual can bring about a desired change; it requires others to act as well. Participation, therefore, is not in itself a guarantee of success, and hence to participate and fail to achieve a desired end is the worst possible outcome. Apathy makes more sense. It makes sense even if the desired result is achieved, since then the individual gains the benefit at no personal cost. Of course, if everyone thinks like this, nothing gets changed. And we know that, in defiance of this logic, people do, in fact, fight for causes. Does this just make them irrational, or is there a way that such participation conforms to rationality? Dunleavy argues for the latter, and in doing so introduces a cultural dimension through his use of the idea of 'group identity'.

Dunleavy's contention is that for participation to be seen as rational we need to add 'something more' into the individual's calculation. The additional ingredient is 'group identity' (Dunleavy, 1991: 55). Group identity is the link forged between subjective interest and 'others who are organized in a group' (Dunleavy, 1991: 57). Without group identity, there is no motive for people to join. For Dunleavy, group identity supplies the information which is necessary for action. It organizes the wealth of political data with which individuals are faced and 'short circuits the information problems in coping with many different interest groups vying for attention' (Dunleavy, 1991: 59). It also supplies a basis 'for the development of other beliefs which sustain group mobilization' (Dunleavy, 1991: 61). In summary, group identity is a key notion in Dunleavy's revised rational choice account of group membership; it supplies the incentives for action. It plays a major part in compensating for the rational apathy that might otherwise obtain. And it does this by supplying information to the actor. In other words, this argument parallels de Tocqueville's view of culture as a device for simplifying political calculations and sorting out political information.

But where in de Tocqueville culture is integral to political life, in Dunleavy culture is 'information' to be used in pursuing pre-existing interests. Dunleavy says little about how group identity is constituted, but it seems to consist of the knowledge that others are similarly placed. This knowledge provides a catalyst for political action. Group identity, therefore, is only of significance because of the interests that people already have by virtue of their plight or perceptions. Group identity does not create those interests. As Dunleavy (1991: 57) writes, group identities are 'a subset of subjective interests'.

Dunleavy introduces the notion of group identity because he wants to break the logic that encourages rational actors to be apathetic. It rests on the idea that 'interests' exist as independent variables. People have interests because of common views or plights; these, as it were, are the facts of political life. But, as I have noted, it is not clear what 'group identity' actually refers to and whether it can perform the task required of it. Essentially, group identity seems to be viewed as information, the information that there are others in a similar situation or with similar views. The key information would seem to be that such-and-such a group exists and caters for such-and-such an interest. Information of this kind is not, however, straightforwardly obtained or communicated. It comes from many sources and is open to many interpretations. Imagine that we were considering political participation on grounds of illness or poverty. The modern world is riven with endless different versions of what it means to be 'ill' (or 'well') or to be 'poor' (or 'rich'). All forms of contemporary culture, whether magazines or advertisements or movies, create different notions of poverty or illness. In other words, the interest we have – to be well, to be rich – cannot be some pre-given state of affairs, but is actually constituted by the group identity people adopt (the kind of poverty or illness that they see themselves as having). This is what I take Friedman (1991: 349) to mean when he says that communication depends upon the use of 'symbols that take on a history of their own'. He makes this point in relation to Wildavsky, but it can apply equally to Dunleavy. Both introduce a cultural dimension into their account of social action, but in doing so they – like the materialists – make culture act instrumentally, rather than expressively. This move returns them to the problem – its mechanistic, behavioural individualism – that afflicted Almond and Verba's original account. Put another way, to take seriously the notion of 'group identity' is to appeal to a different form of social explanation, one in which the focus shifts from interests and rationality to culture.

Interpretative explanations

The fourth and final version of the politics–culture connection is one in which culture is neither determinant nor subservient, neither marginal nor instrumental. Indeed it moves away from the explanatory model altogether, arguing that culture constitutes political thought and action rather than explaining them. It treats seriously the idea that cultural symbols have the power to motivate action, but it does not regard them – as the idealist tends to – as absolutely powerful. Their effect is determined by their context and the constraints imposed by it. This is similar to the position adopted by John Thompson (1990: 122), who writes of the need to understand culture through 'the study of the ways in which meaningful expressions of various kinds are produced, constructed and received by individuals situated in the social–historical world'.

An example of this approach is Robert Putnam's (1994) attempt to explain the survival of democracy in Italy. He argues that the democratic process is the product neither of material conditions, nor of cultural idealism, nor of citizens' attitudes. Rather it is dependent on the existence of certain civic traditions and established cultural practices, which together form the civic community. This community is embodied in such institutions as 'amateur soccer clubs, choral societies, hiking clubs, bird-watching groups, literary circles' (Putnam, 1994: 91). These social networks and institutions forge the habits of mind and action that sustain democracy. But while Putnam's research produces real evidence for a correlation between civic virtue and democratic stability, and thereby provides a much firmer causal link than is supplied by Almond and Verba, it tells us little about why the civic community comes into existence or how the particular character of that community actually makes a difference to the operation of political life. To address this question, we need to turn our attention to the ways in which culture is political, and politics cultural. A focus for this endeavour is provided by the notion of identity, a way of being in the world, which is made possible by engagement with forms of cultural expression.

For political theorists like William Connolly, identity replaces the problem of 'interests' that dominates the other theories we have considered. Identity precedes interests. In his book *Identity/Difference*, Connolly (1991: 64) defines identity in these terms: 'My identity is what I am and how I am recognized rather than what I choose, want, or consent to. It is the dense self from which choosing, wanting and consenting proceed.' Interests are the consequences of identity, and identity is itself formed through the ways in which 'difference' and 'otherness' are established. For Connolly, the politics of identity are what underlie political action. 'Interests' are just a coding of the struggle around identity. Thus, he views the political responses to the environment or to gun control as being motivated by the fact that they touch upon 'the identity of opponents even more than their interests' (Connolly, 1991: 77). What is important is how people's identity is tied to their relationship to nature or to the ownership of weapons. These relations are constitutive of their sense of self and of their politics.

Identity of this kind is not fixed in the way that some accounts of nationalism tend to suppose; identity is not based on some 'essence'. It is constantly being constructed and reconstructed. This process is the product of relations of power and subordination: dominant identities create subordinate ones, and these work to subvert the oppressor in a struggle for recognition (through their 'hidden transcripts', as Scott [1990] calls them). 'If there is no natural or intrinsic identity,' writes Connolly (1991: 66), 'power is always inscribed in the relation an exclusive identity bears to the differences it constitutes.' Joan Cocks (1989: 77) draws out the cultural implications of this position: 'A struggle over the control of culture rather than over the control of the legal–political state becomes logically, although not always chronologically, primary, when the identities of dominant and subordinate social groups turn out to be, at bottom, a function of interpretations imposed on the brute body as if they emanated out of it.' In other words, politics is about the exercise of cultural power. Connolly and Cocks reach this conclusion from their perspectives as political theorists. Inevitably, therefore, they say relatively little about the cultural formation of political identity, despite their explicit and implicit acknowledgement of the role played by (especially) popular culture in the formation of identity. For this, we need to turn to those who place more emphasis on cultural practice in linking identity and political action. I want, in particular, to consider the work of

Lawrence Grossberg and Richard Merelman. Both these writers attempt to show how popular culture engages with political action.

Grossberg asks political questions from within the perspective provided by cultural studies. In particular, he asks how popular conservatism took hold in the USA in the 1980s. His answer points to the 'affective' power of popular culture; that is, the ability of symbols and myths to generate the feelings, emotions and reasons without which political action would not occur. Like Connolly, Grossberg accepts that the adoption of a political ideology cannot be explained simply by reference to people's interests. The idea of 'having an interest' itself depends – as Connolly notes – on the prior existence of an identity, to which the interest can be attributed. Grossberg adds, though, a further term to the equation: passion, the fear and desire that are associated with particular outcomes; the sense that something matters. Terms like 'passion' are typically missing from political explanations, but, says Grossberg (1992a: 82–3), they are essential to accounting for the drives behind action: 'In fact, affect is the missing term in an adequate understanding of ideology, for it offers the possibility of a 'psychology of belief' which would explain how and why ideologies are sometimes, and only sometimes, effective, and always to varying degrees.'

Grossberg's contention is that political action derives from the ideas people have, and these ideas are not simply ways of describing their interests, but ways of expressing them as sources of passionate concern. This, he argues, is achieved through engagement in a culture which shapes and articulates people's feelings, and hence produces their interests. Culture does not simply reflect interests, it generates feelings and gives form to what is otherwise unsaid or unsayable. Grossberg is not, however, an idealist. He is not arguing that we are mere products of our culture; nor is he claiming that culture is the direct expression of fundamental interests. Instead, he offers a theory of 'articulation' as an alternative to both these approaches (Grossberg, 1992a: 48–52). According to this, people construct their lives in the context of many intersecting 'cultural practices' which together form their identities and interests. These cultural practices are themselves part of an intersecting network of social forces, out of which social experience is constructed: 'Such forces, which often seem to have a life of their own but only exist conjuncturally, represent a move-

ment and direction which appears to be independent of the desires of . . . social groups. . . . In determining the configurations of
people and practices, they also create the spaces within which
people can experience and act' (Grossberg, 1992a: 123). For
Grossberg, a key force is represented by popular culture, which is
deeply implicated in the process of articulating the world-view of
individuals and groups. He links this to the notion of fandom.
'No democratic political struggle', he writes (1992b: 64), 'can be
effectively organized without the power of the popular.'

These are, as I understand them, the theoretical underpinnings
of Grossberg's attempt to track the rise of the New Right. His account of popular culture is discussed further in the next chapter.
Here, I want only to note that the underlying political theory is
couched at such a level of abstraction that it is hard to make direct
connections with shifts in political ideology. Although the rise of
the New Right is the ostensible topic of his study, it receives very
little detailed attention either as an ideology or as a political formation.

Merelman's work, by contrast, is more directly empirical in its
attempt to show how popular culture is implicated in political
discourse and identity. Popular culture, he suggests (1991: 193),
'predisposes political narratives towards certain forms of language,
or collective figures of speech'. It does this by providing 'many of
the socially validated cultural images by which we live, including
the narrative of liberal democratic politics in everyday life'
(Merelman, 1991: 36–7). Merelman wants to use popular culture
to account for the creation of meaning and significance that attaches to all political acts. He argues that 'certain qualities of a
society's popular culture subtly prepare people either to seek out
political participation and welcome group conflict or to resist political participation and to reject group conflict' (Merelman, 1991:
8). Merelman wants to show how forms of political practice are
paralleled by dominant popular cultural values or codes. But again,
as with the historical approach of Wiener, to see how popular culture can map onto political practice is only to hint at possible cor-
relations, and not to establish causal (or some other) connections.
Merelman is himself aware of this limitation, acknowledging that
the relationship is hypothesized, not proved.

In summary, both Grossberg and Merelman deploy the broader
concept of culture (making much of its connection to popular culture) to their account of politics. They both, however, fall short of

their ambitions. In doing justice to cultural complexity, Grossberg is rendered relatively speechless on key aspects of politics, while in dwelling on the political context, Merelman is unable to offer any conclusive connection between popular culture and politics. Ironically, this is the problem that, as we have seen, befalls less subtle accounts of political culture and its relationship to political action.

Conclusion

This chapter has been devoted to an exploration of the way culture has been used to explain or understand political thought and action. We began with early attempts to provide empirical evidence for culture's contribution, and the criticism this incurred. These critiques provided the springboard for a broadening of the concept of culture itself and for the development of very different explanatory models (the materialist, idealist, individualist and interpretative). The materialist and individualist models attached relatively little importance to the explanatory powers of culture; and it was left to the idealist and interpretative positions to place culture at the centre. As Hollis (1994) makes clear, there can be no outright 'winner' between the four perspectives. However, given my concerns here, I want to explore further the implication of culture-centred explanatory models for the political salience of popular culture.

If we are to take seriously attempts to link popular culture, political culture and political practice, more attention needs to be paid to the process by which the culture itself features in the relationship. The crucial point of entry is in the mediation of the public and the private (in the contingent construction of identity and of ideology). Mass communication makes private events public, and transforms public events in the process of transmitting them to the home. For John Thompson (1990: 238), this effect on the public–private divide 'has implications for the ways in which political power, at the level of state institutions, is acquired, exercised and sustained in modern societies'. One particular consequence of this is that the content and character of political ideology are not the exclusive province of organized political groupings. Their manifestos or other public pronouncements cannot be treated as self-contained sources of data. Rather, they have to be examined as part of a much wider process of symbolic exchange and interpretation, itself bounded by institutional and material conditions: 'the analysis of ideology should be orientated primarily towards the multiple and complex ways in which symbolic phenomena circulate in the social world and intersect with relations of power' (Thompson, 1990: 265). Thompson's argument places culture at the centre of political action, without at the same time cutting it free of material and other interests. Culture is neither the whole story (as the idealists would have it), nor is it a footnote to deeper forces (as the materialists prefer). Instead, it is something which both shapes and is shaped by political interests. The question we are left with, therefore, is whether this is a plausible approach. Does it make sense to see culture as an expressive, constitutive element in political life, and to see it as something whose character and form must themselves be explained by reference to other interests?

It is evident that there is no return to the old approach. The behavioural view of culture used by Almond and Verba is inadequate as an account both of how culture works and of how it might explain political action. It was this inadequacy that led later writers to develop a fuller notion of political culture, one which encompasses a wider range of sentiments and states of mind, and which sees culture as a discourse that people interpret and use. Culture refers to more than the attitudes people hold towards politicians and political institutions. Rather it is made up of a complex of feelings and images, deriving from the home and work, from manifestos and popular culture. The meaning of terms like 'liberty' is created through the active, passionate engagement with the resources that culture provides, as are the notions of identity and interests that liberty is to satisfy.

Linked to this notion of culture, and people's engagement with it, is the idea that culture is constitutive of political activity, rather than external to it; this, in turn, has implications for the explanatory power and role of political culture. First, it suggests that material conditions do not themselves pre-empt or account for culture. Culture plays a crucial role in the way in which interests are identified and then acted upon. This move, though, creates the tempting possibility that *only* culture explains human action. But rather than returning to this idealist perspective, we need instead to move away from any sense of culture as *explanatory*. We need to think in terms of culture's constitutive role, to the way interests are created through it. This is what underlies our earlier attention to the ways in which culture is itself formed. Culture does not just 'exist', it depends upon institutions and industries, upon money and interests, for it to be produced and reproduced. That is why it is important to acknowledge the making of culture and the organization of access to it, not because it then explains politics, but because it is part of a political process.

The argument of this chapter is that culture constitutes, and is constituted by, politics, and there is no neat division to be drawn between cultural and political activity. This is, I think, what Hall (1989: 128) means, when he writes: 'Culture has ceased (if ever it was – which I doubt) to be a decorative addendum to the "hard world" of production and things, the icing on the cake of the material world. The word is now as "material" as the world.' I think too that histories of punk, and other moments in popular culture, appeal to a similar blurring of the boundary between political thought and cultural feeling. As we have seen, there are theoretical positions which do not share this way of looking at the world, but for those who do adopt this perspective, there is more work to be done. It is not enough to develop a cultural theory of politics; we also need a political theory of culture.

CHAPTER EIGHT

Political theories of culture

There is a need to politicize aesthetics not to aestheticize politics.

Duncan Webster, *Looka Yonder!*

If explanations of political thought and action do depend upon culture, then we need to think more about how culture works, how it moves people (politically and in other ways). The implication of the arguments of Grossberg and Merelman is that popular culture helps articulate particular ideas and ideologies, which in turn inform different judgements and actions. But what needs to be explored further is how variations in culture give shape to political dispositions. This relationship cannot, though, be posed in terms of cause and effect. It may be tempting to assert that a film like *Natural Born Killers* or a TV programme like *The Power Rangers* breeds violence; or indeed that a humanitarian song like 'Do They Know It's Christmas?' creates sympathy for those who are starving. But such claims are themselves premised on a large number of other judgements, not least about how exposure to culture links to thought and action. No amount of empirical work will ever provide a definitive and irrefutable account of how exposure to popular culture produces particular results. Not only are there too many intervening variables, but, as we saw in the last chapter, there are no simple connections to be drawn between culture and action (and even to frame the question this way may be a mistake).

Given this impasse we need to shift the focus, to look at how different political positions (and different explanatory frameworks) read different political significance into popular culture. Rather than asking about the political effects of popular culture, we need to explore the political theories of popular culture. This is to pursue the logic of the discussion in chapter 1 about the definition of popular culture. There it was evident that competing portraits of popular culture were a reflection of competing political values. What I want to do here is to look in more detail at the competing political readings of popular culture. The next section traces out some of the crude divisions within the debate about the politics of popular culture. I have divided the positions along two dimensions. The first dimension distinguishes between *elitists* and *populists*. By elitist I mean those who wish to incorporate a *qualitative* judgement into their account of popular culture, who want to make judgements between examples of popular culture or between 'high' and 'low' culture. Those who eschew such judgements are populists. The second dimension marks the divide between *radicals* and *conservatives*, and is more explicitly political in character. All accounts of popular culture attribute some degree of political importance to it, but they disagree in their view of this importance. What I want to capture here is a division between those who see culture (although not necessarily popular culture) as leading to a beneficial change in society or in individuals within society, and those who see it as threatening the existing (desirable) order. The first group are labelled radicals; the second conservatives. These political positions are derived from the authors' own apparent intention, rather than the unintended consequences of their arguments. The combined dimensions yield four different political perspectives on popular culture: conservative elitists, conservative populists, radical elitists and radical populists. In the last section of this chapter, I shall look at what is missing in all these perspectives, but for now I want to examine each argument in turn.

Four political views of popular culture

Conservative elitists

In his *The Closing of the American Mind*, Allan Bloom (1987) calls passionately for the defence of classical values. These are threatened, he argues, by the pervasiveness of popular culture, although it is not popular culture alone that is responsible for the threat. Much of the blame lies with the educational system within which it circulates (the book's subtitle is *How Education Has Failed Democracy and Impoverished the Souls of Today's Students*). But whatever or whoever is responsible, popular culture has, he suggests, invaded the private space of the home and has colonized the lessons and tastes that were acquired there:

> . . . first radio, then television, have assaulted and overturned the privacy of the home, the real American privacy, which permitted the development of a higher and more independent life within democratic society. . . . With great subtlety and energy, television enters not only the room, but also the tastes of old and young alike, appealing to the immediately pleasant and subverting whatever does not conform to it. (Bloom, 1987: 58–9)

Popular culture is, then, to blame for subverting a stable and valuable order.

Several linked ideas underpin this critique of popular culture. The first idea is that, in a democracy, citizens must be able to form opinions, and must be able to construct visions of the good life. The development of the citizen's capacity for discriminating choice requires knowledge of a particular, classical tradition (the Bible, Plato, Aristotle, Shakespeare, Bach and Wagner). It is this tradition that is being devalued – and with it democracy – by the debased fare of, among other things, popular culture. Hence Bloom (1987: 73) rails against rock music because it has 'one appeal only, a barbaric appeal, to sexual desire – not love, not *eros*, but sexual desire undeveloped and untutored'. But the music's crime has less to do with its behavioural effects than with its intellectual and moral effects (the two are closely connected in Bloom's world view): 'I believe it [rock music] ruins the imagination of young people and makes it very difficult for them to have a passionate relationship to the art and thought that are the substance of liberal education' (Bloom, 1987: 79).

Bloom sees a society in which the intellectual landscape is being narrowed and flattened, the great values and traditions of the past are marginalized and this, combined with the breaking of old ties and authority structures, is creating a generation without the resources to behave as full citizens. Instead they are 'spiritually unclad, unconnected, isolated, with no inherited or unconditional connection with anything or anyone' (Bloom, 1987: 87). Such people, argues Bloom, cannot take on the duties of a progressive democracy, and their predicament is the product of the values inculcated by popular culture. These values extol immediate pleasures over delayed gratification, the easily acquired over the earned.

Bloom's thesis draws a strong connection between the form of a culture and politics, making morality the linking term. Culture is treated as part of the moral order, shaping those who inhabit it and making them capable of political action: 'Culture restores the wholeness of first man on a higher level, where his faculties can be fully developed without contradiction between the desires of nature and the moral imperatives of his social life' (Bloom, 1987: 185). The contrast between 'higher' culture and 'popular' culture is, therefore, a moral distinction, but one which has profound political implications.

Earlier forms of Bloom's argument can be found in the cultural and literary criticism of F. R. Leavis or in the political philosophy of J. S. Mill. And versions of Bloom's argument can also be discerned among his contemporaries, in Neil Postman's *Amusing Ourselves to Death* (1987), for example. They all connect culture to morality and discriminate between forms of culture. Implied in each are theories of political action and views of a proper political order. The sentiments which underlie this conservative elitism form part of a more general common sense. They exist in attitudes to education and child development: not only do we grow out of certain tastes and pleasures (even *Spot the Dog* loses its appeal after a while), but also we learn to like qualitatively better things. In acquiring new tastes and in junking old ones, we are not just changing the objects of our affection, we are developing more refined tastes. Such development, furthermore, is a matter not merely of aesthetic judgement but of moral improvement. We judge people by their taste, by what makes them laugh and cry, by what moves them, by what they are sensitive to. These are guides to what kind of person they are. Tastes are a short-hand account of character. Certainly, these are the intuitions with which the conservative elitist works. This is what Leavis and Thompson (1948: 3) once wrote: 'Those who in school are offered (perhaps) the beginnings of an education in taste are exposed, out of school, to the competing exploitation of the cheapest emotional responses; films, newspapers, publicity in all its forms, commercially-catered fiction – all offer satisfaction at the lowest level, and inculcate the choosing of the most immediate pleasures, got with the least effort.'

To summarize, the arguments of the conservative elitists treat 'popular culture' as a threat to an existing order. They take the view that culture matters in the development of a civilized world, but that it is important that the culture has a particular character, one which popular culture notably lacks. The point is that this position is not simply a product of their conservatism; it is also a consequence of their perspective on culture. By contrast, conservative populists share their political disposition, but do not share their view on popular culture.

Conservative populists

It is possible to detect elements of conservative populism in the pronouncements and policies of Margaret Thatcher and Ronald Reagan. Their political rhetoric constructed a particular view of 'ordinary people', and contrasted them with their 'enemies': the state bureaucracy and the established, liberal elite. Popular culture, as distinct from elite culture, is presented as the 'true' reflection of the people's values and of the good society. Conservative populism is the populism of the tabloid press. It may be homophobic, racist, jingoistic and misogynist, but that is just the way it is. The success of the popular press is a measure of its ability to speak directly to (and for) its readership. The same defence is offered for comedians whose acts are laced with racist slurs. People laugh, and in laughing they are confirming a shared and genuine sentiment (laughter, like embarrassment, is spontaneous).

In this spirit of conservative populism, Prime Minister Thatcher praised the TV situation comedy about politics, *Yes Minister* (later *Yes Prime Minister*), with its cynical view of devious civil servants; President Reagan allied himself with the rugged individualism that he saw in Bruce Springsteen and Sylvester Stallone's Rambo. Their position – as populists – is not legitimated by the content of popular culture so much as by the market which gives expression to it. In principle, if not always in practice, what is good is what is popular.

This approach to popular culture is not, though, confined to representatives of the political establishment. It also inhabits the cultural establishment. Jon Savage and Simon Frith (1993) detect a similar conservative populism in the writing of the style gurus of the 1980s, whose pronouncements were incorporated into the arts pages of newspapers, and who became allied with publishing ventures like *The Modern Review* and *Loaded*, and who appeared in television programmes like the BBC's *Late Show*. Each presented a largely uncritical celebration of popular culture, legitimated by a style of journalism which claimed to speak from within the culture as if from the perspective of the 'ordinary' consumer. But it is a very particular consumer: it is one who mistrusts the liberal establishment and the academic voice that represents it. It is the voice of journalist Julie Burchill and Oxford Fellow John Carey. It is a journalism that celebrates the Hollywood blockbuster over the art movie, the airport page-turner over the Booker winner. In doing so, say Savage and Frith (1993: 109), it lays claim to a specific version of 'the common people' as 'domestic, heterosexual, suburban, middle-class'.

However, though it represents itself as a democratic populism, legitimated by the evidence of the market, it is, in fact, actually engaged in interpreting popular culture and popular taste in particular ways. It is creating rather than reflecting the 'people' and their pleasures. As John Fiske (1989: 24) writes: '"The people" is not a stable sociological category; it cannot be identified and subjected to empirical study, for it does not exist in objective reality.' The people are coloured by whichever artist paints them.

Conservative populism portrays a conservative people, because not only is it celebrating and defending certain tastes, it is rooting them in 'a particular kind of nostalgia: the commonplace acts as a bulwark against all sorts of social change, against a permanent fear of unrest at the margins. Out there aren't just strange ideas but strange people – young, female, foreign, homosexual' (Savage and Frith, 1993: 109). The authority of this reading of the popular is defended through an ideology of 'experience' – this is how 'we' *really* feel (when Dirty Harry stands over his man, when Tarantino choreographs his bloody mayhem). And it is a particularly powerful cultural critique because, as Savage and Frith (1993:

113) comment, 'you can't *challenge* experience' (their emphasis). Ian Macdonald (1995: 30) offers a yet more dismissive view: 'The reason why cultural relativism caught on is not because ordinary people read Derrida but because the trickle-down essence of Deconstruction suits both the trash aesthetic of media hounds and the philistinism of Essex man.' Certainly, this conservative populism was in tune with a public policy programme that gave institutional form to it.

In Britain, it underpinned government policy for broadcasting reform, itself the brainchild of the New Right. The Peacock Committee (1986), set up by Margaret Thatcher to advise on the future of the BBC, was part of a New Right campaign to unseat the elite, liberal establishment. One of their original proposals was the privatization of Radio 1, itself part of a general strategy to deregulate broadcasting. For the New Right, there could be no rational justification for subsidizing commercial success. Although Peacock's proposals were never fully implemented, their impact could be detected in the government's later document *Broadcasting in the 90s* (1988) which had as its subtitle *Competition, Choice and Quality*. The opening remarks made it clear that the intention was to set a populist agenda: 'The Government places the viewer and listener at the centre of broadcasting policy. . . . The Government's aim is to open the doors so that individuals can choose for themselves from a much wider range of programmes and types of broadcasting' (para 1.2). The guiding principle of broadcasting was to be that of 'supply and demand' as determined by the market; this was in accordance with the underlying politics of the right populist's liberalism. There was no duty upon government to subsidize any particular cultural form. Hence, the conservative populist fulminates against the subsidizing of opera *and* pop radio.

The legitimating convention of this populism is, of course, that 'the people' are simply the product of their choices, and as such represent an objective social fact which the market reveals. But as many commentators have pointed out, the rhetoric of populism contains a rich panoply of political values and judgements. Indeed, this was apparent in the Thatcher government's reluctance to embrace the full logic of market liberalism in broadcasting. They were not prepared to tolerate a complete free-for-all, and wanted – for example – to guard against pornography. This caution was itself a product of the fact that they actually worked with a particular notion of 'the people' (that is, those whom they thought would be offended by pornography). Thus, broadcasting policy, while emphasizing the notion of individual choice, also promised to maintain standards on 'good taste and decency' (para 1.2). These standards are those of 'ordinary people', that is, 'ordinary people' as defined by the Conservative Party, the Home Office and organizations like the National Viewers' and Listeners' Association (then headed by Mary Whitehouse). In a similar way, President Reagan's view of the ordinary person was created under the influence of such organizations as the Parents Music Resource Center and its argument that certain rock lyrics and videos offended against common decency. Populism is always the product of a particular ideology and interest. There is, therefore, an ambiguity in the right populist view of the politics of popular culture. Popular culture is celebrated as an expression of popular taste, but it also represents the site of potential danger, which demands that it be regulated as well as applauded. In short, the two conservative perspectives on popular culture analyse it in relation to the existing order, seeing it either as maintaining or threatening that order. The populist seeing it as having the potential to endorse that order; the elitist seeing it as a threat.

Radical elitists

Radical elitism represents those who identify in culture the potential for considerable social change and improvement, but who associate this possibility with elite culture, not with its popular variant. For such writers, popular culture is the expression of those forces which seek to prevent change, or to promote changes that do not benefit the majority of people. Elite culture is radical; popular culture conservative – which is, of course, the reverse of the position adopted by the conservative elitists. The radical elitist places popular culture within the existing social structure (and particularly its capitalist mode of production).

There are three strands of radical elitism. These emerge as a result of the way in which popular culture is judged. One strand compares popular culture unfavourably with 'folk' culture; the second makes an unfavourable comparison with the avant-garde; and the third sets it below traditional classical or high culture. Dave Harker (1980, and 1992) is an example of the first strand. He detects in certain kinds of folk culture a radical spirit that challenges the status quo. Such radicalism is, however, eliminated in the process of commercialization. Serious political comment is replaced by sentimentality. He sees the capitalist process as having deprived popular music of its radical potential. He argues, for instance, that Bob Dylan's politics lost their radical edge with each step taken towards the conventions of rock and away from folk. Harker also attacks those who have claimed to find radicalism within commercialized popular culture, especially those who want to claim that popular music reflected a radical spirit in the late 1960s. It was, he says, just part of the same (commercial) plot. The radical elitism of this position is to be found, first, in the way Harker assumes that popular culture can embody some kind of challenge to the status quo. This claim depends upon the judgement he makes of the relative qualities of the two types of popular culture – the uncommercialized folk versus the commercialized mainstream pop. The former can only survive on the outside.

A variant of this argument appears in the second strand of radical elitism, which again mixes aesthetics and political economy. With regard to the latter, it places weight upon the source of the culture, valuing the product of independent companies and distribution networks over those belonging to the major conglomerates. But the political commitment that mistrusts majors is tied to a particular aesthetic. In popular music, this aesthetic is the defining brief of a magazine like *The Wire* which champions experimental music. The magazine prides itself on pursuing 'all those wild adventures in modern music we all crave so madly' (October 1996), on celebrating 'wayward exploration' in a 'desire to free music from the crippling embrace of the customs and lores that spawn it' (August 1996).

The musician and writer Chris Cutler expands upon this radical aesthetic in his defence of the jazz music of Sun Ra and the Arkestra. First, this is music that stands aside from the commercial realm: 'Sun Ra and the Arkestra cannot be understood as a commodity – as a pack of gimmicks and promises. They aren't simply offering their work for sale – indeed, they clearly don't care what "the market" wants' (Cutler, 1985: 38). These principles of production are also contained in the music itself: 'Music is equated by Ra with Life, with creation and therefore with joy. It is a celebration of discovery and human creativity. Most important, it celebrates the creativity of *Collective* Being, of the ability to distinguish the true colour of things and then to *act rightly*' (Cutler,

1985: 67; his emphasis). This kind of music stands apart from (and above) commercial, popular music which expresses 'consumerist and bourgeois values'. Such music has 'evolved in the primal soup of the marketplace, to sell – vicariously – success, power, romance, sex-roles; to glorify wealth and waste' (Cutler, 1985: 204).

Both these first strands of radical elitism – in their focus on either the folk or the avant-garde ideal – owe a debt to an earlier version of the core argument. This is associated with the work of the Frankfurt School in the late 1930s and 1940s, whose pessimistic reading of modern cultural production saw it as a crucial device in the maintenance of the capitalist order. The key contrast here is between high and popular culture. A classic statement of this argument is provided by Theodor Adorno and Max Horkheimer, and was reiterated and developed by Herbert Marcuse. Together, they explain the maintenance of social order under capitalism by reference to the influence of a culture which reproduces the values and habits of capitalism. Central to their argument is the belief that capitalism's success, its ability to manage the potential threat posed by the exploited, derives from its eradication of the will to revolt. The desire to say 'no', to refuse the demands of capitalism, has been crushed, not by brute force and coercion, but by the erosion of the very instinct to revolt.

The Frankfurt School rejects any mechanistic marxism, in which the material development of capitalism generates increasing levels of misery, out of which springs revolution. Culture is not a straightforward product of material circumstances. This did not mean, however, that it was autonomous – culture was still to be understood in terms of 'its position in the social totality' (Held, 1980: 80). But in recogniszing culture as important in its own right, the Frankfurt School was acknowledging, among other things, the impact of Freud on social theory. The subconscious cannot be viewed as a mere extension of the material realm. Indeed, the subconscious is seen as the site of those desires which inspire criticism of the existing order. Art engages with the subconscious, and with the suppressed desires and ambitions that demand social change. Marcuse (1968: 132) talks of art as 'the moulding of unfulfilled longings and the purification of unfulfilled instincts'.

Rebellion and refusal derive from the capacity to imagine alternative ways of life, alternative forms of being. The ability to conceive of such things is to recognize particular feelings and desires, to identify the expressive dimension in human existence and to break from the instrumental rationality of capitalism. Thus, Marcuse (1972: 79) invests art with the ability to communicate 'the indictment of the established reality' and to represent 'the goals of liberation'. Art becomes a means to freedom: 'The search is for art forms which express the experience of the body (*and* the "soul"), not as vehicles of labor power and resignation, but as vehicles of liberation' (Marcuse, 1972: 82; his emphasis). Technical rationality represents the interests of control and management, not of liberation: 'a technological rationale is the rationale of domination itself' (Adorno and Horkheimer, 1979: 121). It treats the world as an object to be manipulated or administered – nature and people are both exploited. Popular culture is commercial culture: it can be mass produced and it can serve its allotted propagandist purpose. In music, this would be epitomized by muzak.

The vision of liberation, the spirit of revolt, are kept alive only within high art. It is there that our desires find expression. Marcuse (1972: 99) writes: 'On a primary level, art is recollection; it appeals to a pre-conceptual experience and understanding which re-emerge in and against the context of the social functioning of experience and understanding – against instrumentalist reason and sensibility.' Not that all art is equally good; that is, equally capable of giving form to these desires. To be good, art has to produce 'beauty as the sensuous appearance of the idea of freedom', and 'beauty as the negation of the commodity world and of the performances, attitudes, looks and gestures, required by it' (Marcuse, 1972: 117, 121). 'Guerilla theater' or rock music cannot do this. They are commodified and thereby become part of real life, and hence vulnerable to the prevailing order (Marcuse, 1972: 101). Marcuse (1972: 92) is equally critical of 'bourgeois culture', 'which serves to justify and beautify the established order'. Importantly though, he is not rejecting all 'bourgeois art' on the simple grounds of its class character. Despite its role as status symbol or commodity, it may still retain 'that alienation from the established reality which is the origin of art' (Marcuse, 1972: 97). It is this thought – that good art is defined by its ability to evoke an alternative, better order – that underlies the critiques of culture voiced by the Frankfurt School, and in it is contained the need to make *judgements* of the art, to show how popular culture is aesthetically inadequate and politically reactionary.

Adorno and Horkheimer write of the commercialization of culture as a method by which the culture industry propagates 'mass

deception' under the guise of 'enlightenment'. Consumers are given
the illusion of emancipation through art, while they are, in fact,
merely acquiring commercial objects that add to their enslavement.
They *think* that they are being freed, though: 'Art for the masses
has destroyed the dream but still conforms to the tenets of that
dreaming idealism which critical idealism balked at' (Adorno and
Horkheimer, 1979: 125). Events like lotteries or game shows allow
the culture industry to promote the ideas of freedom or opportunity – anyone can succeed. They encourage the idea of individuality (or, at least, 'pseudo-individuality') and promise untold riches.
In his dissection of popular music, Adorno (1990) detects a similar
confidence trick. Audiences are given the illusion of individuality
in jazz improvisation, in the idea that the player is creating sponta-
neously and uniquely. In fact, a standard pattern is being followed.
The sounds may be different but the storyline is the same. The illusion of freedom cloaks the reality of social discipline. Mass culture
not only provides propaganda for the existing order, it also main-
tains discipline within it: 'The tragic film becomes an institution
for moral improvement' (Adorno and Horkheimer, 1979: 152). The
audiences conspire in their own oppression by calling 'for Mickey
Rooney in preference to the tragic Garbo, for Donald Duck instead
of Betty Boop' (Adorno and Horkheimer, 1979: 134). In Donald Duck
they see the triumph of 'technological reason over truth', represented by the way in which 'Donald Duck in the cartoons and the
unfortunate in real life get their thrashing so that the audience can
learn to take their own punishment' (Adorno and Horkheimer, 1979:
138). Mediocrity, the acceptance of the status quo, rather than the
demand for what might be, is celebrated in the 'idolization of the
cheap' which has the effect of 'making the average' appear 'heroic'
(Adorno and Horkheimer, 1979: 156).

   Through mass production and commercialization, culture is
standardized, manufactured to reproduce the logic and rhythms
of capitalism. Culture has become a form of industry, and formal
differences between films or soap operas are no more real than
differences between other categories of product – whether cars or
washing powders. 'Every tenor voice comes to sound like a Ca-
ruso record, and the "natural" faces of Texas girls are like the successful models by whom Hollywood has cast them' (Adorno and
Horkheimer, 1979: 140). Just as technological rationality transforms
the inner nature of humans and the outer nature of the world, so
mass culture becomes 'life': 'Real life is becoming indistinguish-

able from the movies' (Adorno and Horkheimer, 1979: 126). In the same way that technology dictates our responses to the physical world, so film controls our imagination. Works of culture are 'designed' rather than created; they are made to follow set patterns and to elicit set responses. 'The culture industry does not sublimate; it represses,' write Adorno and Horkheimer (1979: 140), and hence 'works of art are ascetic and unashamed; the culture industry is pornographic and prudish.' Marcuse observes a similar process in popular culture itself, where radical elements are made conservative. He writes (1972: 114; his emphasis) of black music as

> the cry and song of the slaves and the ghettos. In this music, the very life and death of black men and women are lived again: the music *is* body; the aesthetic form is the 'gesture' of pain, sorrow, indictment. With the takeover by the whites, a significant change occurs: white 'rock' is what its black paradigm is *not*, namely, *performance*.

And what is true for individual artefacts is true for the culture as a whole. Under the logic of technological rationality, it becomes a form of administration, a way of ordering leisure time. The process which organizes the mass production of culture is dedicated to the systematic promotion of 'rubbish'.

In summary: for radical elitists like Marcuse and Adorno and Horkheimer and those who have echoed them, mass culture is not just a means of disciplining an otherwise recalcitrant people. It is about transforming them into a shallow, supplicant mass. The transformation is a product not of propaganda, but of psychology; it entails the elimination of the will to revolt: 'The most intimate reactions of human beings have been so thoroughly reified that the idea of anything specific to themselves now persists only as an utterly abstract notion: personality scarcely signifies anything more than shining white teeth and freedom from body odor and emotions' (Adorno and Horkheimer, 1979: 167). This is achieved through the propagation of a particular kind of culture, driven by the ambitions of capitalist accumulation.

Radical populists

Radical populism can be viewed as a direct response to the radical elitism of the Frankfurt School. Its most cited exponent is John Fiske. In his book *Understanding Popular Culture* (1989), he talks of

'The Jeaning of America'. His analysis of the iconography of jeans enables him to detect a gallery of political gestures in a pair of trousers. He writes (1989: 4): 'If today's jeans are to express oppositional meanings, or even to gesture toward such social resistance, they need to be disfigured in some way – tie-dyed, irregularly bleached, or, particularly, torn. If 'whole' jeans connote shared meanings of contemporary America, then disfiguring them becomes a way of distancing oneself from those values.' Fiske takes seriously Umberto Eco's remark that our clothes speak for us, and invests jeans with the eloquence of Bernard Shaw and the political insight of Karl Marx. Fiske (1989: 187) is committed to a populist perspective which argues 'that we can learn at least as much, if not more, about resistances to the dominant ideology from studying popular everyday tactics as from theorizing and analysing the strategic mechanisms of power.' Fiske's reason for taking this view is that he attributes 'semiotic productivity' to the business of popular culture consumption. People can make meanings for 'social identity and social experience from the semiotic resources of the cultural commodity' (Fiske, 1992: 37).

Fiske is sometimes represented as the most extreme of radical populists, one who can find a subversive meaning in anything. But this is unfair. He is aware of countervailing commercial forces which constrain the interpretations that any cultural item may acquire, and his position owes a strong family resemblance to the other major strand of radical populism: the work of Birmingham University's Centre for Contemporary Cultural Studies.

In the 1970s, the CCCS group, drawing on an eclectic range of theoretical sources (including Althusser, Gramsci and Bakhtin), sought to recover the meaning of cultural life for its participants, to see reggae and rock as resources around which subcultures made sense of their lives and resisted dominant ideologies. Of course, there was, as Jim McGuigan (1992) points out, no single CCCS position, and no one writer fits neatly into the left populist category. None the less, it is possible to see in writers like Paul Willis, Iain Chambers and Dick Hebdige a celebration of the capacity of cultures to mesh homologously with lived experience (the populism) and to stand in opposition to the status quo (the radicalism).

The argument begins with the claim that people are actively engaged in the consumption of their culture; they are not its passive recipients. In *Common Culture*, Willis (1990: 1, and 6) writes

about the 'vibrant symbolic life and symbolic creativity of everyday life, everyday activity and expression', out of which are formed
'collective and individual identities'. It is in this process of active
consumption that culture acquires, through the use to which it is
put and the way it is reinterpreted, its radical political dimension.
As Chambers (1986: 212) argues, it is through the interplay with
popular culture that people break with any attempt to impose an
all-encompassing ideology: 'We need to disrupt the presumed coherence of ideology, texts and images. . . . That means living inside the signs. It means engaging in the contradictory pleasures of
fashion, style, television soap, video games, sport, shopping, reading, drinking, sexuality.' Through this engagement, 'the sense of the
possible' is changed, and with it the political map. Two processes
are at work. On the one hand, popular culture conveys many, contradictory meanings; on the other hand, people take pleasure
in the way they derive their own meanings from their engagement with it. Thus, Hebdige (1979: 18) issues the following injunction: 'Our task becomes . . . to discern the hidden messages
inscribed in code on the glossy surfaces of style, to trace them out
as "maps of meaning" which obscurely re-present the very contradictions they are designed to resolve or conceal.' In reading the
contradictions in the text, in excavating a subversive subtext, the
radical populists are not appealing to the same standards of judgements as made by the elitists. Although the radical populists want
to look beyond the self-conscious experience of individuals, and
in this sense distance themselves from conservative populism, their
concern is not to distinguish between the quality of different cultural artefacts. It is a matter not of attributing a higher or more
sophisticated politics to one film or song or programme, but rather
of penetrating the complexities of any given example. Popular
culture exists as the imaginative efforts of its audience.

Summary

In this section, I have surveyed briefly four different political
interpretations of popular culture, dividing them crudely along
two axes: conservative–radical, elitist–populist. Presenting them
this way reveals a number of cross-cutting cleavages. Left and right
elitists share the belief that culture has to be judged, rather than
simply observed or understood from within. Similarly, left and

right populists root their arguments in a version of the thought that 'the people know best'. But in each of these alliances there are conflicts. Left and right elitists disagree in the kind of judgements they make about culture, just as left and right populists are at odds over their description of 'the people' and of how any act of cultural consumption should be read.

Rethinking the politics of popular culture

Faced with these cross-cutting cleavages and alliances, it is tempting to conclude that there is some better way of thinking about the politics of popular culture, one which provides a synthesis of all the others. This thought finds further encouragement in the fact that familiar political battle-lines, between left and right, are breaking down in the face of an emergent postmodern politics in which identities and interests are fluid and contingent, in which institutional and material forces are subsumed within the realm of discourses. This temptation to strive for an easy synthesis needs, however, to be subjected to closer scrutiny. I want to begin by looking more closely at the populist reading of popular culture.

In the wake of unbridled enthusiasm for postmodernist theorizing, the populist argument has enjoyed an inevitable ascendency. The challenge to hierarchical systems and established narratives, not to mention the 'death of the author', has legitimated the idea that judgement is largely redundant and that all texts are available to countless readings. It is no wonder, therefore, that popular culture has been designated a prime site of postmodern practice – in the stylistic conventions of the pop video and in the possibilities created by sampling technology.

Popular culture's deployment of these new opportunities is linked to the politicization of consumption. The consumer creates; consumption becomes a form of political activity. Frank Mort (1989: 171) writes: 'Today's consumer culture straddles public and private space, creating blurred areas in between.' Consumption choices become expressions of political concern: 'Consumption is now centre stage in the political battleground over the economy' (Mort, 1989: 161). Via consumerism, popular culture comes to represent direct political empowerment. But this attribution of populist radicalism to consumption is problematic.

Judith Williamson argues that it confuses three distinct elements in culture: the text/object, the way it is produced and the desire with which it is consumed. Writing about the popularity of the Walkman, she observes: 'In analysing these products we can understand more about the society which both produces and uses them. But their forms are fundamentally those of a market capitalism – which they reflect, rather than shape. What *are* potentially radical are the needs that underlie their use: needs both sharpened and denied by the economic system that makes them' (Williamson, 1986: 232; her emphasis). Williamson sees culture as a window onto the economic and political structure. Cultural consumption cannot, therefore, substitute for political action, even if it becomes the focus of the desire for such action. The politics of consumption cannot be assumed. The task of the analyst is to judge as well as detect; it is to discriminate.

Angela McRobbie's (1991) feminist critique of popular culture and cultural studies takes a similarly sceptical line on populism. She notes that, in celebrating the consumption of culture, many of the radical populists marginalize women. The pleasures of popular culture are enjoyed at women's expense rather than in mutual gratification. And indeed the culture itself reinforces sexual stereotypes that promote the oppression of women. The implication of her analysis is that experiences of popular culture cannot be taken for granted – that we need to recognize that the conditions of consumption and the pleasures of consumption are not equal for all. In the same vein, she also insists that the reading of cultural texts must be alive to reactionary as well as radical meanings. Rap can simultaneously be radically critical and conservatively reactionary. The mere fact that a marginalized group has adopted a distinct cultural style does not mean that they now articulate a coherent, critical response to their oppression.

The arguments of Williamson and McRobbie, and the criticisms that they make of populism, establish a case for judgement and discrimination in culture. But does this, therefore, make them elitist? I think not, if only because the traditional forms of elitism are equally problematic. There is a sense in which we are all populists now. Or rather, it is difficult in a secular, non-communist world to defend the elitism of old. Whether it takes the aristocratic ideal of being born to rule, or the Leninist idea of the vanguard leadership, such elitism is left now to religious fundamentalism. In the same way, the notion of absolute, incontrovertible standards, though still the subject of political rhetoric, is difficult to uphold. Standards are based on less sure foundations, maintained by complex systems of legitimation and authority, and as such are constantly vulnerable to erosion and reconstruction. Insofar as elitism is the alternative to populism, it is an elitism established discursively and politically. It is an elitism that owes its legacy to Plato, Rousseau, J. S. Mill and Gramsci. It is an elitism of an 'enlightened leadership', whose interests do not derive from some selfish set of interests or some higher authority, but which is rooted in some view about what is best *for* the people. It is this tradition that echoes in the critique of populist accounts of culture.

Its fullest statement can be found in Jim McGuigan's *Cultural Populism*, itself a critique of the populist strand within cultural studies. McGuigan's survey of the history of cultural studies leads him to the conclusion that it has slid 'into uncritical populism' (1992: 39). McGuigan wants to move away from a concern solely with interpretations of the text and wants to reintroduce political economy into the analysis of popular culture: 'the separation of contemporary cultural studies from the political economy of culture has been one of the most disabling features of the field of study' (McGuigan, 1992: 40). Not that he regards this as a simple move; the old certainties of materialism no longer provide the necessary groundwork.

Tied to the reintroduction of political economy, McGuigan (1992: 76–9) also wants to introduce a critical perspective, a way of discriminating between examples of popular culture and their politics. He argues that cultural analysts, in siding with 'the popular', abrogate their responsibility and deny their skills, to the disadvantage of those they claim to understand and/or represent. They have a duty to use their knowledge and powers of discrimination, just as parents have a duty to deny children an endless diet of sweets and chips. His second reason for introducing a critical perspective is to address what he calls 'the crisis of qualitative judgement'. If cultural critics are going to fulfil their political obligations, then the question becomes one of establishing how this should be done: how we should judge a work of popular culture. This task, argues McGuigan, does not disappear with analysis of the modes of consumption or production of popular culture. There is a need to identify the criteria and means by which judgements are to be made. 'In short,' writes McGuigan (1992: 173), 'the study of culture is nothing if it is not about values.' Frith (1996) reaches a similar conclusion when he argues that aesthetic judgement is an expression of ethical views, and that each is impossible without the other. He also notes that what is important about conservative elitists like Allan Bloom is that they, at least, take the content seriously, that they make explicit what is in fact implicit in all analyses of culture – the making of judgement: 'To deny the significance of value judgement in popular culture (to ignore popular taste hierarchies) is, if nothing else, hypocritical' (Frith, 1990: 105). Everyone makes judgements – to choose one film or record over another is not to engage in some completely arbitrary process. It is to value one thing higher than another, and in doing so not to be thinking only about aesthetics but about a wide range of values – some political, some moral. In other words, both Frith and McGuigan connect their critique of populism to the need to adopt a critical account of the content and creation of popular culture. This position is itself derived from an account of social action which links morality, aesthetics and material conditions.

Reintroducing the element of discrimination to cultural analysis does not, of course, meet with universal approval, especially as it seems to clash with the agnosticism and scepticism that postmodernism heralded and with which cultural studies has then been colonized. John Storey (1993: 183) is especially scathing of McGuigan's concern to reinsert qualitative judgement, seeing it as a return to 'Arnoldian certainties' and the elevation of the university lecturer as 'guardian of the eternal flame of the cultural'. For Storey, there are more interesting questions to be asked than whether a piece of popular culture is good or bad. He accuses McGuigan of being engaged in the 'rhetorical vacuousness' of the 'moral leftists'. It is never quite clear what his other questions are, but Storey's (1993: 200–1) position is one which seeks to marginalize the judgemental issues in favour of a 'critical plurality', although, importantly, he too wants to steer a course between 'a dismissive elitism' and 'a disarming anti-intellectualism'. It is hard to see why, if this is what Storey wants, he does not engage more seriously with the issues of judgement. He seems to imagine that the value of culture can be rooted in the meanings that people produce from it, and that this provides the basis for a radical cultural politics. But that is to assume *either* that all meanings are necessarily radical *or* that there is some independent criterion by which cultural use can be judged. The first is to offer an uncritical populism which defines everything as radical; the second

offers an unvarnished elitism. Storey's own position, then, seems
to push him back into the arms of the very thesis that he begins by
criticizing.

If Storey's criticism fails, then we are faced with the view of
popular culture suggested by Frith and McGuigan. Indeed, we
are confronted with the view of culture with which we ended the
previous chapter. It is for this reason that I want to try to connect
the two approaches, and to draw once again upon Grossberg's
attempt to synthesize cultural and social theory. Like Williamson
and McRobbie, Grossberg (1992a: 22) treats as 'too romanticized'
the radical populist view of culture as constitutive of particular
relations and positions. But he goes further, arguing that cultural
studies has been hidebound by its intellectual grounding in 'the
model of communication [that] assumes a relationship between
two discrete and independently existing entities: whether between
individuals, or between audiences and texts, or between signified
and signifiers (Grossberg, 1992a: 38). Like Frith, Grossberg wants
to integrate culture into social existence. There are two consequences of this. The first is not to confine cultural studies to the
way specific audiences respond to particular texts, but to treat
the object of study – culture – as part of social activity, whether
leisure or labour. The second consequence is not to see culture
simply as the source of 'meaning'. Grossberg wants instead to
acknowledge the full range of responses to, and relationships with,
popular culture. This allows him to suggest that cultural practices
create possibilities for the transformation of reality, and that they
relate our economic and emotional relations, our desires and our
politics.

Grossberg (1992a: 79–80) argues that popular culture works primarily through *affect*, the way it articulates 'the "feeling" of life'.
The importance of affect is the way it is 'organized according to
maps which direct people's investment in and into the world'.
Affect constitutes the form of our passion, itself the drive behind
a belief in how we judge the world. Popular culture's affective
potential helps to organize people's passion, and as such becomes
part of a process of empowerment: 'Affective empowerment involves the generation of energy and passion, the construction of
possibility' (Grossberg, 1992a: 85).

A similar view of people's relationship to culture emerges in
Frith's account of the value of popular culture. He writes, for
example, of how culture does more than reflect or express our

feelings; it actually gives form to our feelings, but it does not dictate those feelings in a manipulative way: 'songs don't *cause* people to fall in love, but provide people with the means to articulate the feelings associated with being in love' (Frith, 1996: 164; his emphasis). Popular culture works as a language, so that songs are modes of expression (Frith, 1996: 166). This argument has important consequences for the way we think about the relationship between politics and popular culture. Popular culture does not substitute for politics, it becomes instead a way we experience our feelings and passions, a way we identify ourselves. As Frith (1996: 169) writes: 'The most significant political effect of a pop song is not how people vote or organise, but how they speak.'

Conclusion

This chapter began by looking at the ways in which popular culture has been analysed politically. My contention was that this analysis was organized around two dimensions: populism–elitism and radicalism–conservatism. In the latter part of the chapter, I have argued that the various positions that emerge from these two dimensions are founded on untenable ideals, primarily because of the impossibility of either elitism or populism. To escape this predicament means, first, rethinking the way in which popular culture engages with politics. This is represented by the way in which culture is understood as an organizing force, a way of articulating feelings. There is, however, one other element to this reintegration of politics and popular culture. This is the connection made between ethics and aesthetics, and by the role played by judgement and discrimination in both the pleasures and the analysis of popular culture. It is here, I want to argue, that the relationship between politics and popular culture is grounded. The next chapter is an attempt to justify this claim.

CHAPTER NINE

The politics of judgement:
from condemnation to commendation

> Culture and politics . . . belong together because it is not
> knowledge or truth which is at stake, but rather judgement
> and decision . . .
> Hannah Arendt, *Between Past and Future*

In practice and in principle, judgement is unavoidable. Whether
deciding how popular culture should be organized or regulated, or
in analysing current arrangements, decisions have to be made about
what is right or reasonable. In passing comment on the 'packaging
of politics', we are forced to discriminate between different types
of package – to say whether they advance or threaten democracy,
to link cultural criticism with political analysis. Judgement featured
prominently in the debates about the politics of popular culture. It
was explicit in the case of the elitists, and implicit in the case of the
populists. Indeed judgement is an inescapable part of any response
to popular culture. Moreover, it is not just a feature of the theory. It
is practised daily in decisions about what kind of popular culture is
to be made available, in what form and for whom. In the next chapter, I want to look at what we mean by 'good' popular culture, and
the way in which politics is connected to the pleasures of popular
culture. But for now, in this chapter, I want to look more closely at
the practice of judgement – how and why it is made. Everywhere
in the culture industry – in broadcasting, publishing, journalism,
media corporations, and so on – judgements have to be formed and

implemented every day – about what to produce, for what market, in what form. In the same way, individuals make decisions about what to watch or listen to or buy. Everyone chooses one thing rather than another because they think it is in some way 'better' than the alternatives. A similar process works negatively in decisions not to purchase or to broadcast. This is most dramatically embodied in decisions to censor popular culture. Here decisions are being taken about what is 'bad' in popular culture. Whether in positive decisions to sign an artist or negative ones to censor them, judgements are being made which affect the content and character of popular culture. In drawing attention to these decisions, I do not want to suggest that they are the result of individual choice, or that they can be seen as discrete moments of deliberation, only that there is a process at work whereby some culture is selected and some ignored, and that we need to look at how and why this happens. This chapter explores the politics of both the process and the principles. The politics of judgement are examined in two distinct ways: (1) how the judgements themselves draw upon a set of political values and assumptions; and (2) how the process of judging is itself an enactment of politics, similar in many ways to the decisions that are the staple diet of politics generally. But to begin with, I want to expand upon points made in the previous chapter, and to explain more fully why judgement is important to understanding the politics of popular culture. To do this I want to eliminate three approaches which seem to avoid judgement: populism, relativism and absolutism. Each entails a particular politics, a way of understanding the value and significance of popular culture, but each is flawed.

Populism, relativism, absolutism

Populism

In the last chapter, we identified two types of populism. For the radical populist, popular culture is an expression of the interests and tastes of those who make use of it. These choices have political significance because they derive from a struggle for recognition and from a desire or need to subvert a dominant ideology. They presume, in other words, an intrinsic oppositional disposition which finds its expression in cultural activity. The focus, therefore, is upon the activities of the users rather than the cultural object itself.For the conservative populist, the tastes of the consumer are pre-given. The market serves to realize those tastes. Popular culture is, therefore, the product of the market and of the laws of supply and demand.

Consumers of popular culture are presented as just that: *consumers*, digesting whatever it is their tastebuds crave. Their tastes are not to be analysed, merely acknowledged. The market responds to their preferences. But to tell the story like this is to overlook the ways in which any given product gets to the market, and once there, how consumers choose between them. Markets are not based on complete information – producers cannot know in advance exactly what consumers want; and competition within the market is rarely perfect – there are monopolies and oligopolies, which seek to manage taste rather than react to it. And even when the market is dominated by vast conglomerates, consumers still have to decide between products – which films to see, which books, records or videos to buy. Many products fail to find a market. Both of these processes – production and consumption – entail some element of judgement and discrimination.

Neither populist approach allows space for the business of judgement. Indeed, they make no attempt to examine the texts, or to explain how and why one is preferred to another, or whether the chosen item (or the evaluation put upon it) represents some kind of alternative and not more of the same. These questions do not arise because of the prior assumptions that culture merely serves as a peg on which are hung pre-existing interests and concerns. But, as McGuigan (1992) and others have pointed out, this position celebrates a romantic sentimentality which allows any taste to be viewed as a genuinely popular expression of a real desire, whatever the product. Apart from the fact that we know little about what actually informs popular taste, the populist approach makes no attempt to discriminate between examples of popular culture. Everything is blanketed in relativism, and unfounded political assumptions substitute for judgement or empirical data.

Relativism

As Frith (1991b: 105) comments, 'the populist assumption is that all popular culture goods and services are somehow the same in their empowering value. . . . The aesthetic discrimination essential to cultural consumption and the considered judgements it involves are ignored.' The populist is reluctant or unwilling to pass judgement. Judgement becomes a mere matter of 'taste', and taste is merely a subjective individual response, no more or less valid than any other. The pleasures of the Smurfs are equivalent to those of the Smiths.

Relativism discounts judgement on the grounds that there can be no vantage point from which to compare the respective merits of any two artefacts. Taste can only be understood as the culturally specific response of an individual, group or society. This approach replaces the romantic politics of the populist with a non-judgemental liberalism. The substitution, however, establishes a politics which denies the idea of progress in taste, that people can learn to appreciate better art. People may change their tastes, but this does not mark 'progress' so much as a change of circumstances or needs. Indeed, the relativist position denies choices and allows only *responses*. In doing this, it contradicts our intuition that we are always discriminating between the good and the bad. It also clashes with the intuition that judgements of culture are indications of a person's character, that it matters when someone we like fails to share our enthusiasm for [fill in your own choice]. In short, the relativist seems to overlook a key aspect of popular culture. 'The essence of cultural practice', writes Frith (1991b: 105), 'is making judgements and assessing difference.' But if we are to avoid the traps set by relativism, the temptation is to introduce some higher, independent standard that provides criteria for discriminating between the good and the bad.

Absolutism

Absolutism appears to offer an escape from the consequences of relativism. It finds advocates – whether explicitly or implicitly – in writers like Allan Bloom or F. R. Leavis who want to establish a set of standards by which to separate the high from the low, the good from the bad in culture. Such standards assert that George Eliot is a better writer than Catherine Cookson, that Schoenberg's music is better than Sting's, that it is more important to read *The Odyssey* than *The Odessa File*. These standards are themselves also rich in political values; first, because the 'standards' in culture are premised upon a set of moral and/or political views about the good society and the good life; and, secondly, because of the implications for how such judgements are reached: they are the province not of popular choice, but of informed expertise, of hierarchy not democracy.

The absolutist position sets itself against the liberal democracy of relativism (in which all choices are equal), and against populist democracy (in which the people's choice is sacrosanct). But is absolutism a coherent position? Is there, in fact, an independent authority from which these standards can be derived? There are, of course, many examples of people acting *as if* there were such standards. History is littered with instances when standards of truth and quality have been imposed. But as many writers – from Charles Taylor (1967) to Michel Foucault (1980) – have pointed out, such standards are themselves the product of interpretation and power. All judgements are partial, formed by the circumstances, culture and interests of those who judge. This is not to deny that judgements are exercised, nor that they need to be, it is just to claim that they cannot be understood as the product of some absolute standard.

Summary

But if populism, relativism and absolutism are flawed, is there any way in which we can talk about judgement in popular culture? This question matters because it allows us to discriminate between examples of popular culture, thereby enabling us to comment on the different politics of different films, records, and so on, and on the processes by which such culture is organized. As McGuigan (1992: 173) argued: 'the study of culture is nothing if it is not about values. A disenchanted, anti-moralistic, anti-judgemental stance constructed in opposition to cultural and political zealotry only takes you so far.' So how are values and judgements to be incorporated? I want first to consider whether there is a theoretical position which avoids the traps set by populism, absolutism and relativism. Secondly, I wish to shift the focus away from the theory of judgement to the practice, to see what can be learnt by looking at how judgements are actually made.

The sociology of judgement

One obvious objection to this project emerges from the work of Pierre Bourdieu. His major work *Distinction* seems to represent a comprehensive denial of the notion of judgement, and an assertion of the need for a material reading of taste. At the very beginning of his book, Bourdieu (1986: 7) summarizes his view that 'art and cultural consumption are predisposed, consciously and deliberately or not, to fulfil a social function of legitimating social differences.' In a similar vein, he claims that the survey work that underpins *Distinction* reveals 'the very close relationship linking cultural practices (or the corresponding opinions) to educational capital (measured by qualifications) and, secondarily, to social origin (measured by father's occupation); and, on the other hand, the fact that, at equivalent levels of educational capital, the weight of social origin in the practice- and preference-explaining system increases as one moves away from the most legitimate areas of culture' (Bourdieu, 1986: 13). Taste is organized according to social attributes and interests.

There is a danger of seeing Bourdieu as a crudely materialist, determinist or functionalist writer. But this is to ignore the role he allows to the *organization of taste*, and the exercise of judgement within the social structure. 'Aesthetic dispositions' are enshrined in institutions – in the repertoire of opera companies, in art galleries, and so on. An aesthetic operates within social groupings (Bourdieu, 1986: 58, 100–1, 173). That these aesthetics are rooted in particular social locations is not to make them the crude product of their habitat. At the same time, the form and focus of taste are not arbitrary. We may eat food out of necessity, but our diet is conditioned by social and economic factors, by class and cultural norms. Why one activity or practice is associated with one class rather than another is a consequence of the operation of intermediaries, not of some pre-determined connection: 'A cultural product – an avant-garde picture, a political manifesto, a newspaper – is a constituted taste', dependent 'on the work of professionals' (Bourdieu, 1986: 231). One implication of this is that there are struggles over the claim to ownership of tastes and practices, struggles which entail competing experiences of the world and which are resolved in a number of ways (Bourdieu, 1986: 250ff). Tastes may be conditioned by material circumstances and class location, but the objects of taste – what is acceptable, what is unacceptable – are not determined by economic circumstances. This is the business of politics. Although Bourdieu devotes relatively little attention to this process, it is clearly important to his argument. The sociology of judgement and taste has to have an accompanying politics.

The politics of judgement

McGuigan (1992) addresses the issue of judgement by reintroducing the concept of ideology, and using it to comment on the fact that popularity is no guarantee of radicalism. Taking the example of the *Sun* newspaper, he draws attention to the way in which 'popular pleasure is routinely articulated through oppressive ideologies that operate in fertile chauvinistic ground. It is populist in the worst sense' (McGuigan, 1992: 184). But there are problems with this approach, not least in the authority which McGuigan claims for his particular ideological readings. He has been accused of relying upon 'absolute standards' (Storey, 1993: 183). Whether or not this is a fair criticism of McGuigan, he has to defend his particular judgements against those who do not share his ideological disposition. In other words, arguments about the politics of culture are no more than the disputes that traditionally animate politics, albeit conducted within cultural studies. It may not simply be a matter of 'I know what I like', but it is still a matter of 'I know what I believe in'. Is it possible, though, to move beyond this, to find an account of judgement that is not simply ideology spoken in a different language?

An alternative approach is suggested by Barbara Herrnstein Smith's *Contingencies of Values*. She accepts that there is no future in attempting 'to establish normative "criteria" ' or in devising 'presumptively objective evaluative procedures' (Herrnstein Smith, 1988: 28). She is dismissive of such ventures because, in her view, values are 'radically contingent', by which she means they are the product of 'social, political, circumstantial and other constraints and conditions' (Herrnstein Smith, 1988: 28–30). Judgement is part of a constantly shifting economy of taste and values. The same spirit informs Frith's (1990: 96) approach to the distinction between the good and the bad in music: 'Arguments about music are less about the qualities of the music itself than about how to place it, about what it is in the music that is actually to be assessed.' In this process, there are competing discourses and interests which have to be differentiated and placed within a hierarchy. This is done through a combination of an art discourse (where the key idea is 'transcendence'), a folk discourse (where the key is 'integration'), and a pop discourse (where 'fun' is the defining term) (Frith, 1991b: 106–7). Frith's point is not that these discourses provide an absolute set of standards, or indeed that they are used consistently and rigorously. They are, he acknowledges, peculiar to the person making the judgement. Equally, he does not view such judgements as the result of deliberations by autonomous, discrete individuals. They are inescapably social. As Frith (1996: 72) writes: 'Whatever the individual bases of our judgements, once made we do seek to justify them, to explain them.' The incentive for defending them is that they describe real feelings, which are as much about morality as aesthetics (Frith, 1996: 72–3).

Included in this contingent notion of values, with its economy of circulating tastes and judgement, is the idea that there are 'institutions of evaluative authority' whose job is 'to devise arguments and procedures that validate the community's established tastes and preferences' (Herrnstein Smith, 1988: 40). These institutions form part of a *process* of evaluation, not a unique act of pure disinterested judgement (Herrnstein Smith, 1988: 42). The distinction made between high and popular culture is a product of an 'institutional setting, rather than the value issues as such' (Frith, 1991b: 110).

These views constitute an attack on the Frankfurt School's approach to mass culture. The argument of Horkheimer and Adorno, Marcuse and others, depends upon the distinction they make between popular and high culture, between the critique implied by the latter and the complacency embodied in the former. But such distinctions, says Herrnstein Smith, trade upon unexamined assumptions about the qualities of either, and the persuasiveness of the Frankfurt argument owes more, in fact, to the language used to describe the 'rival' art forms than to the experiences which they represent (Herrnstein Smith, 1988: 75ff). It is the triumph of rhetoric over reason. The formal terms available to talk about classical music do not, in themselves, constitute proof of higher qualities within the music, and indeed they do not actually describe the experience of hearing the music.

To emphasize the contingency of values and to reject any

notion of absolute standards is not to side with the relativist who says that all judgements are equally valid, or with the populist who infers judgement from political disposition or from given choices. Just because no value judgement can acquire the status of objective judgement, it does not follow that all are equally valid. All that is implied is that notions of an objective standard do not exist and cannot supply the means of discrimination. What it does mean, though, is that judgements and values must be understood in the context in which they operate, in terms of the systems of validation to which they appeal. The focus shifts, therefore, onto attempts to *claim* objectivity, which are viewed as part of a process involving a set of institutions and interests. The business of judging popular culture is part of a political process, one involving the exercise of power and the attempt to legitimate that power. Censorship is a classic example of exactly this.

Censorship and the judgement of popular culture

Censorship makes explicit the linkage of popular culture and politics. Censorship may be less common than is suggested by the attention it receives, but it is nonetheless widespread. Much censorship focuses on the category of 'news/current affairs', but entertainment is by no means immune. In 1992 in the UK, cuts were imposed on 11.1 per cent of all films with an '18' certificate and 18 per cent of all videos with an '18' certificate. In 1994, the Australian Film Censorship Board banned the Spanish film *Tras El Cristal* (In a Glass Cage); in Cambodia, the editor of the *Voice of Khmer Youth* was imprisoned for a year for publishing a cartoon; in Germany, the book *Eye for an Eye* was withdrawn; and in Malaysia, the government issued strict guidelines as to what could appear on TV and on film. But while the practice of censorship is widespread, it is not motivated by a universal set of concerns. In Australia, censorship was directed at the portrayal of child abuse; in Cambodia, it was at the mockery of political leaders; in Germany, it was anti-semitism that provoked censorship; and in Malaysia, it was sex and violence. These variations are overlaid by differences in the system of censorship and its political context. Censorship is traditionally thought to be the province of state-centred communist regimes; and they have, of course, been among its main practitioners. Under Stalin, Soviet film censorship was so strict that in 1950 only six feature films survived the tests. But it is apparent that liberal and capitalist regimes also censor. Tom Dewe Mathews (1994), for example, says of Britain that it 'possesses the most rigorous film censorship system in the western world'. In the United States, fierce battles have been fought over rap music and heavy metal, as well as over film and fine art. US television is more cautious about what it will allow to be shown or said. When the British situation comedy *Men Behaving Badly* was transferred to the States, the swearing and sexual references were toned down. While the USA and the UK operate a similar system of film censorship, based on voluntary cooperation, the USA regime is more liberal. However, rather than dwelling upon the similarities and differences between systems of censorship, I want to explore the circumstances under which censors act – why, for instance, do Mapplethorpe's photos pass unnoticed in one city, but become subject to prosecution elsewhere?

From the brief survey above, it is apparent that censorship emerges in response to four main concerns: sex, violence, security and politics. When dealing with popular culture, the first two are most commonly cited, and turn upon questions of what defines obscenity and what effect portrayals of violence have upon behaviour. The group NWA (Niggaz With Attitude) were threatened by censorship in the USA and UK. An assistant director of the FBI wrote to NWA's record company: 'A song recorded by the rap group NWA on their album entitled *Straight Outta Compton* encourages violence against and disrespect for the law enforcement officer. . . . Advocating violence and assault is wrong. . . . Music plays a significant role in society, and I wanted you to be aware of the FBI's position relative to this song and its message' (quoted in Marsh and Pollack, 1989: 33). As police forces in the States became aware of NWA, they organized to ban the group from playing. Ice T's record 'Cop Killer' provoked a similar reaction – it was banned in Ireland, and removed from live shows in Australia and New Zealand. Most notable, though, was the success of the Washington-based Parents Music Resource Center (PMRC) in getting warning labels attached to records. Among the PMRC's membership were wives of ten senators, six congressmen and a cabinet secretary (Pareles, 1985). The US Senate honoured the PMRC with a hearing to discuss their claims, at which evidence was given by Frank Zappa and John Denver, among others (*Time*, 20 September 1985: 48-9). But while sex and violence are the commonest causes for censorship, it is important not to overlook the explicitly political reasons for bans (although, of course, attempts to censor sex and violence are themselves 'political', in the sense that they form part of a process of policing the body and sexual identity). In the UK, this is typically linked to the situation in Northern Ireland. Songs such as Paul McCartney's 'Give Ireland back to the Irish' or the Pogues' 'Birmingham Six' have been refused airplay. Many television plays or series about the same subject have also been cut or banned: *Carson Country* (1972), *The Folk Singer* (1972), *The Legion Hall Bombing* (1978), *The Price* (1985), *Crossfire* (1987). The Blow Monkeys' 'Celebrate (The Day After You)' was banned for its attack on Margaret Thatcher (Cloonan, 1996). In the United States between 1950 and 1954, the McCarthy witch-hunts were directed at Hollywood screenwriters, directors and actors for their alleged communist sympathies. These were matched and outstripped by the political censorship that characterized the treatment of popular culture in the Soviet Union and in South Africa.

But what is apparent in these examples is the way that the object of attention (the film, record, exhibition, and so on) is only of passing interest. Some would-be censors have not seen the offending item; this was the case in Britain in 1996 when there were calls to ban the film *Crash*. Censorship is the product of particular political circumstances as much as the specific portrayals and images. It is this that helps explain why Martin Scorsese's *The Last Temptation of Christ* or Salman Rushdie's *Satanic Verses* were banned in some places, fêted in others, and treated with indifference elsewhere.

The politics of censorship

To state the obvious: censorship exists only where there is the means and the will to censor. Therefore, part of the explanation of the different responses in different media is whether and how a system of censorship exists, and equally importantly who is implicated in this process. Many countries have quasi-autonomous bodies dedicated to reviewing films; few have equivalents for music. Some countries, like the UK and Malaysia, have strict government guidelines regulating the content of their broadcasting. Others have a more laissez-faire system. These differences are not simply a product of ideology. When the USA and the UK were in the grip of the New Right, it was only the UK that sought to extend its control over the content of TV and videos. Censorship is a product of circumstances and systems as well as ideologies.

The state's ability to censor depends on the cooperation of other interested parties. Film censorship could not operate without the collusion of film-makers and distributors. And such collaboration is itself the product of particular political circumstances. In the United States, the record industry accepted labelling of records partly because this concession was helpful to them in their attempt to lobby the government over another issue. They wanted a bill to eliminate piracy via a tape levy (*Time*, 20 September, 1985: 49); they also wanted another bill to stop 'parallel imports' (that is, domestic releases that were pressed abroad and reimported) (Holden, 1993: 11–15). The (failed) prosecution of a gallery for exhibiting photographs by Robert Mapplethorpe, photographs that attracted little attention at other museums or galleries, was initiated by an alliance of sympathetic local politicians and fundamentalist political organizations. Robert Dole's targeting of rap in 1995 was a by-product of the mid-term elections to Congress, which established a power-base and agenda for the Republicans. When copies of NWA's album were impounded, one record company executive remarked, 'The Establishment is rounding on the industry and wants to make an example of NWA' (*Music Week*, 15 June 1991). The black music writer Nelson George observed that 'The media were using rap as a scapegoat instead of looking at the causes of violence in the black community' (quoted in *The Independent*, 26 July 1989). Grossberg emphasizes the broader context of the right's targeting of popular culture in the 1980s. For him, this was part of an attempt 'to redefine "freedom" and reconstitute the boundaries of civil liberties; to (re)regulate sexual and gender roles . . . ; to monitor and even isolate particular segments of the population . . . ; and to discipline the working class' (Grossberg, 1993: 193). This was achieved through 'regulating the possibilities of pleasure and identity as the basis for political opposition by dismantling the cultural and political field constructed in the 1960s' (Grossberg, 1993: 193–4). Censorship formed part of a larger process of reshaping the political landscape, organizing

some interests and marginalizing other ones. Richard Goldstein
(1989: 30) described it as being driven by a wish to keep people
'uninitiated and unable to assert the extent of their desire . . . to
assure that each of us knows his or her place in the order. And the
order remains unchanged.' Censorship springs from a recognition that culture can embody an alternative order. McClary (1994:
34) talks of how music, for example, provides an opportunity for
the disenfranchised 'to articulate different ways of construing the
body, ways that bring along in their wake the potential for different experiential worlds. And the anxious reactions that so often
greet new musics from such groups indicate that something crucially political is at stake.'

Grossberg points to a variety of different sources for this policing of desire and identity, each one operating with their own
agenda. He sees a fundamentalist attack, based around the Chris-
tian right, who wish to eliminate vast areas of popular culture. A
second attack comes from those – like the PMRC – who want to
regulate, rather than eliminate, popular culture, to (re)mark the
boundaries between the acceptable and the unacceptable. A third
line of attack – the most insidious, says Grossberg – comes through
the incorporation of popular culture into the strategies and propaganda of conservative commercial interests, to use it in corporate
marketing. In 1996, it was announced that Bob Dylan's music, once
the accompaniment to youthful rebelliousness, was to be the
soundtrack for advertisements for the Bank of Montreal.

What all of these reactions to popular culture represent is an
attempt to re-establish or reinvent an old order and the values
that sustained it. Their political impact depends on their various
trajectories coinciding and finding an appropriate embodiment.
In the late 1980s and early 1990s, that embodiment was the Republican senator Jesse Helms. As Goldstein (1989) commented:
'Helms is the point man for a powerful coalition of populists,
nativists, fundamentalists, and neocons whose goal is to alter
American culture, top to bottom – from fine art to rock'n'roll.'
Another figurehead is syndicated columnist and former presidential candidate Pat Buchanan, who has set himself against 'the
explosion of anti-American, anti-Christian, nihilist "art"' (quoted
in Goldstein, 1989). The business of censoring and regulating popular culture is part of the business of sustaining a particular version
of American identity and values. For Grossberg, these acts of censorship are not just a function of political ambition. They are prem-

ised on the power and political potential of popular culture. What is important, though, is that rock does not bear a particular political stamp – it is as much the sound of reaction as rebellion. As Grossberg (1993: 202) notes: 'Rock's politics were firmly located within the commitment to mobility and consumerism . . . that is, rock culture never renounced the normative passion for comfort and success.' For all its posturing, rock remains linked to a conservative consensus, or, rather, its *lack* of politics makes it available to those who want to use it for their own political ends. To this extent, rock's politics come from the outside – whether from the left or the right.

In summary, censorship has to be understood as the particular product of political ideology, political interests and political institutions. It cannot be seen simply as a function of the cultural artefact itself – it is not the film or the music alone that causes the reaction; but equally, it is not the pre-determined result of a particular system. Instead, censorship is the consequence of the way in which judgement is constituted politically, of the way something comes to be seen as 'bad'.

Commendation of popular culture

What is true for censorship is also true for the more positive exercise of judgement in popular culture, when commendation rather than condemnation is involved. An obvious example of judgement in popular culture, and of its politics, is the awarding of prizes. Popular culture has its full quotient of award ceremonies. There are the Oscars, the BAFTAs, the Brits, the Emmies, the Eurovision Song Contest, the Grammies, the Mercury Music Prize, and so on. All manner of reasons can be detected in the creation of such examples – from the commercial interest of the sponsors and of the culture industries, to the self-esteem of the artists (the desire for respectability and publicity). Whatever the reasons, my immediate concern is not primarily with the motives behind prizes, but rather with the process by which such awards are made, although the two may, of course, be connected. How is it that one film or performance is judged better than its rivals?

This interest has to be set against a background of both media attention and media scepticism. There is a widespread view that

popular culture cannot be judged, and that the consequences of
any deliberation is the arbitrary result of randomly distributed
prejudices. Either that, or they are the product of deviousness and
deception, of industry bribes and the like. Even the beneficiaries
of the award have been known to cast doubts on the process. The
group Portishead, winners of the 1995 Mercury Music Prize, said
that they did not understand how music could be judged. (They
took the prize money anyway.) Such scepticism is not confined to
prizes for popular culture. Blake Morrison (1995: 10) hints at the
ulterior motives that seemed to influence the decisions of the Nobel
Prize committee for Literature: 'Wasn't the award to Boris
Pasternak in 1958 a diplomatic manoeuvre in the Cold War? Was
it just coincidence that the Finnish writer Frans Eemil Sillanpää
won in 1939 (when Finland was pluckily resisting the Soviet Union) or that the Polish writer Czeslaw Milosz received the award
in 1980 (the year of Solidarity and the shipyard strike in Gdansk)?'
Morrison also speculates as to why Graham Greene never received
the prize, explaining it not by reference to the quality of his work,
but by reference to Greene's personal conflicts with certain judges.
But is such cynicism warranted? Are prizes awarded arbitrarily
or on the basis of irrelevant prejudices? It is, I think, a mistake to
presume corruption without looking more closely at the processes
which produce such decisions, and to ask whether, in fact, judgement can better be explained by more than either self-interest or
lottery. After all, the instances of judgement – censorship and commendation – that we have considered so far may be regarded as
specific examples of a general phenomenon. This is the routine
business of judging popular culture that occurs within any number
of institutions in the culture industry. Throughout the creating,
producing and consuming of popular culture, decisions are being
taken by television companies, arts funding bodies, radio stations,
and so on; all of them have responsibility for allocating scarce resources (whether money or airtime) to works of popular culture.
Are all of these to be understood as the product of corruption and
chance?

  What we know of decision-making in the arts suggests that,
while it may not be a simple matter of rational choice, it is also not
the result of some corrupt conspiracy. Keith Negus's *Producing
Pop* (1992) is one of the few detailed accounts we have of how
decisions (about how artists are selected and marketed) are made
within the popular culture business. As Negus himself argues,

traditionally our understanding of such decisions was based on the assumption that there were a series of 'gate-keepers'. These operated to admit or exclude particular artists or works of art, and success for either depended upon them gaining entry to the pinnacle of the gate-keeping hierarchy. Such a position gave credence to the view of the industry as a device for weeding out 'unacceptable' ideas and forms, in preference to the bland and the familiar. It also identified sites for corruption and control.

In his portrait of life in the modern record corporation, Negus replaces the hierarchy of gate-keepers with a network. He writes (1992: vii) of the need to understand the industry as 'cultural worlds lived and constantly remade'; the industry is made up of 'the webs of relationships and multiple dialogues along and around which the musical and visual identities of pop artists are composed and communicated'. Drawing upon Bourdieu, Negus (1992: 46) argues that 'record industry personnel can be conceptualised as "cultural intermediaries".' These people are part of a complex network through which circulates information, and out of which are fashioned decisions about whom to sign and how to present them. This model of the record industry, as a complex web in a state of continuous flux, makes talk of cynical manipulation seem less plausible. Instead, the emphasis shifts to the role of intuitions and hunches, to the part played by 'gut feelings', rather than any systematic rational assessment, based on clearly specified criteria. The language of assessment and judgement is couched in the languages of the marketing, sales and A and R departments. In understanding the business of judging we need, therefore, to understand the discourses in which it is conducted. But to leave it like this would be to reach only a partial understanding. We need also to consider the institutions and arrangements that frame these discourses.

The decisions reached by those who preside over arts prizes or arts policy, those who decide what to promote and what to ignore, are the products of political processes. They are not simply or solely the result of such processes, but they cannot be understood independently of them. This is, of course, a central claim of policy analysts, who are also interested in how decisions are reached, but it is not typically or extensively applied to arts policy – despite the similarities. Robert Hutchinson (1982: 12–13), an ex-administrator for the Arts Council, once wrote: 'Allocating arts subsidies is, at best, a complex and subtle process – part science, part art – and the Arts Council's job involving the constant weighing up of like against unlike is invidious and almost absurdly difficult.' This is a world that a bureaucrat working in any policy realm would recognize.

If, then, arts decisions are like other policy decisions, how should they be understood? To return to the example of arts prizes: if we discount the claim that the outcome is the random result of arbitrarily distributed preferences, then there are a number of other possibilities to be considered. The first, and most obvious, is that the result is merely the consequence of one work of art being *better* than the others. If such standards were possible (and our earlier discussion suggested that they were not), their operation might be called into doubt by the examples of those recognizably great artists – like Greene – who fail to get acclaim. Morrison (1995: 10) gives a list of the writers who have *not* won the Nobel Prize: Tolstoy, Ibsen, Zola, Hardy, Gorky, Freud, Lorca, Rilke, Calvino. To claim that the best wins would be to overlook too much evidence to the contrary. We need, instead, to focus on the process of selection. The first stage involves the setting of an agenda by the creation of a shortlist (out of which the 'best' is chosen). In many arts prizes, publishers/record companies have to nominate contenders, and while judges may introduce works not so nominated, much still turns on the decisions reached by company executives. Even if the nominating and shortlisting processes were beyond reproach, this view – that the best wins – is itself premised upon a notion of the best which requires a set of agreed standards. But if such standards did in fact exist, there would be no need for judgement. A computer could do the job. The 'best' is a contingent feature of the selection. This is not to deny the fact of judgement, only to understand the circumstances of its operation.

What, therefore, do we know about the way decisions are taken? One approach concentrates on the regulations and rules that organize those decisions. Put simply, the Chair of any judging panel establishes a code of behaviour and set of procedures which, while crucial to the efficient operation of the committee, also shape the outcome. The Nobel Prize for Literature, for example, is decided by the judges each writing a single name upon a piece of paper, and then placing it in a special urn. The winner is the person whose name occurs most frequently. A different set of rules or voting procedures would produce a different result. The injunction to reach consensus might not generate the same winner that is reached by a secret ballot. Equally, alternative voting rules will alter the result – a simple majority will produce a different winner to a transferable vote system (where the votes of losing candidates are redistributed to the other candidates until the winner has 51 per cent of the votes).

Other analysts have contended, however, that the rules and regulations are themselves only the formal legitimation of a more fundamental truth: the winner is the product of underlying interests. In other words, the outcome of any deliberation is, in a sense, a foregone conclusion. If we know who has power, we can predict what will be chosen. This accords roughly with the notion of 'bureaucratic politics', in which it is assumed that committee deliberations are largely the enactment of a script inscribed by the interests gathered round the table.

This model has typically been applied to standard areas of policy-making, especially foreign policy. There is no reason why it might not also apply to arts policy. Reflecting on Arts Council decisions, Hutchinson (1982: 27) writes: 'Vested interests were fully involved in the Arts Council's decision-making from the outset, not as representatives or delegates, just as vested interests.' Advisory panels were 'advisory' in name only, since they contained leading members of the institutions seeking funds (for example, the Royal Opera House). Again, this is a familiar political pattern: Britain's nuclear power policy was formed on the advice of its direct beneficiaries (for example, the United Kingdom Atomic Energy Authority). Hutchinson even proposes the adoption of social scientific analyses of power to reveal the process of agenda-setting and preference shaping within the Arts Council. But interests alone cannot tell the whole story. Analysing the distribution of interests within the Arts Council would explain how jazz receives funding while folk does not, but it would not explain why this particular distinction – between jazz and folk – was drawn. It would not explain why folk was labelled an 'amateur' art form, and, therefore, allocated to regional funding, while jazz was ascribed to a different category and different form of funding. Interest-based analysis also looks less viable in discussion of arts prizes – at least of those which are not directly linked to the industry involved. The notion of vested interests applies to decision-making where a set of established institutions (or branches of the same institution) meet on a regular basis to allocate scarce resources, and where the outcome has direct consequences for those involved.

Where there is no such connection – as with one-off prize committees – it makes less sense to talk of interests as the determinant of
outcomes.

What prize committees do replicate, though, is the process of
alliance formation. Describing her experience of judging the Booker
Prize, Kate Kellaway talks of having an ally in her colleague Peter
Kemp, and of how this alliance helped to ground their judgements.
It is an arrangement whose importance is revealed at the moment
it breaks down: 'When you disagree with someone whose judgement you ordinarily share, it is like a sudden power failure – and
the worst of it is that you are not sure who has fused' (*The Observer*, 5 November 1995). This example parallels familiar ones
within politics where majorities are forged out of coalitions.

But even where interests and alliances do play a part, they alone
do not tell a complete story. Arguments still have to be made and
claims legitimated. If the discussion within committee does help
determine the outcome, then we need to ask *how* exactly the discussion does contribute to the result. Simon Frith (*The Guardian*,
15 September 1995), reflecting on his experience as Chair of the
Mercury Music Prize, argues that skills of advocacy are crucial to
the outcome. Judges do not make straightforward comparisons
between the competing works: 'What matters is less comparison
than advocacy. It's a pity that no one outside the judging room
will ever hear the wonderful case made (by the same judge) as to
why first *To Bring You My Love* and then *Maxinquaye* should win
the prize; that no one else will get to applaud the speech that swung
it for Portishead.' Judging panels are not a team of experts who
determine which recording (in the case of the Mercury Prize) is
the 'best'. The outcome is, instead, the result of how effectively
the judges marshal their arguments in favour of one or other piece.
Booker judge Kate Kellaway remarked of one of her fellow panel-
lists, Adam Mars-Jones, 'I'm afraid this is a man who could persuade me that a chair was a table, or a turkey a swan' (*The Observer*,
5 November 1995). Advocacy is not the only factor. As I have suggested, the way these items are considered (the setting of the
agenda and so on) is also important, but no agenda can alone determine the outcome. In these circumstances, advocacy, the power
to persuade, matters.

If this is the case, then it is interesting to consider how advocacy
skills are distributed. Are they as randomly distributed as tastes?
The answer would appear to be that they are not. Some people are

better advocates than others, and while this may be a product of class, education and sex roles, it is also a consequence of professional experience. The practice of passing judgement and arguing a case is more commonplace in some professions than in others. In the world of popular music, for example, broadcasters have to decide upon play lists, and have to defend or reject records every day in the company of others (who have to be persuaded). Journalists may also pass judgement, but this is usually done on paper (rather than in committee), and although there are editorial conferences to decide whom to put on the cover or what acts to feature, these battles are conducted at editorial level, and not with the journalists who pass judgement. A similar, but not identical, point is made by Geoffrey Vickers (1968) in his discussion of the 'art of judgement'. He observes that judgement is often a function of role, and that the role one occupies shapes the kind of criteria one applies and the weighting one gives.

But how much importance should attach to advocacy? Certainly if we draw upon insights into other kinds of judging panels, the claims of advocacy may be weakened. If, for instance, we think of prize panels as similar to trial juries (about which we know much more), then the evidence suggests that the internal dynamics of the committee are not decisive, or at least not in the way suggested by the emphasis placed upon advocacy. In *Judging the Jury*, Hans and Vidmar (1986) argue that juries do not actually *decide* anything. Minds are already made up, and majority opinion at the start of the discussion usually wins out at the end. A similar view is taken by McCabe and Purves (1974: 9–10), who also contend that there is very little evidence of jurors altering their views in the course of a discussion. But this conclusion does not make the jury irrelevant. It may not decide the outcome; it does, however, play an important function: 'It . . . helps to clarify and solidify initial positions' (Hans and Vidmar, 1986: 112).

This approach to juries, which concentrates on outcomes and processes, contrasts with those which focus directly on the individual juror. Here the question is how individuals decide, and, according to Reid Hastie (1993: 5), two competing perspectives vie for attention. There is the rational actor model, based on ' "top-down" rational rules', and there is the model which starts with "bottom-up" psychological principles'. These have produced, says Hastie, four models of juror behaviour, three of which are mathematically based and claim to be able to generate predictions of behaviour that owe nothing to the actual cognitive states of the individuals. The fourth model (an amalgam of different methods) focuses upon cognitive processes and the way in which representations and memories feature in the deliberation. Each aspires to a science of decision-making, but they vary in the relevance they attribute to the juror's state of mind. My concern here is not with the comparative strengths and weaknesses of any of these approaches, nor is it with the plausibility of such a 'science'. Rather it is to point to the fact that such analyses are possible; that such decisions cannot be assigned to chance or chaos.

It may, of course, be objected that prize panels are not equivalent to juries insofar as they do not hear the same evidence in advance, and are not therefore arguing about the same things. They do, however, read the same books and listen to the same music. And studies of juries reveal that, even though the evidence is presented in advance, the subsequent discussion brings together entirely different perceptions and uses quite different languages to those deployed in the courtroom (McCabe and Purves, 1974: 11). Whether or not the jury is, in fact, a good analogy for the prize committee is not my main concern. It may be that the seminar is a better one. I want merely to draw attention to the fact that judgements are an important part of popular culture; and if we want to understand how these judgements are exercised, we need to know how they are organized and how the institutions of judgement operate. The politics of judgements are a key part of the politics of popular culture.

Conclusion

These remarks on the workings of the prize committee have been tentative and speculative. We know too little about them to say more. The important point, however, is not to provide a definitive account of any given decision, but rather to draw attention to the way in which judgement is organized. This chapter began with the claim that at crucial moments in discussion of the relationship between politics and popular culture we confront the issue of judgement. The subsequent discussion has been about how the process of judgement might be analysed. We have concentrated here upon the practice of judgement, and I have tried to illustrate the ways in which this practice has been conditioned by politics. Not politics in the sense of behind the scenes deals and corrupt practices, but politics as the playing out of institutional norms and as the business of decision-making. The focus has been on analysis and description, not evaluation. The latter is the concern of the last chapter. What kind of popular culture do we want, and how might it be created? How, ultimately, are politics and pleasure linked in popular culture?

CHAPTER TEN

Political pleasures

For me, the phrase 'Albert King, where y'at?' became more than an invitation to hear him play on the East Side on any given night. When I had problems at work, when romances didn't work out, when I had no money, I'd ask 'Albert King, where y'at?' and play some blues until I felt better. . . . But Albert King offered more than solace for disappointments. In his style of performance, his knowing persona, and the community he called into being through performance, he built bridges between people and showed them life could be worth living.

George Lipsitz, *Dangerous Crossroads*

There are two topics on which it is easy to provoke an argument: popular culture and politics. And once engaged in such disputes, it is easy for them to get personal. You start with a friendly exchange about last night's television or about a current political issue, and, before you know it, your entire existence can seem to be under threat. What you found profoundly moving, they find naïvely sentimental; what they hold to be a basic human instinct, you regard as the failing of a few. The fact that it is so easy, in such disputes, to move from the blandly general to the distressingly personal is, I think, an important defining feature in the relationship between popular culture and politics. Our feelings about popular culture, like our feelings about politics, matter because of what we invest in it, and what it reveals about us. What is more, personal pleasure and politics are inextricably linked. This is what the rock writer Robert Christgau (1994: 226) had to say about pop and politics:

> ... it's my perhaps literalistic belief that a music that includes Mofungo's 'El Salvador' and Y Pants' 'That's the Way Boys Are' and the Ramones' 'Bonzo Goes to Bitburg' and Hüsker Dü's 'Turn On the News' and Thelonious Monster's 'Property Values' and Carmaig de Forest's 'Crack's No Worse Than the Fascist Threat' and the Chills' 'Submarine Bells' and the Mekons' 'Funeral' and L7's 'Wargasm' and Sonic Youth's 'Youth Against Fascism' and the collected works of the Minutemen is more useful politically than one that doesn't contain such songs. For damn sure it's more fun.

Perhaps no two people would choose the same list from popular culture's many artefacts, but lots of people share the general sentiment. That, at least, is the claim I want to defend here. But before doing this, we need to recall some of what has gone before.

This book has been about the links that tie popular culture to politics, about how political choices shape popular culture, about how popular culture shapes political choices. The story began with the various claims made for the political importance of popular culture. And from there, we turned to the (usually cynical) use of popular culture by politicians. These familiar guises for the relationship of politics and popular culture made way for the less familiar, but more important, connection forged in the institutional, legal and regulatory regimes which order the production, distribution and consumption of popular culture. The final part of *Politics and Popular Culture* has been devoted to exploring the theoretical issues that underpin much of what went before. We considered the claim that culture generally, and popular culture in particular, can explain political thought and action. It transpired that, if popular culture played a part in politics, it was not through its explanatory power; it did not fit, in any very significant way, into a causal chain. Rather its importance lay in its ability to articulate the feelings and passions that drive politics. If this is the case, then it was necessary to distinguish different political positions which could be discerned around popular culture. This was why we looked at the alternatives offered by conservative and radical elitists, and by conservative and radical populists. These competing views provided an opportunity to reflect upon the validity of the populist and elitist views of popular culture. It emerged that neither was tenable, and that in making sense of the politics of popular culture, we need to focus on the way judgement and discrimination operate within popular culture. There were two aspects to this. First, there were the ways in which judgement is organized into popular culture, whether in the guise of censorship or of acclaim. The institutions and processes that produce judgements was the topic of chapter 9. But there is a second aspect to judgement: this is the way that it becomes part of our direct engagement with popular culture, part of the pleasure.

There is always a danger, in exploring these dimensions of the relationship between politics and popular culture, that we forget why popular culture matters in the first place. The answer – as Christgau made clear – is that it is fun; if it wasn't, there would be no point taking it seriously. Taking it seriously means recognizing two things. First: not all popular culture is fun; some of it is boring, stupid, reactionary. And secondly: not everyone is able, through lack of resources or opportunity, to share what fun there is. What I want to do here is to discuss the political conditions which make it possible for people to enjoy popular culture and to talk about the political judgements which help distinguish the boring from the brilliant.

These issues can be put another way: what does it mean to talk of the radical and the reactionary in popular culture? What does this mean for both the form and the organization of popular culture? Must popular culture embrace the avant-garde and the anarchic, or the mainstream and the market? These are the questions to which the rest of this chapter is devoted. In their different ways, they emerge from the theme that has persisted throughout the book: the challenge to populism. The populist response to popular culture tends to overlook the ways in which that culture is organized, or assumes that the market alone is its guarantor, that state interference, in any case, has to be avoided at all costs. The populist response is also inclined to avoid judging popular culture, assuming that it is either the direct expression of the people's tastes, or that, whatever the formal content, its meanings are reconstructed through a process of creative consumption. As I have tried to suggest, these positions cannot be sustained. External interference and judgement are part and parcel of popular culture. But as I have also acknowledged, while such processes are indeed integral to popular culture, and while we need to analyse them in understanding the relationship between politics and popular culture, it does not follow that they take one particular form and have one particular set of consequences. It is reasonable to consider alternative forms and effects.

What makes a piece of popular culture 'radical'? Consider a record which, both in its time and subsequently, has been deemed a 'radical' work of art. In 1969, Captain Beefheart and the Magic Band released a double album called *Trout Mask Replica*. It was treated with awe in the rock press, and it has subsequently passed into rock history as a seminal piece of rock art. It is held to represent a bold experiment, one that stretched rock beyond its traditional confines, and in the process opened up new possibilities. Langdon Winner (1979: 58) wrote that *Trout Mask Replica* was the only album he knew that 'deliberately and successfully sets out to devise a special world of its own as if in defiance of the prevailing norms and fashions of contemporary society'. It tried 'to overthrow our somnambulistic habits of hearing, seeing, and touching things' (Winner, 1979: 59).

It certainly had a profound effect on me. I can still remember buying it in Coventry's inner-city arcade, on the day I was visiting the University of Warwick as a prospective student. I remember poring over its cover during the long journey home – on the front: the Captain, his face replaced by that of a trout, photographed against a red background; on the back: the Magic Band decked out in strange clothes, the Captain holding the skeleton of a table lamp, and their outline obscured by the sun, which shone directly into the camera lens. Then there were the song titles, each one promising bizarre delights, or so my adolescent imagination supposed: 'Moonlight on Vermont', 'When Big Joan Sets Up', 'Ant Man Bee', 'Orange Claw Hammer'. I had to wait all day before I could play it, to hear its riotous cacophony of horns, of spidery guitar runs, and Captain Beefheart's bellowing roar. It was exciting and unsettling; I'm not sure that I actually enjoyed the experience, but I know that my friends and enemies at school hated it, and that was enough. I had achieved in that small gesture an element of individuality, albeit one sustained by the thought that out there in the world of rock journalism, in hip circles in London and in America, 'people like me' were nodding appreciatively to 'Ella Guru'. I am not sure any record has ever mattered so much, and been played so little.

Trout Mask Replica was a radical record, but if this radicalism is understood only through individual anecdotes, it is hard to attribute any great significance to this claim. It merely tells how one person at one time was affected by it. Is it possible to make the claim of radicalism in a wider sense, as more than the result of serendipity?

The obvious and easy answer would be to ask what the popular culture is *saying*: is it saying something 'radical'? The assumption is that radicalism takes a clearly defined place along an ideological continuum, and any given text can be mapped on to it. While this may make some sense with party manifestos or polemics (although it may be hard to decide whether certain New Right claims were radical or reactionary), it is almost impossible to do this with any other type of text. It is hard enough when dealing with works of political philosophy; it is far harder when dealing with works of fiction for whom politics is not their explicit or self-conscious concern. Imagine the problem, therefore, when dealing with a text without words (or with very few) like the Prodigy's *Music for the Jilted Generation*. Here was a piece of music designed for dancing and not for earnest contemplation. And yet this record was described as politically radical. If it was, then the reason could not lie with what was said. It lay in how it sounded (the juddering bass, the police sirens, the deranged shouts and a rhythm that beat in anxious fury), and the way the sounds articulated feelings and moments which daily life seemed to deny. Not that music has to sound angry and awkward to subvert and disrupt – think of the unsettling beauty of Smokey Robinson's ballads, or the shimmering melodies of the Go-Betweens' songs of love and doubt. In a similar spirit, Simon Reynolds and Joy Press (1994) rewrite pop history. In those archetypes of rock, the Rolling Stones, the Clash and Bruce Springsteen, Reynolds and Press find sexual confusion where before there seemed to be male rebellion, and fear where there seemed to be freedom.

If the radicalism is not transparent, is not easily mapped onto some established set of criteria, then how can it be identified? With *Trout Mask Replica*, the radicalism was discerned in the noise, in the disruption of accepted norms of how music should sound. This was not music that was easy on the ear. It becomes radical, therefore, in the way that other works of culture acquire that same status, by breaking with convention, refusing the existing rules. Simon Frith (1996: 20, 277; his emphasis) argues that if culture is about change, then it 'must challenge experience, must be difficult, must be *unpopular*'; it must have a 'disruptive cultural effect'. Of course, it is possible, in doing this, to be deemed reactionary if the aim is to recover an older tradition. Breaking convention, in itself, may not be radical. It has to constitute some notion of 'progress'. There are, of course, many problems with the idea of progress – from what? for whom? – but whatever defines it, the assumption is that something has changed for the better. Not that this change can be intended in any obvious instrumental sense; popular culture cannot form part of some Five-Year Plan. The change is a matter of feelings and of moments. Popular culture's radicalism is measured in its power to disconcert, in the way it raises questions rather than answers them, in the way it reveals feelings rather than rational reflections. But even if popular culture is not prescriptive, even if it cannot be 'designed', it would be a mistake to overlook the political processes that make its effects possible (and the other processes that might operate).

George McKay offers a vision of an alternative cultural order in his book *Senseless Acts of Beauty* (1996), in which he surveys the history of free festivals and radical social movements in Britain. He sees them as part of a culture of resistance, through which music and other forms of cultural expression play a decisive part, and he makes an explicit connection between cultural form and cultural organization. As he writes (1996: 44):

> It's my argument that the free festivals and the Fairs of Albion were central and ongoing features of the British culture of resistance, features that originated during hippy times and that were altered and re-energized by successive subcultural developments. These temporary autonomous zones interrogate the limits of majority culture, producing on occasion moments of violent reaction from within and without. Anarcho-punk band Crass, those archetypal hippy–punk crossovers, put it better when they took issue with punk's unimaginative and inaccurate sneer at hippies as 'boring old farts'.

For McKay, therefore, cultural battles are also political ones. But for him culture is not just about artefacts; it is about the way they are produced. McKay believes that to produce cultures of resistance you need alternative forms of life and cultural production.

Where McKay looks for resistance in the organization of popular culture and in the life-styles associated with it, Greil Marcus finds it in disruptive cultural moments. His history of punk, *Lipstick Traces*, is a history of subversive gestures acted out in obscure corners and at overlooked events, but one that provides a

constant sign that things do not have to be this way. This is what
Marcus (1989a: 441) heard when Johnny Rotten sang 'Anarchy in
the UK': 'An unknown tradition of old pronouncements, poems,
and events, a secret history of ancient wishes and defeats, came to
bear on Johnny Rotten's voice – and because this tradition lacked
both cultural sanction and political legitimacy, because this history comprised of only unfinished, unsatisfied stories, it carried
tremendous force.' For Marcus, popular culture – at its best –
speaks with a democratic voice for the people. This does not happen, however, through the working out of deliberate intentions; it
is more often the almost accidental consequence of the artistic endeavour and historical moment. It is true that organization, in the
form of networks and artistic entrepreneurship, was a necessary
concomitant of situationism and punk, but the organization was
not part of the point; it was a necessary means to an end. The
music or the situations were what created the moment, or at least
established its cultural meaning. With McKay (a democrat too,
but of a different hue to Marcus), the organization plays a central
part: it is the point. The art itself, therefore, has a more instrumental role. It serves the goals of the organization. The sounds, style
and attitudes of Crass, McKay's iconic group, connected directly
with the sensibilities and circumstances of their fans. They were
all part of the same free festival network. Thus Marcus and McKay
raise a question about both the type of organization and about
how the art acquires political significance. They appeal to different notions of popular culture and of democracy.

Their cultural politics emerge in the ways they link text and
context. They both recognize that popular culture's power lies in
contingent properties, the product of circumstances. Where they
differ is in how they judge the conditions for, and character of,
these moments. Neither assumes that either the conditions or the
culture on its own is enough. Each matters. They recognize that
one of Bruce Willis' *Die Hard* movies does not articulate the same
politics as a Ken Loach movie, or that Phil Collins cannot evoke
the same responses as Patti Smith. They both acknowledge the
need to react critically to what is seen and heard. At the same
time, they acknowledge that the responses which popular culture
generates are conditioned by the means by which they are produced and experienced. These conditions have also to be judged.
Where McKay and Marcus differ is in their political judgements
and understandings.

However the 'radicalism' is identified and defined, it can never be reduced to some essence which can establish – like some cultural DNA test – the claims of the radical or the reactionary. The culture being created is a product of any number of mediating influences – journalists, broadcasters, and so on. It is impossible and incoherent to separate out popular culture from the process that produces and disseminates it; just as it cannot be parted from its wider social and political context. These all contribute to the meaning and significance which it assumes. But again to recognize this is not to counsel despair, to say that we can offer no judgement, or to treat all judgements as randomly distributed preferences. Rather it is to argue for a perspective in which we look to radicalism in respect of the possibilities it creates. This is to be measured not just by the range of ideas expressed through the work, but also by the range of opportunities available to others in consuming or contributing to it. It is a matter not just of what it sounds like, or looks like, but also of who can participate in it. And if this makes it sound like an exercise in political analysis, that is exactly how it should sound. Judging popular culture is a political act. Just as we distinguish between types of political system (parting the democracies from the dictatorships), so we can distinguish between types of popular culture by reference not to their explicitly stated views, but to the way they are organized. This is to underline the importance of the middle section of this book, where focus turns to the political structures which organize popular culture. There, however, the emphasis was on the way those political structures currently operate. Here the focus is upon the normative rather than the descriptive. The question of how popular culture should be judged is linked to the question of how political institutions and arrangements ought to be judged.

This is not a matter of laying down the law. It is not a matter of simply stating that one film is better than another. It is about the ways in which we argue about films, about the terms we use and the context of the debate. This is a matter of the competence and rights we enjoy in participating in such debates, and this depends upon the relative openness of the dialogue and the absence of barriers to entry. It is also about the opportunity that people have to see or to make the films that are being debated. These opportunities are a product of principle and practice. By the simple expedient of rearranging the furniture in a room it is possible to encourage or discourage conversation, just as alterations in the mode of address can encourage or discourage participation. The ideal conditions for engaging with popular culture, we might suppose, are those that accord with democratic principles (not that these are settled matters either). But the conditions do not determine the outcome; that depends on who has the better arguments, on who can make the strongest case for a particular example.

Arguing about popular culture, like arguing about politics, is a matter of advocacy, about creating particular visions and persuading others to share them. But these arguments are not just *like* politics, they are *about politics*. In arguing about works of popular culture we are arguing about ways of life. And as with all such arguments, the dispute is not simply about competing views of a better world, but also about how it is to be achieved.

Bibliography

Abramson, J. B., F. C. Arterton and G. Orren (1988) *The Electronic Commonwealth: The Impact of New Media Technologies on Democratic Politics*, New York: Basic Books.

ADC (Association of District Councils) Working Party on the Arts (1989) *Arts and the Districts*, London: ADC.

Adorno, T. (1990) 'On Popular Music', in S. Frith and A. Goodwin (eds) *On Record: Rock, Pop & the Written Word*, New York: Pantheon, pp. 301–14.

Adorno, T. and M. Horkheimer (1979) 'The Culture Industry: Enlightenment as Mass Deception', in *Dialectic of Enlightenment*, London: Verso, pp. 120–67.

Almond, G. and S. Verba (1963) *The Civic Culture: Political Attitudes and Democracy in Five Nations*, Princeton, NJ: Princeton University Press.

Anderson, B. (1983) *Imagined Communities: Reflections on the Origins and Spread of Nationalism*, London: Verso.

Archard, D. (1995) 'Myths, Lies and Historical Truth', *Political Studies*, 43(3), pp. 472–81.

Arendt, H. (1961) *Between Past and Future*, London: Faber & Faber.

Art and Power: Images of the 1930s (1995), London: Hayward Gallery.

Barnard, S. (1989) *On the Radio: Music Radio in Britain*, Milton Keynes: Open University Press.

Barry, B. (1978) *Sociologists, Economists and Democracy*, Chicago: University of Chicago Press.

Beck, A. (1993) 'The Arts Policy of British Government in the Thatcher Years', Paper to PSA Conference, University of Leicester.

Bell, D. (1990) *Acts of Union: Youth Culture and Sectarianism in Northern Ireland*, Basingstoke: Macmillan.

Berland, J. (1991) 'Free Trade and Canadian Music: Level Playing Field or Scorched Earth', *Cultural Studies*, 5(3), pp. 317–25.

Bianchini, F. (1987) 'GLC R.I.P.: Cultural Policies in London, 1981–1986', *New Formations*, 1, Spring, pp. 103–17.

Bianchini, F. and M. Parkinson (eds) (1993) *Cultural Policy and Urban Regeneration*, Manchester: Manchester University Press.
Billig, M., D. Deacon, P. Golding, and S. Middleton (1993) 'In the Hands of the Spin-Doctors: Television, Politics, and the 1992 General Election', in N. Miller and R. Allen (eds) *It's Live But Is It Real?*, London: John Libbey, pp. 111–21.
Bloom, A. (1987) *The Closing of the American Mind: How Education Has Failed Democracy and Impoverished the Souls Today's Student* , New York: Simon & Schuster.
Bourdieu, P. (1986) *Distinction: A Social Critique of the Judgement of Taste*, London: Routledge.
Bourdieu, P. (1991) *Language and Symbolic Power*, Cambridge: Polity Press.
Boyle, K. (1991) 'Northern Ireland: Allegiances and Identities', in B. Crick (ed.) *National Identities: The Constitution of the United Kingdom*, Oxford: Basil Blackwell, pp. 68–78.
BPI (British Phonographic Industry) (1991) *Statistical Handbook 1991*, London: BPI.
BPI (1993) *Statistical Handbook 1993*, London: BPI.
Broadcasting in the 90s: Competition, Choice and Quality (1988), Cm. 517, London: HMSO.
Brown, A. (1979) 'Introduction', in A. Brown and J. Gray (eds) *Political Culture and Political Change in Communist States*, Basingstoke: Macmillan, pp. 3–7.
Burleigh, M. and W. Wippermann (1991) *The Racial State: Germany 1933–1945*, Cambridge: Cambridge University Press.
Chambers, I. (1986) *Popular Culture: The Metropolitan Experience*, Basingstoke: Macmillan.
Chevigny, P. (1991) *Gigs: Jazz and the Cabaret Laws in New York City*, London: Routledge.
Christgau, R. (1994) 'Rah, Rah, Sis-Boom-Bah: The Secret Relationship Between College Rock and the Communist Party', in A. Ross and T. Rose (eds) *Microphone Fiends: Youth Music, Youth Culture*, London: Routledge, pp. 221–7.
Clark, T. J. (1984) *The Painting of Modern Life*, London: Thames & Hudson.
Cloonan, M. (1996) *Banned! Censorship of Popular Music in Britain: 1962–92*, Aldershot: Arena.
Cockerell, M. (1988) *Live From Number 10*, London: Faber & Faber.
Cocks, J. (1989) *The Oppositional Imagination*, London: Routledge.
Cohen, S. (1991) *Rock Culture in Liverpool*, Oxford: Oxford University Press.
Colley, L. (1992) *Britons: Forging the Nation 1707–1837*, London: Pimlico.
Commission of the European Communities (1987) *Public Administration and the Funding of Culture in the European Community*, Brussels: Commission of the European Community.
Connolly, W. E. (1991) *Identity/Difference*, Ithaca, NY: Cornell University Press.
Connolly, W. E. (1993) *The Terms of Political Discourse*, 3rd edition, Oxford: Basil Blackwell.
Corner, J. (1995) *Television Form and Public Address*, London: Edward Arnold.
Coyle, D. and R. Ellis (eds) (1994) *Politics, Policy & Culture*, Boulder, Colo.: Westview Press.
Crane, D. (1992) *The Production of Culture*, London: Sage.
Crewe, I. and M. Harrop (eds) (1986) *Political Communications: The General Election of 1983*, Cambridge: Cambridge University Press.

Bibliography 201

Crewe, I. and M. Harrop (eds) (1989) *Political Communications: The General Election of 1987*, Cambridge: Cambridge University Press.

Crosland, C. A. R. (1956) *The Future of Socialism*, London: Jonathan Cape.

Curran, J. and J. Seaton (1991) *Power without Responsibility*, London: Routledge.

Curtice, J. and H. Semetko (1994) 'Does it Matter What the Papers Say?', in A. Heath, R. Jowell and J. Curtice (eds) *Labour's Last Chance? The 1992 Election and Beyond*, London: Dartmouth, pp. 43–63.

Curtis, L. and M. Jempson (1993) *Interference on the Airwaves*, London: Campaign for Press and Broadcasting Freedom.

Cutler, C. (1985) *File Under Popular*, London: November Books.

de Launey, G. (1995) 'Not-so-Big in Japan: Western Pop Music in the Japanese Market', *Popular Music*, 14(2), pp. 203–26.

Denisoff, R. S. (1971) *Great Day Coming: Folk Music and the American Left*, Urbana: University of Illinois Press.

de Sola Pool, I. (1990) *Technologies Without Boundaries*, Cambridge, Mass.: Harvard University Press.

de Tocqueville, A. (1988) *Democracy in America*, New York: Harper & Row. Originally published in 1848.

DGIMT (Development Group for Ipswich Museums Trust) (1988) *European Visual Arts Centre at Ipswich*, Ipswich: Ipswich Museum.

Donald, J. (1992) *Sentimental Education: Schooling, Popular Culture and the Regulation of Liberty*, London: Verso.

Douglas, M. (1992) *Risk and Blame: Essays in Cultural Theory*, London: Routledge.

Douglas, M. and A. Wildavsky (1982) *Risk and Culture*, San Francisco: University of California Press.

Downs, A. (1957) *An Economic Theory of Democracy*, New York: Harper & Row.

Dunleavy, P. (1991) *Democracy, Bureaucracy and Public Choice*, Hemel Hempstead: Harvester Wheatsheaf.

du Noyer, P. (1995) 'Maximum R&B', *Mojo*, June.

Dyson, K. and P. Humphreys (eds) (1986) 'The Politics of the Communications Revolution in Western Europe', Special Issue of *West European Politics*, 9(4).

Elster, J. (1989) *The Cement of Society*, Cambridge: Cambridge University Press.

Eno, B. (1996) *A Year with Swollen Appendices*, London: Faber & Faber

Everett, P. (1986) *You'll Never be Sixteen Again*, London: BBC Publications.

Featherstone, M. (1990) *Global Culture, Nationalism, Globalization and Modernity*, London: Sage.

Ferguson, M. (1992) 'The Mythology about Globalization', *European Journal of Communication*, 7(1), pp. 69–94.

Finnegan, R. (1989) *The Hidden Musicians: Music Making in an English Town*, Cambridge: Cambridge University Press.

Fiske, J. (1989) *Understanding Popular Culture*, London: Unwin Hyman.

Fiske, J. (1992) 'The Cultural Economy of Fandom', in L. A. Lewis (ed.) *The Adoring Audience: Fan Culture and Popular Media*, London: Routledge, pp. 30–49.

Foucault, M. (1980) *Power/Knowledge*, New York: Pantheon.

Franklin, B. (1994) *Packaging Politics: Political Communications in Britain's Media Democracy*, London: Edward Arnold.

Freedland, J. (1996) 'Wanna Be in My Gang?', *The Guardian*, 11 March.

Friedman, J. (1991) 'Accounting for Political Preferences: Cultural Theory vs Cultural History', *Critical Review*, 5(3), pp. 325–52.

Frith, S. (1988a) *Music For Pleasure*, Cambridge: Polity Press.

Frith, S. (1988b) 'Copyright and the Music Business', *Popular Music*, 7(1), pp. 57–75.

Frith, S. (ed.) (1989) *World Music, Politics and Social Change*, Manchester: Manchester University Press.

Frith, S. (1990) 'What is Good Music?', *Canadian Universities Music Review*, 10(2), pp. 92–102.

Frith, S. (1991a) 'Critical Response', in D. Robinson, E. Buck and M. Cuthbert, *Music at the Margins*, London: Sage, pp. 280–7.

Frith, S. (1991b) 'The Good, the Bad and the Indifferent', *Diacritics*, 21(4), pp. 102–15.

Frith, S. (1993) 'Popular Music and the Local State', in T. Bennett, S. Frith, L. Grossberg, J. Shepherd and G. Turner (eds), *Rock and Popular Music: Politics, Policies, Institutions*, London: Routledge, pp. 14–24.

Frith, S. (ed.) (1994) *Music and Copyright*, Edinburgh: Edinburgh University Press.

Frith, S. (1996) *Performing Rites: On the Value of Popular Music*, Oxford: Oxford University Press.

Frith, S. and H. Horne (1987) *Art into Pop*, London: Methuen.

Frith, S. and J. Street (1992) 'Rock Against Racism and Red Wedge: From Music to Politics, from Politics to Music', in R. Garofalo (ed.) *Rockin' the Boat: Mass Music and Mass Movements*, Boston: South End Press, pp. 67–80.

Garnham, N. (1983) 'Public Service versus the market', *Screen*, 24(1), pp. 6–27.

Garnham, N. (1986) 'The Media and the Public Sphere', in P. Golding, G. Murdock and P. Schlesinger (eds) *Communicating Politics*, Leicester: Leicester University Press, pp. 37–53.

Garnham, N. (1990) *Capitalism and Communications*, London: Sage.

Gates, H. L. (1987) *Figures in Black*, Oxford: Oxford University Press.

Gilroy, P. (1993) *Small Acts: Thoughts on the Politics of Black Cultures*, London: Serpent's Tail.

Girvin, B. (1989) 'Change and Continuity in Liberal Democratic Political Culture', in J. Gibbins (ed.) *Contemporary Political Culture*, London: Sage, pp. 31–51.

Gitlin, T. (1991) 'Bites and Blips: Chunk News, Savvy Talk and the Bifurcation of American Politics', in P. Dahlgren and C. Sparks (eds) *Communication and Citizenship: Journalism and the Public Sphere*, London: Routledge, pp. 119–36.

Goldstein, R. (1989) 'Crackdown on Culture', *Village Voice*, 10 October.

Gray, C. (1993) 'The Network for Cultural Policy in Britain', Paper to PSA Conference, University of Leicester.

Grenier, L. (1993) 'Policing the French-language Music on Canadian Radio: The Twilight of the Popular Radio Era?', in T. Bennett, S. Frith, L. Grossberg, J. Shepherd and G. Turner (eds) *Rock and Popular Music: Politics, Policies, Institutions*, London: Routledge, pp. 119–42.

Grossberg, L. (1993) 'The Framing of Rock: Rock and the New Conservatism', in T. Bennett, S. Frith, L. Grossberg, J. Shepherd and G. Turner (eds) *Rock and Popular Music: Politics, Policies, Institutions*, London: Routledge, pp. 193–209.

Grossberg, L. (1992a) *We Gotta Get Out of This Place: Popular Conservatism and Postmodern Culture*, London: Routledge.

Grossberg, L. (1992b) 'Is There a Fan in the House? The Affective Sensibility of Fandom', in L. A. Lewis (ed.) *The Adoring Audience: Fan Culture and Popular Media*, London: Routledge, pp. 50–65.

Gyford, J., S. Leach and C. Game (1989) *The Changing Politics of Local Government*, London: Unwin Hyman.

Hall, S. (1981) 'Notes on Deconstructing "the Popular"', in R. Samuel (ed.) *People's History and Socialist Theory*, London: Routledge, pp. 227–40.

Hall, S. (1989) 'The Meaning of New Times', in S. Hall and M. Jacques (eds) *New Times: The Changing Face of Politics in the 1990s*, London: Lawrence & Wishart, pp. 116–34.

Hans, V. and N. Vidmar (1986) *Judging the Jury*, New York: Plenum Press.

Harker, D. (1980) *One for the Money*, London: Hutchinson.

Harker, D. (1992) 'Still Crazy After all These Years: What *was* Popular Music in the 1960s'?, in B. Moore-Gilbert and J. Seed (eds) *Cultural Revolution? The Challenge of the Arts in the 1960s*, London: Routledge, pp. 236–54.

Hastie, R. (1993) 'Introduction', in R. Hastie (ed.) *Inside the Juror*, Cambridge: Cambridge University Press, pp. 3–31.

Hayward, S. (1993) *French National Cinema*, London: Routledge.

Hebdige, D. (1979) *Subculture: The Meaning of Style*, London: Methuen.

Hebdige, D. (1988) *Hiding in the Light: On Images and Things*, London: Routledge.

Held, D. (1980) *Introduction to Critical Theory*, London: Hutchinson.

Henry, I. (1993) *The Politics of Leisure Policy*, London: Macmillan.

Herder, J. (1968) *Reflections on the Philosophy of the History of Mankind*, Chicago: University of Chicago Press. Originally published in 1791.

Herrnstein Smith, B. (1988) *Contingencies of Value*, Cambridge, Mass.: Harvard University Press.

Hewison, R. (1988) *Too Much: Art and Society in the Sixties 1960–75*, London: Methuen.

Hill, J. (1993) 'Government Policy and the British Film Industry, 1979–90', *European Journal of Communication*, 8(2), pp. 203–24.

Holden, D. (1993) 'Pop Go the Censors', *Index on Censorship*, 5(6), pp. 11–15.

Hollis, M. (1994) *The Philosophy of Social Science*, Cambridge: Cambridge University Press.

Hughes, C. and P. Wintour (1990) *Labour Rebuilt?*, London: 4th Estate.

Hutchinson, R. (1982) *The Politics of the Arts Council*, London: Sinclair Brown.

IFPI (International Federation of the Phonographic Industry) (1990) *World Record Sales 1969–1990*, London: IFPI.

Jackson, T. (1995) 'The New Political Pop', *The Big Issue*, 155, 6–12 Nov., pp. 16–17.

Jamieson, K. H. (1992) *Dirty Politics: Deception, Distraction, and Democracy*, Oxford: Oxford University Press.

Jayaweera, N. (1987) 'Communication Satellites: A Third World Perspective', in R. Finnegan, G. Salaman and K. Thompson (eds) *Information Technology: Social Issues*, London: Hodder and Stoughton, pp. 195–208.

Jenkins, H. (1992) '"Strangers No More, We Sing": Filking and the Social Construction of the Science Fiction Fan Community', in L. A. Lewis (ed.) *The Adoring Audience: Fan Culture and Popular Media*, London: Routledge, pp. 208–36.

Kael, P. (1980) *When the Lights Go Down*, London: Marion Boyars.

Kavanagh, D. (1995) *Election Campaigning: The New Marketing of Politics*, Oxford: Blackwell.

204   *Bibliography*

Kline, S. (1993) *Out of the Garden: Toys, TV, and Children's Culture in the Age of Marketing*, London: Verso.
Laclau, E. (1977) *Politics and Ideology in Marxist Theory*, London: New Left Books.
Laing, D. (1985) *One Chord Wonders: Power and Meaning in Punk Rock*, Milton Keynes: Open University Press.
Laing, D. (1987) 'The Tape Levy', *Popular Music*, 6(1), pp. 93–4.
Laing, S. (1992) 'The Politics of Culture: Institutional Change', in B. Moore-Gilbert and J. Seed (eds) *Cultural Revolution? The Challenge of the Arts in the 1960s*, London: Routledge, pp. 72–95.
Leavis, F. R. and D. Thompson (1948) *Culture and Environment*, London: Chatto & Windus.
Leitner, O. (1994) 'Rock Music in the GDR: An Epitaph', in S. Ramet (ed.) *Rocking the State: Rock Music and Politics in Eastern Europe and Russia*, London: Westview Press, pp. 17–40.
Lewis, J. (1991) *The Ideological Octopus*, London: Routledge.
Lewis, P. and J. Booth (1989) *The Invisible Medium: Public, Commercial and Community Radio*, Basingstoke: Macmillan.
Lijphart, A. (1989) 'The Structure of Inference', in G. Almond and S. Verba (eds) *The Civic Culture Revisited*, London: Sage, pp. 37–56.
Linton, M. (1996) *Election*, London: 4th Estate.
Lipsitz, G. (1982) *Class and Culture in Cold War America*, Amherst, Mass.: Bergin & Garvey.
Lipsitz, G. (1990) *Time Passages: Collective Memory and American Popular Culture*, Minneapolis: University of Minnesota Press.
Lipsitz, G. (1994) *Dangerous Crossroads: Popular Music, Postmodernism and the Poetics of Place*, London: Verso.
Logan, J. and H. Molotch (1987) *Urban Fortunes: The Political Economy of Place*, Berkeley: University of California Press.
Maarek, P. (1995) *Political Marketing and Communication*, London: John Libbey.
McAuley, J. (1991) 'Cuchullain and an RPG-7: The Ideology and Politics of the Ulster Defence Association', in E. Hughes (ed.) *Culture and Politics in Northern Ireland*, Milton Keynes: Open University Press, pp. 45–68.
McCabe, S. and R. Purves (1974) *The Shadow Jury at Work*, Oxford: Basil Blackwell.
McClary, S. (1991) *Feminine Endings: Music, Gender and Sexuality*, Minnesota: University of Minnesota Press.
McClary, S. (1994) 'Same as It Ever Was: Youth Culture and Music', in T. Rose and A. Ross (eds) *Microphone Fiends*, London: Routledge, pp. 29–40.
Macdonald, I. (1995) *Revolution in the Head*, London: Pimlico.
McGinniss, J. (1969) *The Selling of a President*, New York: Trident Press.
McGrew, A. and P. Lewis (eds) (1992) *Global Politics*, Cambridge: Polity Press.
McGuigan, J. (1992) *Cultural Populism*, London: Routledge.
McKay, G. (1996) *Senseless Acts of Beauty: Cultures of Resistance since the Sixties*, London: Verso.
McQuail, D. and K. Siune (eds) (1986), *New Media Politics*, London: Sage.
McRobbie, A. (1991) *Feminism and Youth Culture*, Basingstoke: Macmillan.
Malm, K. and R. Wallis (1993) *Media Policy and Music Activity*, London: Routledge.
Marcus, G. (1975) *Mystery Train: Images of America in Rock'n'Roll Music*, New York: E. P. Dutton.

Marcus, G. (1989a) *Lipstick Traces*, Cambridge, Mass.: Harvard University Press.

Marcus, G. (1989b) 'We are the World?', in A. McRobbie (ed.) *Zoot Suits and Second-Hand Dresses*, Basingstoke: Macmillan, pp. 276–82.

Marcus, G. (1991) *Dead Elvis*, New York: Viking.

Marcus, G. (1993) *In the Fascist Bathroom*, London: Penguin.

Marcuse, H. (1968) *Negations: Essays in Critical Theory*, London: Allen Lane.

Marcuse, H. (1972) 'Art and Revolution', in *Counterrevolution and Revolt*, London: Allen Lane, pp. 79–128.

Marling K. A. (1994) *As Seen on TV: The Visual Culture of Everyday Life in the 1950s*, Cambridge, Mass.: Harvard University Press.

Marqusee, M. (1994) *Anyone But England: Cricket and the National Malaise*, London: Verso.

Marsh, A. (1977) *Protest and Political Consciousness*, London: Sage.

Marsh, D. (1996) 'Look Mam, Top of the World', *Mojo*, May.

Marsh, D. and P. Pollack (1989) 'Wanted for Attitude', *Village Voice*, 10 October.

Mathews, T. D. (1994) *Censored*, London: Chatto & Windus.

Merelman, R. (1991) *Partial Visions: Culture and Politics in Britain, Canada, and the United States*, Madison: University of Wisconsin Press.

Middleton, R. (1990) *Studying Popular Music*, Milton Keynes: Open University Press.

Mill, J. S. (1977) 'Civilization: Sign of the Times', in *Collected Works*, vol. 18 (edited by J. Robson and A. Brady), Toronto and London: University of Toronto Press and Routledge & Kegan Paul, pp. 119–47.

Miller, D. (1988) 'The Ethical Significance of Nationality', *Ethics*, 98(4), pp. 647–62.

Mitchell, T. (1996) *Popular Music and Local Identity*, London: Leicester University Press.

Morley, D. (1986) *Family Television: Cultural Power and Domestic Leisure*, London: Routledge.

Morley, D. (1992) *Television, Audiences & Cultural Studies*, London: Routledge.

Morrison, B. (1995) 'A Prize Worth Writing For', *Independent on Sunday*, Review, 1 October.

Mort, F. (1989) 'The Politics of Consumption', in S. Hall and M. Jacques (eds), *New Times: the Changing Face of Politics in the 1990s*, London: Lawrence & Wishart, pp. 160–72.

Mulgan, G. and K. Worpole (1986) *Saturday Night or Sunday Morning*, London: Comedia.

Murphy, B. (1983) *The World Wired Up*, London: Comedia.

Negus, K. (1992) *Producing Pop*, London: Edward Arnold.

Nimmo, D. and J. Combs (1990) *Mediated Political Realities*, 2nd edition, London: Longman.

Olson, M. (1965) *The Logic of Collective Action*, Cambridge, Mass.: Harvard University Press.

Orman, J. (1984) *The Politics of Rock Music*, Chicago: Nelson-Hall.

Pareles, J. (1985) 'Should Rock-Song Lyrics be Sanitized?', *Herald Tribune*, 18 October.

Pateman, C. (1989) 'The Civic Culture: A Philosophical Critique', in G. Almond and S. Verba (eds) *The Civic Culture Revisited*, London: Sage, pp. 57–102.

Peacock Committee (1986) *Report of the Committee on Financing the BBC*, Cmnd 9824, London: HMSO.

Phillips, A. (1991) *Engendering Democracy*, Cambridge: Polity Press.
Plant, S. (1992) *The Most Radical Gesture: The Situationist International in a Postmodern Age*, London: Routledge.
Postman, N. (1987) *Amusing Ourselves to Death*, London: Methuen.
PSI (Policy Studies Institute) (1993) *Cultural Trends 1992*, London: PSI.
Putnam, R. (1994) *Making Democracy Work: Civic Traditions in Modern Italy*, Princeton, NJ: Princeton University Press.
Raban, J. (1991) *Hunting Mr Heartbreak*, London: Picador.
Redhead, S. (1986) *Sing When You're Winning*, London: Pluto Press.
Redhead, S. and J. Street (1989) 'Have I the Right? Legitimacy, Authenticity and Community in Folk's Politics', *Popular Music*, 8(2), pp. 177–84.
Reporters Sans Frontières (1993) *1993 Report: Freedom of the Press throughout the World*, London: John Libbey.
Reynolds, S. (1996) 'Slipping into Darkness', *The Wire*, 148, June.
Reynolds, S. and J. Press (1994) *Sex Revolts*, London: Serpent's Tail.
Rhodes, R. (1988) *Beyond Westminster and Whitehall*, London: Unwin Hyman.
Rigby, B. (1991) *Popular Culture in Modern France*, London: Routledge.
Robertson, D. (1985) *The Penguin Dictionary of Politics*, Harmondsworth: Penguin.
Robinson, D. C., E. B. Buck and M. Cuthbert (1991) *Music at the Margins: Popular Music and Global Cultural Diversity*, London: Sage.
Rorty, R. (1989) *Contingency, Irony, and Solidarity*, Cambridge: Cambridge University Press.
Rose, R. (1980) *Politics in England*, London: Faber & Faber.
Rose, T. (1994) *Black Noise: Rap Music and Black Culture in Contemporary America*, Hanover, Penn.: Wesleyan University Press.
Ruane, J. and J. Todd (1991) '"Why Can't You Get Along with Each Other?": Culture, Structure and the Northern Ireland Conflict', in E. Hughes (ed.) *Culture and Politics in Northern Ireland*, Milton Keynes: Open University Press, pp. 27–44.
Rutten, P. (1991) 'Local Popular Music on the National and International Markets', *Cultural Studies*, 5(3), pp. 294–305.
Samuels, D. (1991) 'The Rap on Rap', *New Republic*, November.
Savage, J. (1991) *England's Dreaming*, London: Faber & Faber.
Savage, J. and S. Frith (1993) 'Pearls and Swine: Intellectuals and the Media', *New Left Review*, 198, March/April, pp. 107–16.
Scammell, M. (1995) *Designer Politics: How Elections are Won*, London: Macmillan.
Schama, S. (1989) *Citizens*, New York: Knopf.
Schiller, H. (1996) *Information Inequality*, London: Routledge.
Schroeder, A. (1996) 'Watching Between the Lines: Presidential Debates as Television', *Press/Politics*, 1(4), pp. 57–75.
Scott, A. (1997) 'Globalization: Social Process or Political Project?', in A. Scott (ed.) *The Limits to Globalization*, London: Routledge.
Scott, J. (1990) *Domination and the Arts of Resistance*, New Haven: Yale University Press.
Semetko, H., J. Blumler, M. Gurevitch and D. Weaver (1991) *The Formation of Campaign Agendas: A Comparative Analysis of Party and Media Roles in Recent American and British Elections*, Hillsdale, NJ: Lawrence Erlbaum.
Seyd, P. (1990) 'Radical Sheffield: From Socialism to Entrepreneurialism', *Political Studies*, 38(2), pp. 335–44.

Shank, B. (1994) *Dissonant Identities: The Rock'n'Roll Scene in Austin, Texas*, Hanover, Penn.: Wesleyan University Press.
Shepherd, J. (1993) 'Popular Music Studies: Challenges to Musicology', *Stanford Humanities Review*, 3(2), pp. 17–36.
Shiach, M. (1989) *Discourses in Popular Culture*, Cambridge: Polity Press.
Simons, J. (1995) 'The Exile of Political Theory: The Lost Homeland of Legitimation', *Political Studies*, 43(4), pp. 683–97.
Smith, A. (1991) *National Identity*, Harmondsworth: Penguin.
Smith, G. (1996) *Lost in Music*, London: Picador.
Sreberny-Mohammadi, A. (1991) 'The Global and Local in International Communications', in J. Curran and M. Gurevitch (eds) *Mass Media and Society*, London: Edward Arnold, pp. 118–38.
Stanley, M. (1990) 'Why Does the Venue Pressure Group Succeed?', Problems of Politics thesis, Politics/Sociology Sector, UEA, Norwich.
Starr, F. (1983) *Red and Hot: The Fate of Jazz in the Soviet Union*, Oxford: Oxford University Press.
Storey, J. (1993) *An Introductory Guide to Cultural Theory and Popular Culture*, Hemel Hempstead: Harvester Wheatsheaf.
Straw, W. (1991) 'System of Articulation, Logics of Change: Communities and Scenes in Popular Music', *Cultural Studies*, 5(3), pp. 368–88.
Straw, W. (1993) 'The English Canadian Recording Industry since 1970', in T. Bennett, S. Frith, L. Grossberg, J. Shepherd and G. Turner (eds) *Rock and Popular Music: Politics, Policies, Institutions*, London: Routledge, pp. 52–65.
Street, J. (1986) *Rebel Rock: The Politics of Popular Music*, Oxford: Basil Blackwell.
Street, J. (1988) 'Red Wedge: Another Strange Story of Pop's Politics', *Critical Quarterly*, 30(3), pp. 79–91.
Street, J. (1993) 'Local Differences? Popular Music and the Local State', *Popular Music*, 12(1), pp. 43–55.
Street, J. (1995) 'Making Fun: The Local Politics of Popular Music', in J. Lovenduski and J. Stanyer (eds) *Contemporary Political Studies 1995*, Exeter: PSA, pp. 316–23.
Street, J. and M. Stanley (1989) 'Report on Local Authority Support for Popular Music', Centre for Public Choice Studies, UEA, Norwich.
Strinati, D. (1992) 'The Taste of America', in D. Strinati and S. Wagg (eds) *Come on Down? Popular Media Culture in Post-War Britain*, London: Routledge, pp. 46–81.
Tate, G. (1992) *Flyboy in the Buttermilk: Essays on Contemporary America*, New York: Simon & Schuster.
Taylor, C. (1967) 'Neutrality in Political Science', in P. Laslett and W. G. Runciman (eds) *Philosophy, Politics and Society*, Third Series, Oxford: Basil Blackwell, pp. 25–57.
Thompson, J. (1990) *Ideology and Modern Culture*, Cambridge: Polity Press.
Thompson, J. (1996) *The Media and Modernity: A Social Theory of the Media*, Cambridge: Polity Press.
Thompson, M., R. Ellis and A. Wildavsky (1990) *Cultural Theory*, Boulder, Colo.: Westview Press.
Toop, D. (1984) *Rap Attack: African Jive to New York Hip Hop*, London: Pluto Press.
Toop, D. (1993) 'No, Minister, the Party's Over', *The Times*, 26 March.
Topf, R. (1989) 'Political Change and Political Culture in Britain, 1959–87', in J. Gibbins (ed.) *Contemporary Political Culture*, London: Sage, pp. 52–80.

Tunstall, J. and M. Palmer (1991) *Media Moguls*, London: Routledge.

Veljanovski, C. (ed.) (1989) *Freedom in Broadcasting*, Hobart Paperback 29, London: Institute of Economic Affairs.

Vickers, G. (1968) *The Art of Judgement: A Study in Policy-Making*, London: Methuen.

Wachtel, D. (1987) *Cultural Policy and Socialist France*, New York: Greenwood Press.

Wallis, R. and K. Malm (1984) *Big Sounds from Small Peoples: The Music Industry in Small Countries*, London: Constable.

Walzer, M. (1992) 'On the Role of Symbolism in Political Thought', in T. Strong (ed.) *The Self and the Political Order*, Oxford: Basil Blackwell, pp. 64–76.

Ward, M. and P. Pitt (1985) 'Introduction', in *The State of the Art or the Art of the State?*, London: GLC, pp. 5–7.

Waters, C. (1990) *British Socialists and the Politics of Popular Culture*, Manchester: Manchester University Press.

Webster, D. (1988) *Looka Yonder! The Imaginary America of Populist Culture*, London: Routledge.

Welch, S. (1993) *The Concept of Political Culture*, Basingstoke: Macmillan.

Wiatr, J. (1989) 'The Civic Culture from a Marxist-Sociological Perspective', in G. Almond and S. Verba (eds) *The Civic Culture Revisited*, London: Sage, pp. 103–23.

Wicke, P. (1992) ' "The Times They are A-Changin": Rock Music and Political Change in East Germany', in R. Garofalo (ed.) *Rockin' the Boat: Mass Music and Mass Movements*, Boston: South End Press, pp. 81–93.

Wicke, P. and J. Shepherd (1993) ' "The Cabaret is Dead": Rock Culture as State Enterprise – the Political Organisation of Rock in East Germany', in T. Bennett, S. Frith, L. Grossberg, J. Shepherd and G. Turner (eds) *Rock and Popular Music: Politics, Policies, Institutions*, London: Routledge, pp. 25–36.

Wiener, M. (1981) *English Culture and the Decline of the Industrial Spirit 1850–1980*, Cambridge: Cambridge University Press.

Wildavsky, A. (1987) 'Choosing Preferences by Constructing Institutions: A Cultural Theory of Preference Formation', *American Political Science Review*, 81(1), March, pp. 4–21.

Williams, R. (1981) *Culture*, London: Fontana.

Williams, R. (1989) *Resources of Hope*, London: Verso.

Williamson, J. (1986) *Consuming Passions*, London: Marion Boyars.

Willis, P. (1978) *Profane Culture*, London: Routledge & Kegan Paul.

Willis, P. (1990) *Common Culture*, Milton Keynes: Open University Press.

Wilson, E. (1985) *Adorned in Dreams: Fashion and Modernity*, London: Virago.

Winner, L. (1979) 'Trout Mask Replica', in G. Marcus (ed.) *Stranded: Rock and Roll for a Desert Island*, New York: Knopf, pp. 58–70.

Wolff, J. (1983) *Aesthetics and the Sociology of Art*, London: Allen & Unwin.

Worpole, K. (1992) *Towns for People*, Milton Keynes: Open University Press.

York, P. (1984) *Modern Times*, London: Futura.

Young, S. (1991) 'Local Service Delivery', *Contemporary Record*, 4(3), February, pp. 15–17.

Zhao, B. and G. Murdoch (1996) 'Young Pioneers: Children and the Making of Chinese Communism', *Cultural Studies*, 10(2), pp. 201–17.

Index